Annie Sacerdoti

The Guide to Jewish Italy

photographs by Alberto Jona Falco

Guide Marsilio

Thanks to Piero Campi, Aldo Izzo, Pietro
Meggiorin, Benedetto Zitoli, Associazione
Nazionale Fotografi Professionisti – Tau Visual,
Studio Olimpic – Milan.

Photographs
The photos in this guide are by
Alberto Jona Falco and are the property
of the artist.
No reproductions, even in part, may be made.
© 2003 Photo by Alberto Jona Falco –
STUDIO OLIMPIC
www.studioolimpic.it

Other photos in the book are by
Paolo Zappaterra (pp. 112, 113, 114, 115, 116,
117, 119, 120, 121, 122, 131, 186, 187, 188);
Pietro Meggiorin (p. 194);
and Vivi Papi, who took the photos (pp. 10, 67,
73, 134, 135, 167, 168, 180, 181) of the Passover
Haggadah published in Venice by the printers
Pietro, Alvise, and Lorenzo Bragadini in 1609
(Milan, private collection).
The photos on pp. 43 and 64 are from
the Marsilio archives.

The photos of the interior of the church
of Santa Maria in Scolanova, Trani (p. 188)
are courtesy the Ufficio Diocesano
Arte Sacra e Beni Culturali, Trani.

Thanks to the Ente Risiera di San Sabba
and the Mausoleo delle Fosse Ardeatine
for their permission to take photographs.

Translation by
David Kerr

Cover:
Mantua, synagogue interior

Design
Tapiro, Venice

© 2003 by Marsilio Editori® s.p.a.
in Venice
First Edition: July 2004
Third Edition: September 2008
ISBN 978-88-317-8471-4

www. marsilioeditori.it

Contents

Jewish Italy is one of the European diasporas that has attracted great interest from scholars or people who simply wish to know more. It is neither the oldest nor the largest — nor does it have the strongest traditional connotations. But over the centuries the diaspora in Italy has preserved some special features that make it unique in the world. This is especially true of its artistic and cultural heritage, found throughout the Italian peninsula, even in the southern Italian regions, where there have been no Jewish communities for more than 500 years. But interest in the Jewish past has been growing stronger, particularly in these regions. Experts are conducting in-depth research and are expecting new discoveries. But naturally most interest is focused on the regions where Jewish communities engage in an active daily life in which Italian Judaism still has much to say and those who offer a fascinating world for anyone wishing to explore it further. For over 2,000 years its culture and language have been an integral part of Italian history and culture. These communities attract attention because they offer examples of the artistic output of Italian Judaism (illuminated manuscripts, printed Hebrew books, kettuboth, *to mention a few), which are almost without equal in other countries. The Italian Jewish heritage also has a good deal to offer as regards to synagogue architecture (from the small concealed prayer rooms before emancipation to grandiose buildings after 1848), its furnishings (from the Venetian school to the baroque Piedmontese synagogues), and the great variety of ornaments for* Sefarim, *the Scrolls of the Law (crowns, trays, pointers, and embroidered capes), or the objects for festivities (the lamps for the Sabbath or* Hanukkah) *and family life. All of these are on view in the various Jewish museums.*

Ultimately, what this guide illustrates is Judaism. It does so by accompanying the reader to the various places where Jewish life is expressed most fully. This means not only visiting monuments, museums, libraries, and archives with their important treasures of the Jewish past, but also going to places where traditions, stories, and relatively unknown figures can be discovered. It means being able to purchase Judaica and taste the best kosher cuisine with the awareness that every culture is multifaceted and vital and that a true knowledge of a culture can only be gained by exploring every aspect.

Amos Luzzatto
President of the Union of Italian Jewish Communities (UCEI)

Foreword

The heritage of Jewish art and culture is an important part of the overall Italian cultural riches. In Italy there are close to seventy synagogues dating from the Middle Ages to the 20th century, and two from Ancient Roman times (at Ostia Antica, near Rome, and Bova Marina, in Calabria). Found throughout the country, there are Jewish museums that house precious objects, furnishings, books, stelae, gravestones, and documents from all the historical periods.

For a long time, to protect its cultural identity, the Italian Jewish world adopted a guarded approach to the outside world. The many years of racial persecution and war accentuated this tendency to reservedness, mainly due to the need for self-defense. Over the last few decades, however, things have begun to change. On the one hand, many Jews have rediscovered a pride in their own roots and identity, and on the other, non-Jews have begun to look at the Jewish world with a genuine desire to explore it in more depth, encouraged by a greater diffusion of culture and information.

In this positive climate of rediscovery, the *Guida all'Italia Ebraica* ("The Guide to Jewish Italy"), conceived and written by Annie Sacerdoti and Luca Fiorentino was published in 1986. For the first time the Jewish places and memories scattered throughout Italy were brought together in one volume. That book marked the beginning of a reassessment of the Italian Jewish heritage, which was given an equal artistic standing and was acknowledged as an integral, indispensable part of the rest of the Italian cultural heritage. For readers it was surprising to discover that in all the Italian regions there are monuments, historical evidence, and more or less significant traces left by Judaism — many not even known to the Jewish people. This was also true of the southern Italian regions, despite the fact that all Jews had been expelled over five centuries ago at the time of the great expulsion from the Iberian peninsula in 1492.

The success of this first book led to the idea of providing more in-depth works on the heritage in the individual regions. Thus the creation of *Jewish Itineraries – Places, History and Art*, a series of nine volumes (six translated into English), edited by Annie Sacerdoti, who also wrote some of the volumes together with Annamarcella Tedeschi Falco. The others were written by experts on the various regions: Dora Liscia Bemporad, Francesca Brandes, Maria Luisa Moscati Benigni, Bice Migliau, Micaela Procaccia, Silvio Cusin, and Pier Cesare Ioly Zorattini. The present book has been possible thanks to the studies conducted by these researchers over the years.

This new *Guide to Jewish Italy*, published almost twenty years after the first, however, is based on a different logic; the texts and photographs are equally important. Alberto Jona Falco's images enable the reader to be visually immersed in the Jewish world. The photographs show the architecture through a focus on details, which may otherwise go unnoticed by the casual visitor. The rooms and the furnishings, fabrics and objects, have been captured and portrayed by the photographer's lens without a hint of rhetoric. On the contrary they have the fond familiarity of someone who has lived in the Jewish world since childhood, and now revisits it with the eye of a professional seeking to highlight the intentions of the various artists who created the objects being studied.

The guide contains essential historical and practical information about the many places that can be most easily visited. Covering the whole of the Italian peninsula, the texts and photographs invite the reader to enter and explore the richness of the Italian Jewish cultural world, for far too long overlooked or neglected. [A.S.-A.J.F.]

אהרן

יהודה אריה ממודינא בכהר יצחק זל

הקדמה לפירוש צלי אש :

מיום באת על פני חוץ הגדה זאת תמה ונברה ופותר יפ אותהי כלם דמות תכניתה ובורו לבב
כל איום הרחיבו. עד כי כל אחד במעטהו הטפנים הרבה מקינותי ולא מותרה כבת ולחקוק
אותה פנים ירדו רבים נעלה מחד נעלה היקר כמ'גרשון בן נסוה פני נטכר כמ'משה מארדנ'ך ובו'לטוב ולחתקון
וכל הנבדר להרדפה . כבי לאמוסיף מן דולים מירות דברי החבובה על תתכמכתי . כי איום אם כבר
באו בה ביורים וכומוכים תחלה לעבוים הנגמכיים הנה מה טוב כי יהיו בה ביחורים ובומות מחמד
כל רוחני ואם יתרחם בתנהה סתרין המעלים לעבוים בלתי כל ה'ללמוכו כגוייים לחמינ'וים ולממלי
הרעת נכון הדבר להאבד בה בתבאור מים חיים הבדר לזניקים ויורדעים ויהיו ודבריים עני ומתיני
ויחרתי בקם לבחר לזה אהיה פירוים כפי ראות עיני . והנב על אני בעני הכינ'ויום זה כמה מני'מירות
עלי על ההבדיה קרלחזי . כמו באון . יהודה (כי'יובאת מכרים תפארת ונאון יל ערתנא היא) אמר
בחולי אם אריפוכו לא יהיה לבוד' לא רביית לראות חבה לעבוד . ויבעתי אותו להתלות בחולן גדול
הסר הרב אברבניל יל אמר בכל ביאורי העלוה עצה הגדיל סבריי על כל . וגם פה בביאור החבד
מספרין הלז . ירדתי לבד מכה לא כי כמהו . אמנם כי ראמתי היום קטן ותקנ'היות כמים התמהים
קוסיחתיו ותי אם בה לא נמאלו ותאתחמ לא הוסכמו מהני' . אמר את פני תבין חכמה תחבא ולא תלאחם
להחיותו במעט את התרובה . קראחתי בכמטו צלי אש כי כן קרבן הפסח בהיותו כאכל בלי היה תרכוין
מיתחיתעטו אך בטבעטו ויפה לו בטעב. כן וגבה פסח אמר בקרא חבורו הרב זל הבתחי בספור על
רמוזי ותאבסהו כלי והגמיקתיו אך לטובה וטעם לבמח . כי אם כל המרובה לפרד בו'מה'אין כי מבוכה
לזה ביה וסף לקח וידבא אחרים העלוה הזה על פטמיית מלות ההגדה וכלו אם הכבר בלוליה
זה בלי אש' זבת פסח הוא לה' . וההומוב בתזניז בו עורך מכבל ואוכל ואוכל את חקם לרצון לפני
ה' עד אמר גלכה נזבחה לאלהינו בירושלם הבכוניה מהרה אמן ;

קומטה דילה פארינה

קו אימפּאסטנו איל פ'וֹרדילה פארינה
אי פוני'ל פורני'ל סינ'פאן קונ'ינארי

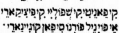

משה

Italian Jews: over two thousand years of history

The history of the Italian Jews begins in Rome in 168 BC. This was the year ambassadors from Judaea, accompanied by merchants and craftsmen, arrived in the city. In 63 BC they were followed by Pompey's prisoners of war, after the fall of Jerusalem. There were soon to be many more: 30,000 in Rome alone, and 50,000 throughout the Italian peninsula (out of a total population of 5 million). Although, because bound by religion, rites and customs, they felt "different," they were well integrated in Roman society and at times protected, for example, by Julius Caesar.

After the destruction of the Temple of Jerusalem in AD 70, thousands of other prisoners arrived in Rome but in an adverse climate due to the spread of Christianity and the continuous disputes between Jews and Christians. Roman tolerance gradually wore thin, especially after Emperor Constantine embraced the Christian faith in 313, recognizing it as the state religion. The emperor forbid conversions to Judaism and mixed marriages. He prohibited Jews from owning Christian slaves and levied special taxes from them. In the meantime groups of Jews had formed throughout the peninsula — in Bologna, Ferrara, Trieste, Turin, and smaller towns.

The invasions of Italy by the Goths, Vandals, and Huns also brought death and plundering to the Jews, who only reacquired some tranquillity after the arrival of the Ostrogoth king Theodoric in the early 6th century. But on his death, Italy once more became a land to be conquered by any comers.

In the 7th century the Jews left the Frankish-Lombard kingdom in the north to seek refuge in the south where they created some groups, at times culturally very lively, especially in Sicily, initially under the Arabs, and then under the Normans. The struggles between the papacy and the empire indirectly affected the Jewish groups: in 1120 Pope Callistus II issued a bull limiting their rights. In 1231 Frederick II of Swabia guaranteed them equality with other citizens, but three decades later Pope Clement IV goaded the Dominicans and Franciscans against them. In the early 14th century there were 40,000 Jews in Italy out of a total population of 8 million. In 1348 a terrible outbreak of the plague decimated the population of Europe in only a few years. Accused of having spread the plague, the Jews were expelled by many states, and thousands sought refuge in Italy, mainly in Lombardy, Trentino, Piedmont, the Veneto, and Emilia.

In the mid-15th century Renaissance Italy was divided into a host of small states. Some gravitated in the papal orbit, while others came under imperial influence. These states thus had different attitudes towards the Jews. The overall climate of openness during the Renaissance, however, was favorable for study and the arts in the growing Jewish groups, which were especially numerous at some courts of princes or dukes, such as the Este in Ferrara and the Medici in Florence.

Then in 1492 a major change occurred: the complete expulsion of Jews from the Iberian peninsula led to the arrival of huge numbers of refugees in Italy. At the same time the Kingdom of Naples, which had come under Spanish rule, forced Sicilian, Calabrian, and Neapolitan Jews to leave the south of Italy. Around 40,000 Jews left Sicily, after a continuous presence on the island going back fifteen centuries.

In 1500 there were 50,000 Jews out of a total of 9 million inhabitants in Italy. This century, characterized by the Reformation and Counter-Reformation, saw the introduction of heavy restrictions, such as the enclosure in ghettos, imposed in 1555 by Pope Paul IV in the bull *Cum nimis absurdum*. This segregation was to last for over three centuries. The Jewish population rose from 20,700 in 1600 to 34,300 in 1800.

After the French Revolution and the arrival in Italy of Napoleon's army, the Jews obtained equal rights with other citizens. This, however, was soon revoked by the restoration of the monarchy which, after the Congress of Vienna in 1814–15, reintroduced discrimination and segregation.

From the mid-19th century the history of Jewish communities became increasingly closely bound up with that of Italy, as it struggled to win independence from Austria and the Bourbons. Jews enthusiastically took part in the uprisings of the Risorgimento, and patriots like Mazzini and Cattaneo openly fought anti-Semitism. There where 200 Jews in Garibaldi's ranks in 1848–49. Count Camillo Cavour's private secretary was Isacco Artom from Asti. He was flanked in the Savoy government by other Jews, such as Ottolenghi, Todros, Vitta, and Leonino. Their presence was a sign of important recognition, and the consequence of the act of emancipation of 1848, with which King Charles Albert of Savoy had granted Piedmontese Jews equal rights with all his other subjects.

The fall of Rome in 1870 marked the end of the Church's temporal power and finally brought the abolition of the ghettos as well as freedom and equality for all Jews in the new state. In the legislation of 1889 all religions were admitted and defamation of any professed religion, including Judaism, was a punishable crime.

The process of urbanization in Italy in the early 20th century encouraged many Jews to leave small towns and rural areas to go and settle in the large cities, where they were actively involved in the nascent industries, liberal professions, and public life. In 1871 the Italian Chamber of Deputies included eleven Jews. From 1907 to 1913 the mayor of Rome was Ernesto Nathan. Six percent of the university teaching staff was Jewish. Triestine Jews, led by the writer Italo Svevo, played a key role in the Irredentista movement to free the city still under Austrian rule. While, on the one hand, emanci-

Rome, Arch of Titus, detail of the frieze with a menorah. The arch was erected after the destruction of the Temple in Jerusalem as a symbol of the Roman victory over the Jews. Until 1948, when the State of Israel was founded, Jews refused to walk under the arch.

pation meant freedom for Jews after centuries of injustice, on the other, it also contributed to changing the face of conventional Judaism, leading to assimilation and the neglect of ancient traditions preserved for centuries.

In the First World War (1914–18) Jews fought in the trenches alongside other Italians and there were many among the death toll of 600,000. When the Fascists rose to power in 1922, the Jews were perfectly integrated and had harbored no suspicions about the possible anti-Semitism of the new regime. Even Mussolini had an

ambivalent position on the question. In 1929, with the Concordat between Italy and the Holy See, Catholicism became the state religion and the life of the Jewish communities was regulated by the so-called Falco Law (1930).

But Fascism soon began to show its true face: in 1931 university lecturers were called on to swear an oath of loyalty to the regime. Out of one thousand professors only twelve refused to sign. They included five Jews: Giorgio Errera, Giorgio Levi della Vida, Vito Volterra, Mario Carrara, and Fabio Luzzatto. Some Italian Jews began to form underground groups of resistance to the regime, such as the "Justice and Freedom" movement founded by Carlo and Nello Rosselli, which included prominent figures like Carlo, Mario and Riccardo Levi, Max Ascoli, Leone Ginzburg, and Gino Luzzatto.

But the real anti-Jewish persecution and discrimination began when Fascism adopted the doctrine of the biological basis for differences of race, previously alien to Italian traditions. In 1938 Mussolini ordered the publication of the *Manifesto on Race*, aligning the country with the Nazi ideology, and declaring the existence of a pure Italian race to which the Jews did not belong. From September the same year a series of increasingly restrictive laws were decreed: foreign Jews were expelled from the country and Italian Jews were barred from schools, military service, public employment, and could not own assets or companies. By now to all effects and purposes the Jews were second-class citizens. On December 31, 1938, the "racial census" counted 45,270 Jews.

Around 5,000 members of the Italian Jewish community went into exile, but many remained and had to endure humiliation and restrictions.

In June 1940 Italy entered the war on the side of Germany. The wave of anti-Semitic feeling grew stronger and the Jewish communities and their synagogues were raided and plundered. In the period 1943–45 these persecutions eventually became a witch-hunt and 8,500 Jews were arrested and deported to the extermination camps.

PIEDMONT
1. Alessandria
2. Asti
3. Biella
4. Carmagnola
5. Casale Monferrato
6. Cherasco
7. Cuneo
8. Ivrea
9. Moncalvo
10. Mondovì
11. Saluzzo
12. Turin
13. Vercelli

LOMBARDY
14. Mantua
15. Milan
16. Sabbioneta
17. Soncino

LIGURIA
18. Genoa

VENETO
19. Padua
20. Venice
21. Verona

TRENTINO-ALTO ADIGE
22. Merano

FRIULI-VENEZIA GIULIA
23. Gorizia
24. Trieste

EMILIA ROMAGNA
25. Bologna
26. Carpi and Fossoli
27. Ferrara
28. Modena
29. Parma
30. Reggio Emilia
31. Soragna

TUSCANY
32. Florence
33. Livorno
34. Pisa
35. Pitigliano
36. Siena

MARCHES
37. Ancona
38. Pesaro
39. Senigallia
40. Urbino

LAZIO
41. Rome

CAMPANIA
42. Naples

APULIA
43. Trani

SICILY
44. Syracuse

SARDINIA
45. Alghero

Only a few hundred were to return.

After the allies landed in the south of Italy and the armistice was signed on September 8, 1943, in the north — still under Fascist control — the Italian Social Republic was declared. In the days before the German invasion, thousands of Jews managed to reach Switzerland, while others passed the front line to reach the liberated south of Italy. Some younger Jews joined the partisans. Many also tried to hide. Others, however, such as the Jews in the Rome ghetto were caught by surprise: on October 16, 1943, the Germans burst into the ghetto and in a few days, going from house to house, they arrested 1,259 people.

There was a very active Jewish participation in the resistance. Around one thousand Jews fought in the ranks of the 200,000 partisans. Ninety-seven Jews died in combat out of a total of 70,000 dead. Among the 355 martyrs massacred at the Fosse Ardeatine in Rome (March 21, 1944) in German reprisals, there were seventy-five Jews. After the end of the war on April 25, 1945, the Jews counted their dead: out of a total of over 45,000 in 1938, 17,000 were missing. They had either been killed in Italy, disappeared in the extermination camps, or were living in exile.

As in the rest of the country, reconstruction also began for the Italian Jews. They were encouraged by the birth of the State of Israel on May 15, 1948, giving new hope to the Jews of the Diaspora after the extermination of 6 million in Europe. Relations between the Italian Jews and the Catholic Church also saw considerable changes. In the declaration *Nostra Aetate*, at the Vatican Council II of 1965, Pope John XXIII officially condemned any accusations of deicide made against the Jewish people. On April 13, 1986, Pope John Paul II visited the Temple in Rome. This was an unprecedented move. Never before in history had a pope crossed the threshold of a synagogue. This act, and the words addressed by John Paul II to his "elder brothers" the Jews, meant the Catholic Church's critical revision was irreversible.

Today there are around 30,000 Italian Jews enrolled in the communities, out of a total Italian population of 57 million. Almost half are concentrated in Rome and Milan. Others live in medium-sized communities (from 500 to 1,000 members) in Turin, Florence, Trieste, Livorno, and Venice, or in small or very small communities (a few hundred or even dozen people) in Ancona, Bologna, and Naples.

Each community is run by a council, elected by community members. The communities are represented politically by the Union of Italian Jewish Communities (UCEI — Unione delle Comunità Ebraiche Italiane), based in Rome. The Union's tasks include managing political relations with the Italian State, governed by the Agreement (*Intesa*) of 1987, which replaced the law of 1930. The Agreement guarantees official recognition for Jewish organizations, independence of confession and law, and the right, in the widest sense possible, to profess the Jewish religion.

In 1490 Abramo Vitale de Sacerdoti was the first Jew allowed to settle and run a loan-bank in Alessandria, at the time under the Duchy of Milan. His family became the largest and most important in the community: in 1684, 170 of the 230 Jews were called Vitale (the second part of the surname, de Sacerdoti, soon fell into disuse). This family became so influential that it decided if and whom among their fellow Jews could settle in the town. The Alessandria community became increasingly powerful. Indeed, in the 16th century it managed to stop the creation of a ghetto, also avoiding the expulsion, decreed in 1597 for all Jews in the duchy, by then under Spanish rule. In the 18th century, as a consequence of the War of the Spanish Succession, Alessandria passed to the Savoys, who eventually introduced the ghetto in 1724 and the wearing of the badge. A 1761 census recorded the presence of 420 inhabitants in the ghetto. After the Napoleonic period and the subsequent restoration of the monarchy, the community enjoyed the benefits of the age of emancipation (introduced by Charles Albert of Savoy in 1848). The relations with the rest of the town improved further, although there was already a good degree of integration, as is demonstrated by a tragic accident in 1835: when the floor of the synagogue collapsed during a wedding, among the forty-two dead there were seventeen Christians. At the beginning of the 20th century many Jews left Alessandria to go and live in the cities, especially Turin. Under Fascism forty-eight people were deported. Today the community is a section of Turin.

The ghetto created in 1724

The ghetto was bounded by Via Milano, Via Migliara, Via dei Martiri, and Via Vochieri. Set up in 1724 in an area already inhabited by Jews, it consisted of houses linked by courtyards, with ground floor shops (selling fabrics, silks, and hats). Known as Contrada degli Ebrei (the "Jewish District"), the area was altered in the 19th century. Today, however, some old buildings have survived with their original structure: galleries, balconies, and internal passageways.

Small ground-floor prayer room. This room was used by the community for daily prayers and in winter.

Large synagogue interior. Officially opened in 1871, the square-plan synagogue with three orders of stained-glass windows is enhanced with Neo-Gothic motifs. Built at the height of emancipation, it soon turned out to be too large for the requirements of the dwindling community.

The emancipation synagogue

The old synagogue was in an internal courtyard in Via Migliara. Today it is no longer there. The present synagogue at no. 7, Via Milano, was opened in 1871, at the height of the euphoria after emancipation. But it immediately turned out to be too large for a dwindling community.

The monumental brick façade is Neo-Baroque in style. The three orders of windows have strip pilasters and white frames. Over the entrance are the Tablets of the Law and, on one side, a plaque commemorating the deportees. On the ground floor inside the building is the small winter temple and, on the first floor, the large synagogue. With a rectangular plan and three orders of windows with polychrome stained glass, the interior is embellished by Neo-Gothic motifs; there are galleries with arches along the short sides of the room. Next to the ark are choir stalls (an element introduced after emancipation, imitating churches). The present furnishings (ark and *bimah*) come from the synagogue of Nizza Monferrato, now demolished; the previous furnishings were destroyed when the synagogue was sacked in 1944. The women's gallery has two floors. On the second floor of the building is the recently restored small room once used for the *Talmud Torah*.

A long-standing presence

The first Jews settled in Asti as early as 812. There was only a permanent group in the town, however, from the end of the 14th century, after the expulsions from France, Germany, and Spain. To stay in the town the Jews had to practice money-lending and put up with many restrictions. The first prayer room was opened in 1601, in the same building as today, part of the ghetto area in 1724. A census ordered by the Savoy rulers in 1761 reveals there were 200 Jews present in the city; their numbers rose to 360 in 1843, and 450 in 1866.

Perfectly emancipated

Two views of the holy ark. Built in 1809, it has a door divided into eight gilded carved panels depicting the furnishings of the Temple in Jerusalem. The cornice is inscribed with the name of the donor and a psalm. The synagogue was remodeled in its present form in 1889.

A special statute (*Statuto Albertino* — 1848) abolishing all religious discrimination allowed the inhabitants of the ghetto to come and go as they pleased and to enter the liberal professions, the universities, and army with the same rights as the other subjects in the realm. The Asti Jews were so completely emancipated that one — Isacco Artom (1829–1900) — even became prime minister Cavour's secretary. After emancipation many went to live in the cities and the community witnessed the process of assimilation and a decline in synagogue attendance. The racial laws of 1938 caught the by then few dozen Asti Jews ill-prepared. In 1944 thirty of them were deported to the extermination camps and only three came back. Since 1984 the Asti community has been a section of the Turin community.

Daily life in Contrada degli Ebrei

The ghetto stretched from Via Aliberti (formerly Contrada degli Ebrei) to Via Ottolenghi (formerly Via San Bernardino), and was closed at each end by gates. The right-hand house at the entrance to Via Aliberti was once inhabited by the Artom family. It has a Baroque painting of the *Sacra Conversazione* attributed to Giancarlo Aliberti (1662–1740). Tradition has it that the Artom family commissioned this painting so that they could open a window in the same wall looking out of the ghetto, thus obviating the prevailing legislation. No. 5 was the house of the chaplain Stefano Incisa (1742–1819), a local historian of Jewish Asti: his diaries enable us to reconstruct life in the quarter. No. 39 was the Jewish school, called the Clava Institute, after its benefactor. The small school courtyard was used for the tabernacle at *Sukkoth*. There are commemorative plaques in the women's gallery of the synagogue in Via Ottolenghi (no. 8). This building has stood on the same spot since 1601, but was extended and altered: its present appearance is due to redevelopment work carried out in 1889. Before you come to the building there is a rectangular opening with two fine period gas lamps. On the left-hand side, a plaque commemorates the deportees. The façade has horizontal bands, while the entrance portal has four Ionic columns with wide grooves. The architrave is inscribed with a psalm in Hebrew. The entrance hall, containing a bust of Elia Moise Clava, has three doors: the right-hand door leads up a stair to the women's gallery; the middle door to the prayer room; and the left-hand door to a small museum.

The large prayer room

The almost square-plan room (11 × 11.5 m [36 ft. 1 in. × 37 ft. 8 3/4 in.], plus 4.75 m [15 ft. 5 in.] of the women's gallery), is divided up by painted marble

columns with, in between, two rows of 18th-century benches. Some other benches run along the walls. Daylight is provided by large windows on two sides and a central skylight. On the eastern side, bounded by a marble balustrade, is the *bimah*, set in front of the gilded portal of the holy ark. Made in 1809, the ark shows the name of the donor on the cornice, inscribed with some verses of a psalm. The doors are divided into eight gilded carved panels depicting the furnishings of the Temple of Jerusalem. The ark is lit internally by a skylight. In front of the doors hangs the eternal candle, while to one side is a brass *Hanukkiah*. An embroidered floral carpet on the right wall was made by Regina Ottolenghi Artom (1883). The hall leads to the museum, originally the winter temple. Since 1984 it has displayed ceremonial objects, vestments, period photographs, and Asti-rite liturgical manuscripts. Practiced by the communities of Asti, Fossano, and Moncalvo (hence the name *Appam* rite, from the Jewish initials of the three localities), the Asti rite continued old French liturgical traditions, even after they had been abandoned in France. Asti is the only surviving community of the three: the site of the old cemetery at Fossano can still be made out today, and at Moncalvo a plaque was raised in 2001 on the façade of the synagogue (no. 29, Piazza Castello). The Moncalvo synagogue was closed in 1939 and the furnishings taken to Israel.

An unusual cemetery

The cemetery is in Via Martiri Israeliti. Opened in 1806, it was the community's second burial place. Large family tombs, at times enhanced with statues, commemorate some great men (like Isacco Artom), enabling visitors to reconstruct two centuries of the community's history.

According to documents of 1377, at a place called Biella Piazzo, a certain Giacomino Giudeo exercised the profession of innkeeper. This fragmentary piece of documentary evidence is rather tantalizing because the profession of innkeeper was not commonly exercised by Jews. Later information mentions there was a continuous Jewish presence from 1577 — mainly money lenders and merchants. In 1723 a tiny ghetto was established between Vicolo del Bellone and Corso del Piazzo where, according to the census ordered by the Savoy in 1761, twenty-six people lived; their number rose to around one hundred at the beginning of the 20th century.

At that time Biella was a flourishing textile center and the Jews played a leading role in its industrial development. The recurrent surnames were Jona (and the Italian version Colombo) and Olivetti (the family moved to Ivrea, where it founded the well-known manufacturing company of the same name), Vitale (originally from Alessandria), Levi, Sacerdoti, Clava, Morel, and Vallabrega. The typical leading figures at the time of emancipation were liberal-minded and well integrated into society, as is demonstrated by some illustrious men: Emanuele Jona, an engineer at Pirelli; Giacomo Debenedetti, literary critic and writer; Vittorio and Vittoriano Olivetti; and Umberto Diena.

Only one Jew, Giuseppe Waimberg, was deported from the city under Fascism. After the war, the already small community dwindled further and was absorbed by the Vercelli community.

The ghetto with a handful of houses

The heart of Jewish life consisted of two streets: Vicolo del Bellone and Corso del Piazzo. These streets have preserved their original 15th-century architectural feel. They consist of long two- to three-story buildings with courtyards and lengthy internal galleries, in some cases converted into passageways for the purposes of safety when moving between houses or to reach the synagogue without going into the street.

The hidden synagogue

The Biella synagogue holds some pleasant surprises in store for the visitor. Situated inside one of the long ghetto buildings, it has an anonymous façade and is entered from a courtyard (no. 3, Vicolo del Bellone), like all the synagogues at the time of the ghetto. The prayer room is rectangular and its arched windows, draped with large red curtains, are on the right and opposite. The arch pattern is echoed on the left wall by a trompe l'œil with festoons like those of the windows. The dominant colors are red and gold.

Altered for the last time in 1893, the internal arrangement of the synagogue has preserved the original layout common to synagogues built before emancipation: the ark is opposite the entrance, while in the middle of the room is the round walnut *bimah*, surrounded by the prayer benches along the long walls. The central position of the *bimah* meant that everyone could participate in the service. After emancipation, synagogues were given a different internal layout, imitating churches, with the *bimah* in front of the ark, at the back of the room, and the congregation standing opposite, more like onlookers than active participants in prayer. In recent years there has been a tendency to return to the older tradition, also in synagogue architecture, and the arrangement with the *bimah* in the middle of the room, the benches around it, and the ark opposite.

The holy ark dates from around 1780. Contemporary with the arks of

Cuneo, Mondovì, and Cherasco, it is in late Baroque style. Painted green and gold, it is framed by two pairs of columns and surmounted by a crown joined to two lunettes with inscriptions of the Tablets of the Law; the red curtains are also embroidered in red and gold.

The simple decoration may be seen as part of the new architectural trends at the end of the 18th century, when French Humanism arrived in Piedmont imposing more sober lines for furnishings (see also Carmagnola). The ark is lit by two side windows and a third above it: the light illuminating the most sacred piece of furniture in the room (because it contains the Tablets of the Law) comes from the east, as if it had arrived directly from Jerusalem.

From the vestibule a short flight of steps leads up to the women's gallery overlooking the prayer room. The synagogue has not been in use for many years now.

The cemetery with photos of the dead

The Biella Jewish cemetery is now a part of the town cemetery in Via dei Tigli. Many of the gravestones have photos of the dead, as in other Piedmont cemeteries (e.g. Asti and Alessandria). Forbidden by the Jewish religion, this practice reveals how far the small group was assimilated after emancipation. Among the graves is the tomb of Camillo Olivetti, who died in 1943 and was buried in the Jewish section despite having converted to the protestant Unitarian Church in 1934.

Synagogue interior. The synagogue was altered in 1893, but maintained the original structure of pre-emancipation temples: an anonymous façade, a central plan inside with the bimah opposite the holy ark and surrounded by benches.

At the end of the 15th and beginning of the 16th century, Jewish money-lenders settled in Carmagnola. After having been ruled by the Marchese of Saluzzo for centuries, the town passed to the House of Savoy in 1588. The Savoy census of 1761 reveals there were 110 Jews in the town, in twenty-three families. The group grew to 171 people in 1801, and then gradually began to wane. Now there are no Jews left in town and the synagogue and cemetery are cared for by the Turin community.

A harmonious prayer room

Carmagnola boasts one of the finest and most harmonious synagogues in Piedmont (no. 8, Via Bertini), and arguably the whole of Italy. The anonymous façade of the 18th-century building gives no inkling that inside there is a place of worship. From the ground floor, a spiral staircase leads up to the first-floor hall. A laver (wash basin) stands beside the entrance to the room. Another flight of stairs leads up to the women's gallery on the second floor, screened by a close-knit wooden grate. Restoration work carried out by the Piedmont Region has been underway on the building for over twenty years and is still not complete. The foundations have been restored, the furnishings renovated, and the room with all its decorations refurbished. Long meticulous work by craftsmen and architects has restored the synagogue to its former glory, highlighting the rich exuberant Piedmont Baroque style.

The almost square-plan prayer room (8.5 × 10 m [28 × 33 ft.]) has a terracotta floor and is lit by seven windows framed by stuccoes. Other decorations along the walls include cartouches with Biblical verses. Since the Jewish religion does not allow the use of images, Hebrew writings are used here as decorative elements. Five 18th-century gilded wood chandeliers hang from the exposed beams of the ceiling. Set along the perimeter walls, the benches are 17th century and probably came from an earlier synagogue.

The octagonal bimah and a detail of its decoration. Dated 1766, the bimah stands in the middle of a square-plan room, lit by seven windows framed by stuccowork. Opposite is the ark from the same period, decorated with twisted columns at its sides and doors with symbolic images.

Dated 1766, the Ashkenazi-type octagonal *bimah* is made of painted wood with inlaid work. The small twisted columns support a baldachin: each beam starts from a medallion on which is painted a word. When run together the individual words recreate a passage from the Bible (Ezekiel 11, 16): "Yet will I be to them as a little sanctuary in the countries where they shall come." The holy ark is enhanced by two twisted columns at the sides. Its doors are decorated both inside and outside with inlaid work depicting symbolic images: the Temple of Jerusalem, the seven-branched candelabrum (*menorah*), the Tablets of the Law, and the Sacrificial Altar. The pediment is decorated with gilded spiraling acanthus leaves surmounted by the crowned Tablets of the Law and covered by a small baldachin. At either side of the baldachin two oval windows rest virtually on pilasters set against the walls at the sides of the ark. Hebrew epigraphs run along the walls between the windows as an ornamental motif, while copper and glass chandeliers hang from the ceiling.

Via Bertini — together with Via delle Cherche, Via Benso, and Via Baldessano — is in the area where the ghetto was created in 1723. Called L'Isola delle Cierche ("Island of Chains"), this area was chosen because it was off the usual route of Christian processions.

First used in 1863, the cemetery (the Carmagnola Jews' second burial place) is now part of the town cemetery in Via Papa Giovanni XXIII.

A town at the heart of battles

A group of Jews settled in Casale Monferrato after the expulsion from Spain due to the Inquisition in 1492. At that time the town was part of the feudal Marquisate of Monferrat, ruled by the Paleologi, who remained in power until 1533. In 1536 Casale passed to the Gonzaga, Dukes of Mantua, and then to the minor branch Gonzaga Nevers. Lastly, in 1708 it was annexed to the Duchy of Savoy. For almost two centuries the Monferrato area was plagued by wars, and the Jews partly funded the defenses in order to stay on in the town. The community was always subject to a number of restrictions. In 1611 there was even a case of a ritual murder. Initially moneylenders, the Jews also engaged in commerce (jewels, lace, brocades, and spices), and obtained the monopoly for the sale of playing cards and the tender for salt. In 1643 they also won the tender to supply wheat to the French army billeted at Casale Monferrato and for the construction of the fortifications. In 1724 the Savoy enclosed the Jews in the ghetto where, according to the 1761 census, 673 people lived. After the French Revolution and during the Napoleonic occupation (1799–1814) the gates of the ghetto were demolished. Reintroduced with the restoration of the monarchy, they were eliminated for good in 1848 with the emancipation ordered by Charles Albert of Savoy. At that time there were 850 Jews at Casale Monferrato, but by 1931 their numbers had fallen to 112 and today there are only a dozen. The community continues to function, although the synagogue is only opened for services a few times a year. In 1995 the synagogue celebrated five hundred years of life.

The pulpit was added in 1896 to emulate those found in Christian large churches. It was reached by a stair (now demolished) and today simply has a decorative function.

Synagogue interior. The rectangular room is lit by fourteen large windows. The two-story women's gallery runs around three sides and is closed by embellished lacquered grates. Richly decorated, this temple is the finest example of Piedmontese Baroque synagogue architecture.

The Piedmontese Baroque synagogue

The synagogue at no. 44, Vicolo Salomone Olper, is the community's third temple in chronological order. Used since 1599, the prayer room was extended and underwent radical alterations.

Similar to the other houses in the quarter, the synagogue exterior has an anonymous look. Only a high row of windows reveals the presence of the synagogue inside. Before you come to the prayer room there is a large hall (3.7 × 13.4 m [12 × 44 ft.]) continuing into a colonnade (16.8 × 3.3 m [55 × 10.5 ft.]) round a small internal courtyard (16.8 × 5.7 m [55 × 18.5 ft.]).

The prayer room (18 × 9 m [59 × 29.5 ft.]; 9 m [29.5 ft.] high) is roughly rectangular in shape. Daylight is provided by fourteen large windows (seven on each long side). The two-story women's gallery runs round three sides and overlooks the prayer room with twenty-one large windows screened by gilded and lacquered wooden grates: fourteen date from the 17th century, while the seven forming the long wing of the gallery on the first floor are 18th century. These two floors now house a museum. The lunetted barrel-vault ceiling, from which gilded chandeliers hang, rests on the eastern and western walls, which contain the windows and grates of the women's gallery. The ceiling and window bays are decorated with paintwork and stuccoes gilded with pure gold leaf and partly with the more economic "Mecca-like" gilding, i.e., transparent gold-colored paint on a green-blue background, imitating the sky.

When restoration work began in 1968, the walls were covered by a layer of grime, but also some dark bands that the Jews of Casale Monferrato had painted in sign of mourning for the death of Charles Albert. The restoration work has re-created the original colors for the walls and decorations. As a point of

interest for visitors, one small dark section has been left intact, to show what the color was like before the restoration.

The area dedicated to the officiants (with the *bimah* and ark) is raised from the floor. The area is closed by a wrought-iron gate, painted green with some parts in gold leaf. Modified through the addition of a marble balustrade, the area is now entered by small side gates. In the middle is the *bimah* (1765), set in front of the Neoclassical holy ark (1761). Decorated with precious wood and capitals, the *bimah* was given its present appearance after being further embellished in 1787, endowing it with a clear late Piedmontese Baroque influence.

The central body is surmounted by a pediment and supported by wooden columns. The Corinthian capitals and the oak branch and leaf decorations in the tympanum are made of gold. The doors are made of darker wood and inside are painted light blue. Above them is a decoration with the Ten Commandments in Hebrew, the seven-branched candelabrum, and the Ark of the Alliance. Used as a cupboard for ceremonial objects, the ark interior is upholstered in red damask, with gilded sections including figures in relief.

On the side walls of the room are two large brown-tinted stucco decorations: on the right is Jerusalem and, on the left, Hebron with the Tombs of the Fathers. A third stuccowork indicates the original entrance to the temple. On the left of the ark is a pulpit designed by the architect Lucca in 1896. This element is not part of the Jewish tradition and was added after emancipation to imitate Christian churches. The pulpit was once reached by steps, which have now been eliminated, and it has become a decorative element. Two rows of walnut benches face the *bimah* and the ark, according to the arrangement in synagogues after emancipation. At the sides of the ark are two 10th-century candelabra made of embossed bronze with eighty candle-holders each. The gilded stuccowork and Hebrew inscriptions on the walls in the temple interior create fine decorative elements, together with the curved wooden grates

concealing the two women's galleries. The decoration of the walls is exuberant: alongside friezes and cartouches are white Carrara marble stones with Hebrew inscriptions. Arranged in three rows, the inscriptions may be divided into those quoting Psalms (first and third row) and those dedicated to historical events and information connected with the construction and embellishments of the synagogue (second row). Lastly, from the historical point of view, there is a very interesting stone plaque concerning the emancipation of 1848. It is the only inscription in both Hebrew and Italian.

The Jewish museum

Opened in 1969, the Museum of Jewish Art and Ancient History occupies the two floors of the women's galleries and some of the adjacent rooms. A modern section, called the Museum of Light, has recently been added in the basement floor. It features works made by contemporary artists illustrating the festivity of *Hanukkah*. The overall museum is divided into various sections: the prayer and the Sabbath room; the silver objects and fabric rooms; and the education rooms dedicated to festivities and the cycle of life. Consisting of donations and loans, the whole artistic heritage of the museum is on show: i.e., mainly furnishings connected to worship and prayer as well as objects from daily life and study. There are many silver objects that local craftsmen made by copying originals or from designs. Initially not all of these works could have been by Jewish craftsmen, since Jews in Piedmont were only allowed to exercise the crafts of goldsmithry, silversmithry, and weaving in 1754. The furnishings often bear the embroidered signature of the artists or donating family, a dedication, the year of their execution, and the occasion for which they were presented to the synagogue.

Archives from the origins of the community to the present day

In 1989 the historical archives of the community were installed and re-organized in the south-west wing of the building in two large rooms dedicated to the memory of Livia Pavia Wollemborg. In addition to documents, the rooms house a library collection made up of ancient manuscripts and religious texts. The archives enable us to reconstruct life in the community of Casale Monferrato from the origins up to the present day. They consist of 168 bundles made up of one or more folders (totaling 817), arranged in chronological order. The archives also contain the documentation for the Moncalvo community, which died out before the Second World War.

The streets of the ghetto

The synagogue is at the heart of the ghetto, created in 1741. It was bounded by Via D'Azeglio, Via Balbo, Via Alessandria, and Piazza San Francesco. Today the houses still preserve their original features, such as communicating courtyards and long balconies. These buildings already existed before the ghetto. When they were assigned to the Jews, they were modified to create more living space and to open new passageways so that people could move from house to house without going into the street. In Via Alessandria, on the wall opposite no. 16, you can still see one of the hinges for the gate to the ghetto. A few meters before this, there is a small shrine with a Madonna, probably intended to exorcise the Jewish presence.

The two surviving cemeteries

Casale Monferrato has two cemeteries. The older one at no. 10, Via Negri was used from 1732 to 1893, when the more recent one — still in use — was opened in Via Cardinal Massaia. The first burial in this square-shaped cemetery was recorded in 1904.

The Neoclassical holy ark has a central body with a pediment resting on Corinthian capitals. At the top, the Tablets of the Law are surmounted by a large crown.

A 19th-century embossed silver plate. A pair of blessing hands were chosen as the symbol for the Casale Monferrato Jewish museum.

A well-integrated community

From 1543 the Debenedetti family ran a loan-bank in Cherasco. For many years it was the hub of what was always a small community: fifty-one people in the 1761 Savoy census, and ninety-three in 1842. The Jews engaged in moneylending, silk spinning and weaving, and pottery. In 1723 the ghetto was established in the only building at the corner of Via Marconi and Via Vittorio Emanuele. Some families moved into this building but others continued to live elsewhere. When there was talk of enlarging the quarter from 1831 to 1841, some families (Debenedetti and Jona) still lived outside, while others (e.g., the Levi brothers) were even granted the right to attend fairs and markets. The community was well integrated. Indeed, in 1803 the hundred largest tax-payers in the town included Abramo and Donato Debenedetti. In 1813 Abramo was on the town council. Some Jewish names from Cherasco became famous: the Leone Segre Bank, opened in 1930, lent farmers ten lire interest free from autumn to the following Easter; the engineer Emilio Debenedetti electrified the town and in 1946, at the age of eighty, donated a bell for the town hall tower, asking that it be tolled three times on his death, which eventually took place in 1953.

The holy ark and octagonal bimah (late 18th century) are set opposite each other in the small room overlooking the internal courtyard of the ghetto, created in 1723. The walls of the room are decorated with Hebrew inscriptions of the names of the around fifty families once in the community.

The courtyard ghetto

At no. 4, Via Marconi, a 17th-century building with an anonymous façade houses the small synagogue. A steep stair leads up to the hall, where a stone plaque above a laver (wash basin) bears the names of the benefactors and the date 5557 (1797), possibly a reference to the construction of the synagogue (in which case the group probably already had an earlier synagogue), or the year it was renovated.

An intimate prayer room

The small intimate prayer room is lit on two sides by windows overlooking an internal courtyard. As in the synagogues in Cuneo and Mondovì, the central-plan *bimah* is late Baroque (end of the 18th century), when French Humanism exercised a great influence in Piedmont. This took the form of furnishings with much simpler and classical lines compared to the previous tradition. The *bimah* has an Ashkenazi-type octagonal structure with a baldachin made of brilliantly colored carved wood supported by twisted columns. Also late 18th-century, the holy ark has gilded doors with an inscription of the Ten Commandments, surmounted by crowns. Set against the eastern wall of the room, it receives light from the two windows at its sides. The benches run along the walls, and some lamps hang from the ceiling. Round the perimeter walls are Hebrew inscriptions with the names of the families who once lived in the ghetto. Overlooking the room, the women's gallery is framed by thin painted columns. Opposite the entrance there is a small room once used as the school; its benches and old furnishings are still intact. A side room of the building houses the panels from the exhibition entitled "Jewish Life and Culture — Photographic Documentation of the Jewish Presence in Piedmont in the 18th and 19th Centuries," curated by Giorgio Avigdor in 1984.

The cemetery at the town entrance

Situated at Salita Vecchia, the cemetery only has a few headstones lying flat on the ground.

A group of Provençal Jews had already settled in Cuneo by the early 15th century. Others then followed from Avignon, descendents of the so-called *Juifs du Pape* (Pope's Jews), the Jewish bankers taken by the popes from Rome during their time in Avignon (1308–77). By 1436 the group had already been forced to live in a quarter called an *angulo* at Santa Maria della Pieve, where there were 400 Jews and 1,500 Christians. This quarter was then chosen in 1723 for a ghetto. The 1761 census recorded the presence of 134 inhabitants. Moneylenders and merchants, the Jews were always well integrated into town life. Indeed on the grounds of special merit (i.e., for having saved Cuneo during a siege), they managed to have market-day moved from Saturday to Friday. In the 19th century the community was an important center of Jewish culture thanks to the work of Rabbi Lelio della Torre. Moreover, until 1922 he edited the magazine called the *Vessillo Israelitico* (The Israelite Banner). Today, although small, the group is very active. From 1943 to 1944 there was an internment camp at Borgo San Dalmazzo near Cuneo. Thirty Jews were imprisoned in the camp before being deported to Mathausen.

The synagogue at the heart of the ghetto

The Cuneo synagogue has always been at no. 18, Contrada Mondovì, although over the years it was transformed from being a small prayer room into a large building. The present synagogue is the outcome of 19th-century remodeling.

The sober elegant façade is enhanced by Corinthian strip pilasters. Two small arched doors made of dark wood with stone decorations are surmounted by windows echoing the same motifs. A Hebrew inscription from Exodus runs along the cornice. Set back compared to the rest of the façade, the top floor has three windows separated by columns. From the hall there is a stair up to a small school on the first floor, complete with benches, abacus, and books. The second floor houses the prayer room. Another flight of stairs leads up to the women's gallery, which looks out over a balustrade.

Just before the entrance is a *tzedakah* box, half ripped out, as it was left by vandals during the Second World War. Inside the prayer room, behind the benches, is an old panel with the names of the members of the community. A leather lace hanging beside each name stands for a sum of money that was offered on the day that money could not be physically handled.

The synagogue interior

The square-plan synagogue interior is lit by gilded bronze chandeliers with crystals refracting the light in all directions. The walnut benches are arranged in two rows and face the *bimah* and ark, which are in a raised position. A small wooden balustrade bearing a lamp with a floral decoration encloses the officiants' area.

The late Baroque holy ark dates from 1783: as in the Mondovì ark, the doors are gilded with a stylized *menorah* at the center. Down lower are reproductions of the instruments for sacrifices (Aaron's rod, the olive branch, and a manna pot, on the left). The simple *bimah* is made of dark walnut. On the left of the ark is a pulpit, which is not part of the Jewish tradition, but was placed in the room after emancipation to emulate Christian churches. It is no longer in use.

Under the pulpit you can see a cannonball: on November 8 , 1799, during a siege, it impacted into the wall without exploding. Since then the community has celebrated the "Purim of the bomb," a thanksgiving ceremony for

Synagogue interior. The square room is lit by bronze and crystal lamps. The late Baroque holy ark (dated 1783) has gilded doors decorated with a large stylized menorah.

having been spared. The whole building has recently been renovated. The old unleavened bread oven in the internal courtyard was also restored.

The two streets in the ghetto

The synagogue is situated in the heart of the ghetto, which consisted of two streets closed at the ends by four gates: Contrada Mondovì and Chiusa Pesio. Now all restored, the buildings still have their original low structure with courtyards, passages and long internal balconies.

The cemetery

Situated in Via Bassa San Sebastiano, the modern cemetery, a section of the town cemetery, has been in use since 1936. Urban growth has wiped out all traces of the previous two cemeteries: the earliest (1610–1730) was along the River Gesso, while the second (1730–1936) was situated in Calà degli Ebrei (today Via della Pieve).

The first mention of Jews in Ivrea was in 1443. Then a document of 1547 refers to a loan-bank run by four brothers from Nizza Monferrato who had moved to the town. When the group became larger, it met at Borghetto, near the church of San Grato. But life was often difficult, especially because of the anti-Semitic preaching of the Frati Zoccolanti (the "Sandled Friars" — followers of Bernardino da Siena). After King Henry II of France (1547–1559) conquered Ivrea, he ordered the expulsion of Jews from the city in 1556, but to no avail. The community had always been small and only grew in 17th century under the Savoy, who, however, decreed the creation of the ghetto in 1725. It was established at the foot of the castle in Rua Coperta (which soon became Contrada degli Ebrei, then Rue Napoléon, Via Palma, and lastly today, Via Quattro Martiri). According to the 1761 census, only fifty-seven people lived in the ghetto. In 1801 the ghetto was almost devastated by a plundering peasant rabble, but the local populace came to the Jews' rescue. This event is commemorated by a special Purim. In the 19th century the Jews designed a new synagogue and a cemetery. In 1869 there were 160 (the most ever). Their number had grown due to the nascent industrial development of the town with the creation of the Olivetti typewriter factory. Then decline set in. Today the community only consists of a few people and is a section of the Turin community.

The two synagogues

In a building at no. 24, Via Quattro Martiri, the only street in the ghetto, there are two synagogues, built by the community in the wake of the euphoria after emancipation. The Jews had previously met in a rented room on the fourth floor of an old house. The new synagogue was officially opened on September 24, 1875. At the time the community was around one hundred strong, but the new building almost immediately turned out to be too big and was never used. Having been created by restructuring a preexisting building, by the postwar period the synagogue was already crumbling. In 1980, therefore, the community of Turin ceded the large synagogue to the Ivrea town council in exchange for the restoration of the whole building, leaving the Ivrea community the smaller synagogue. This formula meant the building could be restored (completed in 1999) and the large synagogue reopened to host cultural events in the town.

Now accessed by two separate entrances, the synagogues are on the first floor. The small one, originally intended to be a winter temple, is tiny. It is dominated by a glided carved wooden holy ark, draped in mourning since the death of Charles Albert; alongside is a seven-branched wooden candelabrum.

The large rectangular-plan synagogue has a high-vaulted ceiling and walls decorated with painted marble. Two rows of benches look towards the *bimah* and holy

A 15th-century brass lamp for Hanukkah. *The* hanukkiah *was one of the objects in Jewish art that inspired the most imaginative use of materials, forms, and decorations.*

The prayer room in the large synagogue now hosts cultural events. For services the community has a small adjacent room once used only for daily prayers and during winter.

ark in a raised position. The *bimah* is round and made of walnut. With windows on either side, the ark has two sliding doors made of wood, painted green and gold. On opening, the doors slide back into the wall. They are decorated with sculpted images: the donation of the twelve loaves, the sacred fire, and the Ark of the Alliance. Four columns on either side of the ark conceal two stairs leading to gallery boxes, possibly for use by members of the choir. On the left there is still a pulpit, which is not part of the Jewish tradition. An external flight of stairs is enhanced by majestic cast-iron railings and some lamps, also made of cast iron.

The cemetery

The cemetery at no. 30, Via dei Mulini, the second to be opened in chronological order, has been in use since 1863 and is a section of the town cemetery. A plaque in the cemetery commemorates the Polish Jewish soldiers who died in the hospital of Ivrea during the First World War.

Refugees from France

In 1394 many of the Jews expelled from France crossed the Alps and settled in Piedmont, where many small Jewish centers sprang up, even in rural areas. Moncalvo is one such rural locality.

Proof that the group had distant French origins comes from the fact that the Moncalvo Jews always followed the *Appam* rite in their prayers — a combination of the ancient French and German rites also used in another two Piedmont communities — Asti and Fossano. The name *Appam* seems to derive from the Hebrew initials of these three localities.

A second small group of refugees fleeing the Iberian peninsula in 1492 joined the French group, but despite this addition, overall they were still few in number.

At Moncalvo the Jews ran one of the eighteen loan-banks scattered throughout the Monferrato area in the 16th century. But they also engaged in crafts and were traveling merchants.

In 1732 the ghetto was created between Via General Montanari and Via IV Marzo, near the Castle. According to the 1761 Savoy census, 218 people lived in the ghetto. The streets were set up in the higher part of the town, where the low buildings may still be seen today. Entered directly from the surrounding houses, the synagogue was restored and embellished again in 1860. At this euphoric time of emancipation, an entrance was also created in the main square of the castle (no. 29, Castello) and a Hebrew inscription taken from Isaiah was set on the no longer anonymous façade.

The already small community continued to dwindle until it died out altogether in 1939. The prayer room was first closed and then completely dismantled; in the 1950s the furnishings were taken to Israel.

To commemorate the long Jewish presence in the area, in 2001 the Moncalvo town council raised a plaque on the walls of the old synagogue, for years now a warehouse. The cemetery along the panoramic road for Grazzano, however, is still in use. The earliest graves date back to the 18th century.

Gravestones in the cemetery used since the 18th century. There has been no Jewish community in the town since 1939. Now marked by a plaque on the wall, the synagogue was in the upper part of the ghetto, created in 1732. The synagogue was closed in the 1950s, and the furnishings were taken to Israel.

The Judeo-Piedmontese dialect

In Piedmont, as in other Italian regions like Lazio, the Veneto, Tuscany, and Emilia Romagna, Jews introduced Hebrew expressions – often distorted and Italianized – to the local dialect. This created some original languages with their own independent literatures. Such languages used Hebrew and Aramaic words taken from prayers and scriptures and combined them with expressions from the local dialect. It was a cryptic way of communicating, especially between co-religionaries in order not to be understood by non-Jews, such as servants or shop assistants.

But this language then often became so common that even non-Jews used it.

The writer Primo Levi gives a masterly description of the Judeo-Piedmontese dialect in the short story "Argon" in the collection entitled *The Periodic System*: "It has a remarkable comic force arising from the contrast between the texture of the discourse — the rough, laconic Piedmontese dialect — and the Hebrew additions, ripped from the remote language of our forefathers, sacred and solemn, geologically smoothed by the millennia, like the bed of a glacier."

Many of these dialects were used for plays, verse, and ballads, like *La gran battaja dj' abrei d'Moncalv* ("The great battle of the Moncalvo Jews"). This work in perfect Montferrat dialect mixed with Judeo-Piedmontese expressions describes in detail a great brawl in the Moncalvo ghetto. Everyone was involved until the fight suddenly stopped when the guards arrived. Having survived intact to the present day, this ballad is one of the most interesting examples of the Judeo-Piedmontese dialect from the linguist point of view.

Most of the dialects were no longer spoken after emancipation, when, albeit unwittingly, Jews abandoned everything that set them apart from other Italians.

A Jewish group formed in Mondovì at the end of the 16th century round the family of the banker Aron Sacerdote (1584). A small prayer room was almost immediately opened in the town, also frequented by Jews who lived scattered in the surrounding rural areas, where they worked in the production of silkworms and spinning. In 1724 a ghetto was created at Mondovì Piazzo, in the upper part of the town, and the Jews were forced to quit the countryside and take up residence in the ghetto. The backbone of the small Jewish quarter was Via Vico, from Vicolo Pizzo to Piazza d'Armi, but it also included some houses in Vicolo Pizzo and Via delle Orfane, and one house in Via Massacrà. Possibly because Via Vico was so wide, the ghetto was never closed by gates.

According to the 1761 Savoy census, twelve Jewish families lived in Mondovì, totaling sixty-four people. By 1839 there were 147 Jews and in 1867, the figure peaked at 200. Today there are no longer any Jews in the town and the synagogue and cemetery are cared for by the Turin community.

The quarter in the shadow of the cathedral

The buildings in Via Vico, a long uphill street behind the cathedral, still have an 18th-century appearance. Rows of two- to three-story houses form a single backdrop.

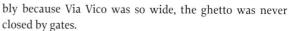

Halfway down the street, at no. 65, there is a small prayer room on the third floor of a building with a totally anonymous façade, giving no outward signs as to what is inside. Next to the large entrance door there is a plaque commemorating Felice Momigliano (1866–1924), a scholar of Italian literature buried in the small Mondovì cemetery.

By going up three flights of narrow stairs, encased between apartments, you come to a small square-shaped synagogue designed at the end of the 18th century, at the same time as the prayer rooms of Cuneo, Biella, and Cherasco.

The prayer room

At the center of the room is an octagonal Ashkenazi-type *bimah* with a baldachin. It is made of carved wood and is enclosed by railings with columns and gilded capitals. Late Piedmontese Baroque in style, this *bimah* is less richly decorated than some others in the area (such as those at Carmagnola or Chieri, made around 1760), but certainly has elegant lines. In addition to the external contemporary influence, the sober decoration may also have been due to the community's lack of financial resources because of the dwindling population in the ghetto.

The gilded holy ark is set against the eastern wall. Twisted columns frame the doors depicting a large single *menorah* (as in the contemporary ark in the Cuneo temple). Above the doors the ark is embellished by the Tablets of the Law. It is lit by two side windows, deliberately positioned so as to cast light from the east — and therefore symbolically from Jerusalem — on the most sacred part of the room (the cabinet containing the Scrolls of the Law). These two windows are the only real external apertures in the room: in fact the window on the left on entering communicates with the women's gallery, while those on the right with painted curtains are trompe l'œil.

From the ceiling hang eight oil lamps and five crystal chandeliers, providing a diffuse light. Along the perimeter walls are inscriptions of Hebrew verses from Isaiah, Psalms, and Leviticus. The dark walnut benches are set against the perimeter walls.

The women's gallery and the school room

Beside the entrance door to the prayer room there is a second door leading to a long balcony. The balcony wall was used for a draining system (it no longer exists) to carry rainwater from the roof to the underground level containing the *mikveh*, or ritual bath. The same balcony provides access to a small room used as the women's gallery, which has an internal window overlooking the main room. The adjacent room was once used as a school. By going out onto the external balcony of this room you can enjoy the extraordinary panoramic view of the surrounding hills.

The cemetery

The Mondovì Jews used the Cuneo cemetery for burying their dead until the period of the ghetto. Then after the population had grown, they were given a cemetery. The first (now demolished to make way for military use) was along the bastions of the citadel. Then from 1865 a section was set aside for Jews in the town cemetery at Mondovì Breo (Viale Cimitero), in the lower part of the town. At the entrance a plaque commemorates the Jews deported from the Mondovì area.

Synagogue interior and the holy ark. The small prayer room is on the third floor of a building in the main street of the ghetto, set up in 1724. An overall impression of wealth is created by the late-Baroque octagonal bimah *in the middle of the room, the gilded ark decorated with twisted columns and a* menorah *on the doors, and the mock drapery painted on the walls.*

The first Jews settled at Saluzzo in 1484. They had come from the nearby town of Piasco, after being expelled by the Marchese Ludovico II. This small group then became the reference point for all those living in the surrounding rural areas. In 1631 the Marquisate of Saluzzo passed to the Savoy. The new rulers established close contacts with Jewish bankers, especially the Calvo brothers, Sabbato di Viterbo, and Joseph Segre. Moneylending was not the only activity exercised by the Saluzzo community. It was also celebrated for its jewel makers (the Segre family) and textile merchants. In 1724 Victor Amadeus II created the first ghetto, whose whereabouts, however, is unknown. A second quarter called Ghetto Nuovo was opened in 1795, near the cathedral, in an alley called Vicolo Venezia, later Chiossetto Venezia and now Via dei Deportati Ebrei to commemorate the twenty-nine deportees (out of a total of forty-two Jews in the town). The Saluzzo Jews eagerly took part in the first wave of emancipation. Raffaele Segre, a town councillor, gave a speech under the Tree of Liberty in 1798. In 1848 lamps in honor of Charles Albert were set up at the entrance to the ghetto with inscriptions in Hebrew and Italian. The Saluzzo community is now a section in the Turin community.

The octagonal bimah is raised on a platform in front of the ark. The two pieces of furniture are 18th-century and come from an earlier synagogue. The rectangular prayer room is lit by eight large windows. It is entered from the courtyard of the old ghetto, created in 1724.

The prayer room. Remodeled in its present form in 1832 on the site of an earlier synagogue, it was restored in 2001. At that time some frescoes were found on the ceiling with four symbolic images, unique in their kind in Italian synagogues.

The synagogue with frescoes

The large courtyard at the center of the houses in the old ghetto seems almost to be in a time warp. With no outwards signs, the synagogue is on the top floor in one of these houses (no. 29, Via dei Deportati Ebrei). The outcome of restructuring an existing 18th-century building in 1832, the synagogue was last restored in 2001. Entered through a gilded wooden door, the large prayer room (with a capacity for 300 people) has a rectangular plan, eight windows (five open onto the street and three onto the courtyard). The parallel rows of benches face the raised *bimah* and holy ark (both 18th century). These two pieces of furniture came from an earlier synagogue, while an 18th-century holy ark, the Tablets of the Law carved in marble, lamps, and various other objects were taken to Israel in the 1950s. The remaining ark is made of gilded carved wood and has internal and external mirrors. It is the only holy ark in Piedmont with curved — as opposed to straight — doors. An octagonal raised platform links it to the *bimah*. The vaulted ceiling has 18th-century frescoes, uncovered by chance in recent restoration work. This is the only example of frescoes in a synagogue in Piedmont, or Italy for that matter: four symbolic images (from Exodus and the Book of Kings) stand out from a sky-blue background. Above the ark are the Tabernacle, red curtains tied by gilded chains and, on the right, a seven-branched candelabrum, the Ark of the Alliance, and the altar for the twelve loaves. Hebrew inscriptions and a floral fascia complete the whole. Another Hebrew inscription runs all the way round the ceiling perimeter. The gilded bronze and crystal chandeliers spread a diffuse light. Screened by an undulating wooden grate, the women's gallery rests on four columns and is reached by a stair up from the entrance. Alongside the women's gallery there was once a small school.

The cemetery

The community's third cemetery is at no. 5, Via Lagnasco. At the entrance is a plaque to the twenty-nine deportees (there is also one in the town hall).

A small group of Jews had settled in Turin by 1424, a little later than elsewhere in Piedmont. Since then Jews have always lived in Turin. At first they were concentrated in the area called Studium, i.e., the "university" area. They soon grew in numbers, as evidenced by the presence of a cemetery and kosher butcher.

Jewish life was governed from 1430 by the "Savoy Statute" introduced by the Duke of Savoy, Amadeus VIII. Although, on the one hand, these laws did grant some concessions, on the other, they also introduced heavy restrictions: wearing the badge was compulsory (but Christians were forbidden from striking or insulting Jews); they had to live in separate quarters, closed by gates, but this rule was never enforced for over two centuries; and there was a ban on constructing new synagogues. Later regulations extended and modified the initial rules. In 1679 it was decided a ghetto should be created. This was the first and only ghetto in Piedmont until 1723: called Vecchio Ghetto ("Old Ghetto"), it occupied the area of the former hospice of the Carità, bounded by Via Maria Vittoria, Via Bogino, Via Principe Amedeo, and Via San Francesco di Paola. In 1702 the population of the old ghetto was 752. By 1724 the area was too small for such a large community, which had grown to over a 1,000 after the arrival of Jews from Cuorgné. The nearby street block of San Benedetto was added and entered from Via del Moro (now Via Des Ambrois).

After emancipation in 1848, the ghetto emptied and in the euphoria of their recently acquired freedom, the Jews decided to express their new status by building a synagogue intended to become a major landmark in the city's architectural heritage. In 1859 they turned, therefore, to Alessandro Antonelli, the leading architect of the day, who began to build what was supposed to be the symbol of emancipation: the Mole Antonelliana. But the building never became a Jewish place of worship. Unable to meet the spiraling costs, in 1875 the community ceded the building, while still under

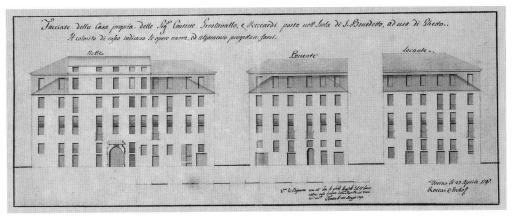

The large synagogue was designed by Enrico Petiti and opened in 1884, when the community abandoned the construction of the building known as the Mole Antonelliana, originally intended to be the emancipation synagogue.

Design for an extension to a ghetto building, late 18th century. Created in 1679, at its largest, the ghetto consisted of five courtyards with a total of 527 rooms.

construction, to the city council in exchange for the land where today's synagogue stands.

After emancipation and until the two World Wars the Turin Jews were increasingly well integrated into the city's social fabric. They included leading intellectuals, writers, artists, university professors, businessmen and, during the Fascist period, a large group of active anti-Fascists who later became partisans. Deportation decimated the community. But after the war, community life picked up again with new vigor. Today the thousand-strong Turin community is a medium-sized community on the Italian Jewish scene, responsible for the sections of Alessandria, Asti, Acqui, Carmagnola, Cherasco, Chieri, Cuneo, Ivrea, Mondovì, and Saluzzo.

Jewish Turin offers visitors two main attractions: the old ghetto, giving a good idea of the past environment in which Turin Jewish life grew and developed for around a century, and the community building (with two synagogues, a library, social center, community offices, school, and rest home), representing the present. These two elements — past and present — are complementary and help visitors to reach a deeper understanding of both.

The ghetto with five courtyards

Not far from Piazza San Carlo, the ghetto area has preserved its original structure, even though all the buildings have been restored or restructured. Initially there were five courtyards (Cortile Grande, Cortile dei Preti, Cortile della Vite, Cortile della Taverna, and Cortile della Terrazza), linked to each other by covered passageways called the "dark porticoes." The buildings originally had a total of 527 rooms, which were then also divided vertically to exploit the space better and create more rooms. On the ground floor were shops. Some of them became dwellings when the population in the ghetto was at its height (1,300 people in 1794).

A gate is still easily recognizable at no. 5, Via Maria Vittoria (formerly Via San Filippo) and the secondary entrance in Via San Francesco di Paola led into Cortile Grande ("Large Courtyard"), the heart of the ghetto, containing the Italian-rite temple, the school, and, in the basement, the ritual bath. This adjoined Cortile della Vite ("Vine Courtyard"), and ended at Via d'Angennes, the street with the Spanish-rite synagogue. The next courtyard was Cortile dei Preti (Priests' Courtyard), the former cloister of a convent, leading by means of stairs and passages to the Cortile della Terrazza (Terrace Courtyard), where the oven for the unleavened bread was located. The

Ghetto Nuovo ("New Ghetto") also had a gate (still recognizable) at no. 2, Via Des Ambrois (formerly Via del Moro). This was the site of the third (a German-rite) synagogue. These two large street blocks were abandoned by the wealthy immediately after emancipation, while for obvious reasons the poorer inhabitants left more slowly.

The synagogue

While exploring the ghetto area gives the visitor a great insight into Jewish history, a visit to the synagogue provides glimpses of modern Jewish life. Situated not far from the Porta Nuova railway station, between Via Sant'Anselmo and Via San Pio v, the main entrance to the synagogue is on a small square recently renamed after the great Turin writer Primo Levi.

Designed in Moorish style by Enrico Petiti when the community gave up building the Mole Antonelliana, it was officially opened in 1884. In 1942 it was struck by a bomb, leaving only the outside walls and the two towers in the façade intact. The temple was rebuilt in 1949, and enhanced with marble and stuccowork. The most recent restoration was in 1994.

The building has a three-part façade: at the center a large rose window is set above the entrance with arches; two crenellated corner towers (there are four of these towers, 27 m [88 ft.] high) are capped with onion domes. Two side walls, made of two-tone stone, have arched porticos.

Beyond a massive gate, a few steps lead up to the interior. The prayer room measures 35 × 22 × 16 m [114 × 72 × 52.5 ft.] and has a capacity of 1,400 people: 1,000 on the lower floor (700 seated and 300 standing) and 400 in the women's gallery on the upper floor. Resting on two large granite columns, the women's gallery runs round three sides and is reached by

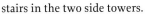

The small synagogue was built in 1972 in the basement of the large temple to a design by the architect Giorgio Olivetti. The central-plan room has furnishings from Chieri.

Three hand pointers for reading the Torah. Used to follow the readings of the Torah without touching the sacred scriptures with the hands, these ceremonial objects inspired craftsmen to work in a highly imaginative, artistic way.

stairs in the two side towers.

The holy ark is set against the eastern wall, while the *bimah* now stands in the center, surrounded by benches, in the traditional arrangement. The large synagogue is only used for major festivities. In 1972 a small Italian-rite temple was created in the basement for everyday purposes.

The small synagogue was designed by Giorgio Olivetti in the form of an amphitheater with vaulted ceilings and walls made of rough exposed brick. Like synagogues before emancipation, it has a central plan. The furnishings are from the former prayer room at Chieri. At the center is an Ashkenazi-type *bimah*, varnished in gold and blue lacquer with a baldachin resting on small twisted columns. Made around 1760, it is late Baroque in style and contemporary with the Carmagnola *bimah*, and in all likelihood by the same craftsman.

The holy ark also comes from the Chieri synagogue and is similar to the ark from Trino Vercellese (now in Israel). It is embellished with blue marble-like columns and gilded Corinthian capitals. When the doors are closed there is a perspective view of a prayer room; at the center the image is complemented by two columns supporting a small arch, with, behind, a rolled-up curtain like a raised drop-curtain. The overall effect is to suggest the wings of a stage. The picture in perspective probably depicts the Temple of Jerusalem: the two columns, Jachin and Boaz, set at the entrance to the Temple, while the dome is reminiscent of the Dome of the Rock of Jerusalem, held to be the image of the destroyed Temple in the Diaspora.

A wall made of perforated bricks separates the central area from a small prayer room containing the 18th-century ark from the German-rite temple in Ghetto Nuovo. It had previously been in the old rest home in Piazza Santa Giulia. In 1963, when the rest home was closed, the ark was moved to the small temple. The doors of the ark are darkened in sign of mourning for the death of Charles Albert (1849) and have two gold pictures alluding to Jerusalem.

The building also houses the Benvenuto and Alessandro Terracini Archives of Jewish Traditions and Customs. This important library of Judaica is in the rooms of the social center.

Four cemeteries

The Turin community has had four cemeteries since the 15th century. The first was situated at the end of what is now Via Tommaseo (formerly Porta Marmorea). In 1668 it was transferred to a site just off the street going from the citadel to the Arsenale Nuovo, now Via Matteotti. Closed in 1772 at the orders of the king, it was replaced by a third cemetery near Porta di Po, now the Vanchiglia area. After this cemetery was also closed, the first Jewish section was created in the city cemetery in Corso Regio Parco (no. 80/90) in 1867. Today there are seven Jewish sections in the cemetery.

A small community with a large synagogue

A small Jewish group lived in the area of the church of San Lorenzo in Vercelli as early as the 15th century. Only after 1492 did the number of inhabitants in the town rise with the arrival of refugees from Spain. In fact one of the most commonly found surnames among Vercelli Jews was Segre, after the Spanish river of the same name. The twenty-four families in the community were concentrated in the area between Corso della Libertà and Via Ponti and Via Garrone. They engaged in moneylending and trading. In 1727, when the ghetto was about to be created, this area was not taken into consideration because it lay on the route of Christian processions. In 1740, after discussions and protests, an area was chosen between Via Foa, Via Gioberti, Via Castelnuovo

Two views of the synagogue interior. Designed by Marco Treves and built by Giuseppe Locarni, the synagogue was officially opened in 1878, but immediately turned out to be too large for the needs of the community, which at the time numbered 600. The basilica-plan building with a nave and two aisles is currently being restored.

delle Lanze, and Via Morosone. Twenty-nine families (a total of 158 people) had to move to this area. With the arrival of Napoleon in Italy, the gates of the ghetto were pulled down, but only to be raised again with the restoration of the monarchy, until emancipation in 1848 finally ended the period of segregation. In the ghetto area there was an oratory that functioned until 1863, when the community decided to build the present synagogue. At this time there were 600 Jews living in Vercelli. Their number gradually fell and by the time the synagogue was actually opened in 1878, the building was already too big for the community. Fifteen Jews were deported from Vercelli during the Second World War. They are commemorated, together with four from Biella, in a plaque in the cemetery. In the postwar period the community began a slow but inexorable decline.

The old ghetto and the Neo-Moorish synagogue

The four streets where the Jews were once enclosed have preserved their original appearance. Walking down these streets in the historic center, we can reconstruct the position of the gates: the first was at the crossroads between Via Foa and Via Gioberti; the second was where the street narrows in Via Foa, before giving onto the square of San Giuliano; the third was halfway down Via Castelnuovo delle Lanze; and the fourth (called *la portina* — "the small door"), at the time always closed, was in the bottleneck of Via Morosone. The synagogue is situated at no. 56, Via Foa. Neo-Moorish in style, it was constructed on the site of an earlier oratory. Designed by the architect Marco Treves, who was born in Vercelli but an adoptive Florentine (he took part in constructing the more or less contemporary temple in Florence), the synagogue was built by Giuseppe Locarni. The central section of the façade is dominated by a sculpture of the Tablets of the Law, surmounted by a rose window with above, a crenellation, and to the sides towers crowned with onion domes. The two side sections are also crenellated and have domed towers. The building is clad in two-tone strips of stone. A portico leads into the interior, which has a basilica-type plan with a nave and two aisles. Supported by columns, the women's gallery is above the aisles and parallel to the nave. The benches in the nave face the *bimah* and holy ark, situated to the rear of the synagogue in a raised position. Hebrew inscriptions run along the perimeter walls beneath the women's gallery. Large stained-glass windows and the dome skylight filter light, contributing to the majestic overall atmosphere. The synagogue has been closed for several years for restoration work.

Jewish art and ceremonial objects

Books have always been important objects for the Jews, a people that has made study, writing, and literature the pillars of its existence. From the 13th century, manuscripts, and especially illuminated manuscripts, were one of their most interesting art forms. Jews usually had to commission them, however, from Christian artists. In addition to the illuminated books, some marriage contracts were real masterpieces (such as the illuminated *ketuboth* made at Lugo di Romagna), and the decorations and techniques evolved over time.

Resorting to Christian craftsmen was a constant feature in the whole of Italian Jewish art. In fact the Jews were not allowed to enroll in the medieval arts and crafts guilds and, therefore, could not work as craftsmen. Moreover, the fact the Jewish religion forbade representing human figures conditioned, but did not effectively limit artistic production. There was an art, however, which was typically the domain of all Jewish women: embroidery. It spread and developed among Jewish women out of necessity, since one of the few trades the men were allowed to practice during the ghetto centuries was that of second-hand cloth merchant. The women, therefore, had to wash and mend old clothes, before they were put up for sale. Thus the art of mending became the very refined and professional art of embroidery. The embroidered fabrics were signed and dated and often particularly precious, because they had come from ceremonial clothes that the nobles frequently exchanged or threw out. The embroidered fabrics became decorative elements in homes but especially in synagogues, as ornaments for the Scrolls of the Law, that is the books of the *Pentateuch*, the typical example of scriptures kept in the holy ark. Always made of silver, the ornaments embellishing the sacred texts were the real treasures of the synagogues. Conversely, the synagogue walls were bare and decorated only with biblical inscriptions and simple friezes. The scrolls are covered by an ornamental cape called the *meil*, made of precious fabrics. The exteriors are embellished with three objects: a large crown or *keter*, resting on the upper section, and two large ferrules projecting from inside the crown. These ferrules are called the *rimonim* and are shaped like towers or small bells. On the side is an ornamenta

Wooden table with inlaid work. Constructed by cabinetmaker Francesco Pucci in the mid-18th century, this table is now in the Civic Museum, Cagli. The same craftsman also made the furnishings for the Urbino synagogue.

Embroidered curtain for the holy ark, detail. The curtain was placed in front of the ark containing the Scrolls of the Law and is considered to be one of its ornaments.

The *aron* in turn is closed by a curtain or *parocheth*, finely embroidered with various motifs: the two columns from the Temple of Jerusalem, inscriptions, decoration of leaves and fruit, and often the date and name of the family which presented it the synagogue.

The Jewish artistic heritage is also the outcome of a tradition, thousands of year old, whereby religious ceremonies were held in houses with the whole family r united. These ceremonies required that the rite be honored with particularly valuab and beautiful objects, such as the two candelabra lit on Shabbat, the lamps with a oil vessel in the form of a star with seven or more branches, and other items, inclu ing the cup for *Kiddush* (the blessing over wine). The form of the cup is prescribed tradition and is so old that it is even found in medieval manuscripts. In addition the *Kiddush* cups, glasses in the form of goblets were also used. They had four "fee and were decorated with Hebrew citations dictated by the rite. There are also som very original decorations, like those on the early 19th-century examples produced i Eastern Europe by Jewish goldsmiths: one cup of repoussé silver has a view Jerusalem and the Wailing Wall as well as Hebrew inscriptions. To mark the end the Sabbath, elegant scent-holders for *besamim* are used for the ceremony of *Ha dalah*, when perfumed essences are scattered to bless the week about to begin.

The scent-holders are usually made of silver and shaped like towers to remind the Tower of David, described in the Song of Songs. But some Central European exam ples are shaped like small fish, symbols of fecundity, and others like birds alluding t the popular Yiddish song of the Sabbath evening in which birds sing the glory of th Lord.

The lamp of *Hanukkah* is what has most caught the imagination of artist enabling them to create lamps with very varied forms and decorations: some ar enhanced by biblical citations, others with vegetal or animal decorations, and some violating for once the orthodox rules, with human figures. They all have one el ment in common: the number of branches. It must always be eight plus the *sham

Embroidered bands for wrapping the Scrolls of the Law. The fabrics were made and embroidered by the women of the house and presented to the synagogue on special occasions such as a birth, Bar-Mitzvah, or marriage.

mash, called the "server," because it was used to light the individual candles in the eight days of the feast. There are also various dishes and objects used for the Passover meal or *seder*, when the whole family sits at the table for the ritual dinner. The most interesting piece is the *Seder* plate with the symbols of the dinner, arranged in a preestablished order: the shank bone, bitter herbs, *charoset*, and *karpas* (vegetable).

A medallion called the *shaddai* is hung on a newborn baby's cradle to protect it from Lilith, Eve's rival, who might send evil spirits to kidnap the child. This is a lucky charm, usually made of silver, but also of tin or poorer alloys. The inscription *shaddai*, means the Almighty, one of God's names. On the doorposts of Jewish houses there is a small case, called a *mezuzah*, containing two passages from Deuteronomy on parchment, recalling the sacred nature of the house. Made of silver, brass, carved wood, or even poorer materials such as bamboo, the *mezuzoth* are always suitably decorated – some with the holy ark containing the Scrolls of the Law.

All of these objects have remained unchanged over time in terms of form and material. Only after emancipation did the Jews begin to express new artistic forms (such as monumental synagogue architecture) by following those artistic trends in painting and sculpture which they had previously ignored.

Today the Jewish artistic heritage is jealously guarded in museums and libraries as tangible evidence of their high artistic standards, often achieved even at the times of greatest hardship and discrimination. Many of the furnishings once in Italian synagogues now live on in Israeli temples, such as the Italian synagogue in Jerusalem, which was reconstructed in 1952 with original 18th-century furnishings from the temple of Conegliano Veneto. This is not an isolated example. In the postwar period many Italian communities, annihilated by deportation and emigration, could not revive normal community life. At that time the head of the Italian Jewish communities – with the memory of destruction still painfully fresh – chose to send to Israel the furnishings and objects from those places where there was no longer any community life. This seemed the best way to avoid losing them forever.

At the court of the Gonzaga

The golden age of Jewish life in Mantua was during the Duchy of the Gonzaga. Under their rule in the 16th century, there were so many Jews in the duchy (over 3,000) that they accounted for seven percent of the entire population. For about a century the community gravitated round the splendid Renaissance court. There were celebrated Jewish physicians (the Portaleone family), actors (Leone de' Sommi and his sister Madame Europa), and musicians (Salomone Rossi). But then in 1612, the political situation changed radically and the Jews were forced to live in a ghetto. This marked the beginning of a period of poverty, made even more dramatic by the sack of Mantua by the Austrians (1620–1630), and an ensuing outbreak of the plague, which the Jews were accused of spreading. The continuous fierce insults drove many of them to leave the city: some (around 600 people) were offered refuge by the Prince of Bozzolo; but others (around a 1,000) tried to cross the River Po on rafts and drowned after being carried away by currents. After these tragic events the community was almost halved, and it began a slow inexorable decline.

In 1708 Mantua became part of the dominions of the Habsburgs of Austria. In 1791 the imperial authorities issued *Patenti* (letters patent) granting initial freedoms to the Jews. When the Napoleonic army arrived, Jews actively engaged in the struggle against the old regime, and shared the new French ideals; a rabbi from the Mantua community, Abraham Vita Cologna, took part in the proceedings of the Napoleonic Synedrion.

Other localities in the Mantua area

From the 16th century there was a flourishing widespread Jewish presence in the rural areas around Mantua, and in some places it continued until the beginning of the 20th century. In the golden age of the Gonzaga, there were small groups in forty-eight localities in the area bounded by the rivers Oglio, Mincio, and Po, where the Jews ran loan-banks. Two centuries on there were only about ten such localities. Many still have some obvious reminders of the Jewish presence: synagogues, as at Sabbioneta; curious details, as at Rivarolo Mantovano, where the old synagogue prayer room, now a bar, is frescoed with a portrait of Garibaldi; or a crumbling rabbi's house at Ostiano, and likewise at Revere. There are also cemeteries at Pomponesco, Bozzolo, and Viadana. Lastly, some synagogue furnishings survive, like the two holy arks from Sermide – one is now in the Eastern Sephardic oratory in Milan, and the other in the Italian synagogue in Jerusalem, Israel.

Patriots and martyrs

After having been involved in the Risorgimento wars (Giuseppe Finzi from Rivarolo Mantovano was one of the Belfiore martyrs), the Jews gradually began to abandon the rural areas and then Mantua itself. By the early 19th century many had moved, especially to Milan, to form the nucleus of the new community there.

During the persecutions in the Second World War, a group of Jews — mostly old people from the Milan rest home — were locked up in the community building in Via Giovi and then, a few days later, deported to the Nazi extermination camps. Today the community numbers a few dozen people.

The reconstructed synagogue

The ghetto area was radically transformed by demolition work in 1904. The perimeter, however, can still be made out as well as the position of the four gates: the first was at the corner of Via Giustiziati; the second in Piazza Concordia (formerly Piazza dell'Aglio); the third in Via Spagnoli (formerly Contrada degli Orefici Ebrei); and the fourth in Via Bertani (formerly Contrada del Tubo).

In Piazza Concordia there were once three synagogues, all German rite: the Porta synagogue (1588), and the synagogues of Ostiglia and Beccheria (or the "large synagogue") both dating from 1595. The first two were closed for worship in 1846, and the third in 1900. They were then all demolished during the redevelopment of the quarter.

The main artery in the ghetto was Via Bertani. At the corner of this street and Via Scuola Grande there were also two Italian-rite synagogues: the Norsa

Synagogue interior. Opened in 1902, this synagogue is a copy of the Norsa Torrazza synagogue built in 1513 but then demolished when the ghetto was redeveloped. The room has the same plan, structure, and decorations as the earlier synagogue, whose furnishings it inherited.

Torrazzo synagogue of 1513 (rebuilt in 1751) and the large Italian synagogue of 1635 (rebuilt in 1749). The former was faithfully reconstructed at no. 11, Via Giovi from 1899 to 1902 and is still in use. The large Italian synagogue, on the other hand, was demolished in 1938 and its furnishings were taken to the Yeshivah Ponevez, at Benei Brak, Israel, in 1956 and are still there today.

There was also a third synagogue in Via Bertani, at the corner with Via San Francesco di Paola. Called the Cases synagogue, it was built in 1595 and demolished in 1929. Its holy ark was also taken to Israel and is now in the chief rabbinate offices at Heichal Shlomo, Jerusalem.

The Rabbi's House

The building at no. 4, Via Bertani is commonly referred to as the "Rabbi's House." Possibly once inhabited by rabbis, it is completely decorated with friezes and masks. Its fine 17th-century façade is enhanced by six panels with images from Biblical stories. Over the entrance door is a small balcony with wrought-iron railings.

Some streets — like Via Governolo, Piazza Bertazzoli, Via Norsa, and Piazza Sermide — give a much clearer idea of the old structure of the ghetto. In this area the buildings have been renovated leaving the original architecture intact. Immediately outside the perimeter, at the edge of Piazza Sermide, the Via della Dottrina Cristiana ("Christian Doctrine") almost seems to have been deliberately placed in this location to exorcise the Jewish presence in the quarter.

The modern synagogue

The modern synagogue is at no. 11, Via Giovi, in the three-story community building which, in 1825, was a rest home. In the internal courtyard from 1899 to 1902 a copy of the Norsa Torrazzo synagogue was built, and only just avoided being demolished shortly afterwards when the ghetto area was redeveloped.

Now the only synagogue left in the city, it is a faithful reproduction in terms of plan, structure, and decorations of the earlier Norsa Torrazzo synagogue, whose furnishings it inherited. The plan is rectangular. Several windows run along the two long sides interrupted halfway down by two circular niches, in turn, lit by windows. These niches contain the 18th-century holy ark and *bimah*. Both made of finely decorated wood, they are set opposite each other in a raised position and are reached by going up three steps.

The doors of the ark, decorated with vegetal motifs, are framed by twisted columns, further enhancing this already rich piece of furniture. The dark wood benches are arranged in two parallel rows on both sides of the prayer area. The women's gallery is set on columns in the entrance wall, and overlooks the room from an open balustrade, also with columns. Wrought-iron chandeliers hang from the ceiling. The largest central chandelier was electrified at the beginning of the 20th century.

By using negative molds, the original stuccoes were reproduced, since they could not be detached from the old prayer room. In addition to verses from Psalms, they allude to the munificence of the Norsa Torrazzo family, which in 1751 commissioned the building of the prayer room.

Smaller than the original, the present building houses the community offices and the historical archives with books and documents dating from 1522 to 1810, state registry books from 1750 to the present day, the administrative archives since 1910, the rabbinical tribune archives, and other manuscripts and printed books.

A large part of the old community library is preserved in the Town Library (Biblioteca Comunale, Via Ardigò) and in the Dioceses Archives.

The cemetery outside the town walls

The cemetery (Via Legnano) dates from 1797, when the preexisting cemetery was moved outside the town walls. Headstones from the nearby town of Sermide were also brought to the older part of the new cemetery.

The painting and the Norsa family

There is a painting with an unusual story in the historic center of Mantua. In 1496 the banker Daniele Norsa acquired a house near the church of Santa Maria della Vittoria in Via Claudio Monteverdi. When he bought the building he was given permission, on paying compensation, to wipe out a sacred image adorning the façade. The local populace immediately rebelled and Francesco Gonzaga had to force the banker to demolish the house and replace it with a church, dedicated to the celebrated victory of the Gonzaga over the French at Fornovo (1495). This episode is described in a painting in the basilica of Sant'Andrea by an anonymous artist from the school of Mantegna. The work is a *Holy Family* with St. Jerome holding a model of the church, while at his feet is Daniele Norsa, wearing the badge on his cloak.

A recent community

The Milan community was only founded as late as the 19th century. This can be explained by the fact that the Duchy of Milan — ruled first by the Visconti and then the Sforza — only ever gave Jews permission to stay in the city for three consecutive days to deal with their business. That is why they lived in nearby towns like Monza, Abbiategrasso, Melegnano, Lodi, Vigevano, and Binasco, and went up to Milan every day. This "commuting" continued until 1597, when they were expelled from the whole duchy. For over two centuries, there was thus no longer a Jewish presence in the city or the duchy. They returned, however, in the early 19th century and became a section of the Mantua community, the only community in Lombardy that had survived without interruption. The Milanese group grew rapidly: the seven family groups in 1820 already numbered 200 people in 1840, and 700 in 1870. When the Milan community eventually became larger than the "mother" community of Mantua, it created its own independent organization (1866). In 1890 the by then 2,000 Jews decided to build an imposing synagogue in the heart of the city, in Via della Guastalla, to replace the modest oratory at no. 4, Via Stampa, actually a room in the house of the rabbi, Prospero Moisé Ariani.

The portal of the large temple, detail. Built by Luca Beltrami in 1892, the temple was struck by a bomb in 1943. Although rebuilt in 1953 and greatly altered inside, it still has the original façade.

The community continued to grow: Milan was becoming increasingly industrialized and attracted Jews from Italy and Europe. By the 1920s the community numbered 4,500 people and reached 8,000 in the 1930s, when it welcomed German and other European Jews fleeing from the Nazis. In 1938, when the racial laws were promulgated, the community had 12,000 members. Of these, 5,000 escaped the persecutions by fleeing to Switzerland, Palestine, and the Americas. But 896 were deported and only 50 came back.

In the immediate postwar period, the community helped refugees who had survived the extermination camps and became an important center for clandestine emigration to Palestine. In the 1950s groups of Jews expelled from Arab countries (Egypt, Syria, Libya, Lebanon, Iraq, and Iran) after the Arab-Israeli wars arrived in Milan, as well as groups from Turkey, Romania, Bulgaria, and Hungary. Today there are 6,000 Jews living in Milan with origins in fifteen different countries. Many of them have preserved the rites, uses, and customs of their country of origin and have organized independently with their own prayer rooms (there are thirteen in the city with various rites: Italian, Sephardic, Eastern-Sephardic, German, Persian, and Lebanese). All the children come together, however, to attend the same schools — from nursery to high school.

The temple designed by Luca Beltrami

The central synagogue, Hechal David u-Mordechai at no. 19, Via della Guastalla, is the largest Jewish monument in the city. It was built by Luca Beltrami, an illustrious late-19th-century architect. In line with the eclectic Neo-Baroque movement, the design reveals Byzantine and Arab-like influences, thought at the time to be stylistically more suitable for synagogues.

Beltrami organized the interior space (1,150 square meters [12,378 sq. ft.], with a street front of 37 m [121 ft.]) by following the model of two aisles and a nave. The holy ark is set in the apse of the eastern wall with the *bimah* in front of it, and there is also a pulpit and organ loft: this spatial arrangement is typical of classic church design. The architect also designed the façade — the only part of the building that has survived to the present day. It is divided vertically in three parts: a broad central section, originally corresponding

to the nave, and two side sections, corresponding to the aisles and side galleries above. The central section is delimited at the corners by two strip pilasters running up the whole front and joined by a great arch. Flanked by two windows providing light for the hall, the main entrance door is under the arch. Above the door, at the level of the women's gallery, is a three-arched loggia, with a stone framed window above, providing light for the nave. The central section ends with a tympanum, interrupted by an aedicule containing the Tablets of the Law. In each of the two side sections, on the first floor, are two biforate windows lighting the stairs of the women's galleries.

No expense was spared on the construction. The Italian State gave the community a loan of 75 million lire, covering fifty percent of the total cost, to be paid back in thirty years. The synagogue was officially opened in 1892.

In August 1943 an incendiary bomb hit the building, seriously damaging the main room. After the war the community decided to rebuild the synagogue and in 1947 announced a competition for Jewish architects. The joint winners were the designs by Manfredo D'Urbino and Eugenio Gentili Tedeschi. Both architects were then appointed to carry out the project. They were to construct the building from scratch, after completely demolishing the surviving parts, including the façade. But at the last moment, on economic grounds, the façade was preserved (the demolition alone would have cost 1.5 million lire).

Scrolls of the Law with their ornaments. Bound inside by embroidered bands, the scrolls are covered by precious fabrics. At the top they are also adorned by a large crown, while inside are two protruding tower-shaped rimmonim (ferrules) with bells. On the side is the tass (ornamental tray).

Large temple interior after the 1997 restoration. At that time the interior was remodeled and some windows were reopened and enlarged to let more daylight in.

The new building was completed in 1953. The architects chose the form of a great prism, broken up at the rear by some offices and services. Two side bodies were added to the façade to join up with the adjacent buildings. At the center of the pitch roof is a square skylight covered by a dome. The exterior was clad in rough concrete; the frame and base for the windows were made of Serizzo marble. Twenty-four narrow long windows were opened on the two sides. The interior had three levels: the ground-floor prayer room; the first-floor women's gallery, and a small oratory in the basement. The outcome was a typical example of Rationalist architecture.

Recent restoration work

In 1997 the building underwent some radical changes. The external volume remained unaltered but the façade was restored and the two large windows reopened, in keeping with the original design (they had been closed in the postwar reconstruction work).

The street front was delimited by a wrought-iron gate, made to the original designs: a series of stylized rods, joined at the top by a continuous Greek cross, ending in small spikes, some with volutes at the bottom and, at regular intervals, ornamental roses containing four concentric rods, like thin swords. The main entrance door to the central nave was also completely rebuilt according to Beltrami's designs: the outside has panels made of wood and bronzed steel, while the inside is made of dark walnut to match the prayer room furnishings.

The interior was completely redesigned by Piero Pinto and Giancarlo Alhadeff. Light and color are the main elements. There is much more light thanks to the newly reopened large windows in the façade and the extension of the existing windows that now stretch up high in the side walls of the building; large new windows in the central dome also add more light.

The ceiling in the central section of the women's gallery was raised: it now gradually slopes down from the dome in three broad cornices to the walls along the two sides of the women's gallery, thus eliminating all the sharp edges.

The colors red and gold dominate in the prayer room. The preexisting gold was maintained and strengthened in the central section of the rear wall with the large holy ark, whose gilded tesserae contrast with the dark red of the side walls. The balustrade round the ark and the inside of the dome are also painted gold. The ceiling in the prayer room is white, while the side walls, with a rusticated pattern reminiscent of rough stone, are made of light hazel wood, as is the *bimah*. The floor is the same as the postwar reconstruction, and is made of red Trani marble and pearly white Sicilian marble. Covered in dark red fabric, the seats (453 on the ground floor and 402 in the women's gallery) are made of light beech wood with patterns echoing the three arches in the large windows in the façade. The twenty-three stained-glass windows by New York artist Roger Selden have very lively colors. They are like a great collage of Jewish symbols and letters, repeated in all the windows in different hues and forms.

The synagogue is not used for everyday purposes. This function is fulfilled by a prayer room called the "Scola Shapira in Centro Nessim Pontremoli," to the rear of the large synagogue. In this room, where the Italian rite is practiced, the 18th-century furnishings originally belonged to the now extinct community of Fiorenzuola d'Arda in the Piacenza area. In the basement is the Jarach Room, where a museum is planned, and the Eastern-Sephardic oratory, whose furnishings came from Sermide (in the Mantua area), which also once had a community.

Oratories and archives

In Milan there are several other modern oratories attended by Persian and Lebanese groups. Another two can be found in the school and building at no. 8, Via Eupili, and there is one in Galleria Vittorio Emanuele, with the windows overlooking the square called Ottagono.

The same building at no. 8, Via Eupili, houses the CDEC — a center for contemporary Jewish documentation. This foundation gathers material on Jewish persecutions and deportations and the history of the Jews right up to modern times. The center has an archives, a newspaper and periodical library, video library, and specialized library open to the public.

The cemeteries

The Milan community has a separate section in the monumental city cemetery and some graves in the Musocco cemetery. In fact in 1870 some headstones were brought to Musocco from the first Jewish cemetery of Fopponino (in Piazzale Aquileia), when it was eliminated because the land was used for the expanding city center.

The printers at the court of the Gonzaga

Sabbioneta, the "Gonzaga's Little Athens," achieved its greatest fame during the reign of Prince Vespasiano (1531–1591), who founded the town and established his court there. This was a time of great prosperity, also involving the Jews, who had lived in the city since 1436, exercising the trade of money lending. They were soon followed by others, including the printers Tobia Foà and Salomone Forti. They and their families contributed to the extraordinary Jewish printing output in the Mantua area. The Jewish printing works were situated in what is now Via della Stamperia (formerly Via Fabio Filzi). Since the splendor of Sabbioneta was mainly due to Vespasiano Gonzaga's own personal achievement, on his death, the town fell into inexorable decline. Many Jews left, and by 1773 the group only numbered sixty-three people, although this figure did rise to 113 by 1821. In 1820 the Mantua community, then under Austrian rule, suggested that the smaller rural Jewish communities pass under its auspices. The Jews of Sabbioneta not only refused this offer but decided to enlarge their synagogue. The commission for the work was given to Carlo Visioli, a well-known architect in his day. Visioli was a native of Sabbioneta, and worked in Mantua, Milan, and Cremona. The Jewish group from the neighboring town of Viadana also sought his services, but the project for their monumental temple was never completed. The Sabbioneta synagogue immediately turned out to be too big for the group's requirements. After a few years it was closed and abandoned. There have been no Jews living in Sabbioneta for many years now, and the synagogue building belongs to the Mantua community.

The old synagogue interior. Built in 1820 by the architect Carlo Visioli, the synagogue immediately turned out to be too large for the community of 113 people. When the community died out, the synagogue remained closed until 1994. Today it can be visited on a guided tour of town monuments.

The 19th-century synagogue

Of their own accord the Jews of Sabbioneta settled — there was never a ghetto — in the area between Piazza San Rocco, Via Campi, and Via Pio Foà. A prayer room (the third in chronological order) was installed in a 17th-century building, entered from Via Campi. This building was extended and restructured in 1824 by the architect Visioli, who had been commissioned to redevelop the whole urban block. The prayer room is situated on the third floor. Rectangular in shape, it is preceded by a spacious hall containing some information panels illustrating Jewish life in general and that of Sabbioneta and Mantua in particular. The entrance door bears the date "5584 (1823–24)" and the Hebrew writing: "I shall dwell between his shoulders" (Deut. 33, 12). The holy ark and *bimah* are set against the eastern wall of the room, opposite the entrance. The stone ark has the form of a temple. A pediment, adorned with a crown, bears the Hebrew inscriptions: "A law shall proceed from me" and "Happy is everyone that retaineth her" (Isaiah 51, 4 and Prov. 3, 18). The pediment rests on two columns of painted marble ending in Corinthian capitals. The two wooden doors have six square panels and two half lunettes, decorated in green and gold. In a raised position, the ark is reached by going up a few steps. At the foot of the steps is a small *bimah*. The whole complex is enclosed by a wrought-iron gate and railings. Two lamps hang to the sides. Together with the dark walnut benches, they are the only furnishings to have survived from the old synagogue. The ceiling is decorated with stuccoes, divided in panels, made in 1840 by the Swiss craftsman Pietro Bolla. Resting on columns, the women's gallery overlooks the room through a closely-knit wooden grate opposite the prayer area. It is reached by an external flight of stairs. After decades of neglect, the prayer room was restored by the Brescia Department for Fine Arts (1994) and is now included in guided visits to the town.

Some points of interest

A number of interesting Jewish items have survived in Sabbioneta. Under the porch of the church of the Incoronata is a walled plaque commemorating Leone Donato Forti. In 1826, out of "patriotic love," Forti gave the church back to the religious authorities, after it had been deconsecrated in 1810 following the Napoleonic closure of churches and monasteries. In the 1990s during restoration work on the buildings once inhabited by Jews three intact *mezuzoth* were found in the doorposts of some houses. The *mezuzoth* are blue glass jars with a prayer scroll inside. They are now in the Museum of Sacred Art, near the parish church, at no. 6, Via Pesenti.

The cemetery outside the town gate

The Jews had two cemeteries at Sabbioneta. The whereabouts of the earlier burial place is unknown, but the 19th-century cemetery is outside the town gate called Porta Imperiale.

German printers in Lombardy

A Jewish family of German origin called Da Spira opened a printing works at Soncino some time between 1483 and 1490. According to the custom at the time, they then acquired the same name as that of the town. The main focus for Jewish history in this small Lombard town is in fact the Soncino family and its printing output. In the mid-15th century, a member of the family settled in Soncino, where he had been granted permission to open a loan-bank. The bank flourished and the family decided to stay on, extending its activities to printing, which soon became its main business. In only seven years, from 1483 to 1490, the Soncino family printed thirty books: the first complete edition of the Bible in Hebrew, a series of treatises of the *Talmud*, the *Machzor* (a prayer book containing holy day rituals for the Italian rite) and other works. The most celebrated member of the family was Gershom Soncino, who set new standards in printing. A pioneer of Hebrew printing, he was very industrious and his output was huge — 150 books in

his lifetime. Considered the "prince of printers" and the only Jewish printer in Italy in the late 15th and early 16th century, he was a very careful craftsman who refused to accept anything but perfect printing. To do so, he used refined paper and punches, specially made by the most skilled engraver of the day, Francesco Griffo from Bologna. Only because of such care over these details have his books survived to the present day. Gershom stayed in Soncino from 1488 to 1490, before moving on to various other cities — Brescia, Fano, Pesaro, Ortona, and Rimini. But he never achieved his greatest ambition of working in Venice, because for several years the Venetian Republic prevented Jewish printers from coming to the city and gave the exclusive right to print Hebrew books to the Dutchman Daniele Bomberg. Disappointed, Gershom left Italy to go and live in Constantinople. He died in 1534 in Salonica, where he had lived with his son Mosè, who opened a printing works in the town in 1521.

A press in the Printers' Museum. This perfectly functioning copy is a reproduction of the 16th-century press. A small museum has been installed in the two-story 14th-century building.

Books published by the Soncino printing works. The Da Spira family had come from the Palatinate and took the name of Soncino after the Lombard town where they lived and worked from 1483 to 1490.

The Printers' Museum

According to the historians, Via degli Stampatori is where the Soncino family lived and had its printing works. Today in this street there is a small museum housed in a two-story 14th-century building, which seems to have been the Soncino house-workshop. On the ground floor there is a copy of a 16th-century press and examples of some typefaces used by the printers. The press is in perfect working order and is set in motion to make some samples of printed sheets for visitors. In the showcases there are copies of some books the Soncino printed in their local works. These are books both in Latin and Hebrew as well as some representative works from the art of printing, which took such great steps forward thanks to this family. In recent years some rooms in the Rocca (Castle) have housed conferences dedicated to illustrious printers with accompanying exhibitions of rare examples of their work from libraries all over the world. In Piazza del Municipio, next to the entrance to the Town Hall, there is a plaque commemorating Israel Nathan Soncino.

nun N mem M heaph C
נון ן מם ם כף ך
Zzadi ZZ ph
צדי ץ ף

Ex supraſcriptis litteris,Quattuor,pnũciant pala to,ut. ג ghimel. י. iod. כ. caf. ק. cof.

Quinq; pnũciant ligua,& détib⁹.ut. ד.daleth. ט.teth. ל. lamed. נ.nun. ת.tau.

Quattuor pronunciantur gutture. ut.א. aleph. ה.he, ח.heth. ע.hain.

Quinq; pronunciátur détibus tantũ, ut. ז. zain. ס.ſamech. ר.res. ש.ſcin. צ.zadi.

Quattuor pferuntur labiis, ut. ב.beth. ו.uau. מ. mem. פ.pe.

Item ſunt ſex litteræ,quæ ſi habuerit ſupra ſe uir gulam hanc quæ רפא raphe dicitur. remittũt ſonum,ac diminuunt.ut. ב.uet. ג ghimel. ד.da leth. כ.caph. פ phe. ת.thau,quæ continentur in his duab⁹dictiõib⁹. בגד.begad. כפת.chephath

Pretærea fere omnes litteræ & ſupradictis admit tunt intra ſe paruum punctũ,qui dicitur. דגש. daghes,& tunc augent ſonum

ut.ב.bet.ג.ghimel,ד.dalet.מ. mẽ,& ſic cætere

Itẽ.ה.ideſt he. Quãdo habet intus punctũ tunc ponit infine dictionis & eſt foeminini generis.

Prætetea penultia littera quæ.ש.ideſt ſin.uocat Quando habet hoc punctũ.ש. aſiniſtra.ponitur pro.ſ.littera:& uocatur ſin ſmol Quãdo uero eſt adextra.ש.põit p gemini. ſſ.& uocat ſingemin.

Characteres uocalium.quæ punctis.ac li neis notantur.ſunt duodecim. ut

ſegol zzere pathah camezz
סֶגוֹל ֶ צֵרִי ֵ פַּתַח ַ קָמֶץ ָ
ſciuruch holẽ hirich ſceua
שׁוּרוּק וּ חוֹלֶם ֹ חִירִיק ִ שְׁבָא ְ
hateph camezz ſceloſſa necudoth
חֲטַף קָמֶץ ֳ שְׁלֹשָׁה נְקֻדּוֹת ֻ
ſegol hatef hataſpathah
חֲטַף סֶגוֹל ֱ חֲטַף פַּתַח ֲ

Quorum ָ camez & ַ pathah faciunt.a Camezz pro a longo pathah uero pro a breui. ֵ zere,& ֶ ſegol,& ְ ſceua faciunt.e.Zzere pro e. breui Segol pro e longo.Sceua uero quando eſt in principio dictionis ponit pro e.quando eſt in medio dictionis nõ profert,& ſic in fine dictiõis.

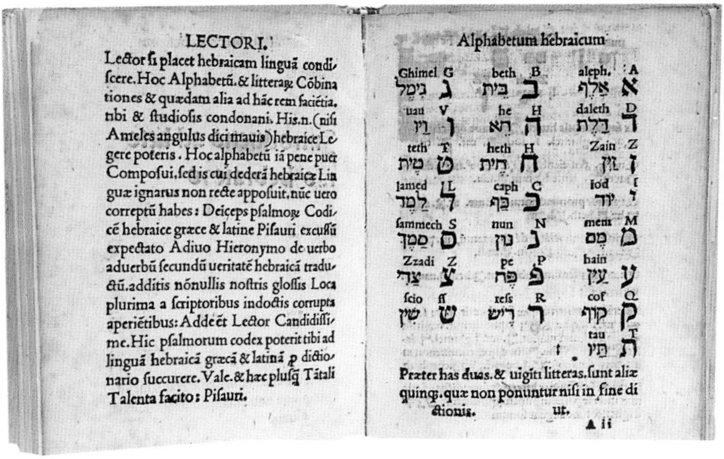
LECTORI.

Lector ſi placet hebraicam linguã condi ſcere.Hoc Alphabetũ.& litterarũ Cõbina tiones & quædam alia ad hãc rem facietia. tibi & ſtudioſis condonani. His.n.(niſi Ameles angulus dici mauis)hebraice Le gere poteris. Hoc alphabetũ iã pene puer Compoſui,ſed is cui dederã hebraicæ Lin guæ ignarus non recte appoſuit.nũc uero correptũ habes: Deiceps pſalmorũ Codi cẽ hebraice græce & latine Piſauri excuſsũ expectato Adiuo Hieronymo de uerbo aduerbũ ſecundũ ueritatẽ hebraicã tradu ctũ.additis nõnullis noſtris gloſſis Loca plurima a ſcriptoribus indoctis corrupta aperiẽtibus: Adde ẽt Lector Candidiſſi me.Hic pſalmorum codex poterit tibi ad linguã hebraicã græcã & latinã p dictio nario ſuccurere. Vale.& hæc pluſq̃ Tãtali Talenta facito: Piſauri.

Alphabetum hebraicum

Ghimel G גִּמֶל ג	beth B בֵּית ב	aleph. A אַלֶף א
uau V וָיו ו	he H הֵא ה	daleth D דָּלֶת ד
teth T טֵית ט	heth H חֵית ח	Zain Z זַיִן ז
lamed L לָמֶד ל	caph C כַּף כ	iod I יוֹד י
ſammech S סָמֶךְ ס	nun N נוּן נ	mem M מֵם מ
Zzadi Z צָדִי צ	pe P פֵּה פ	hain עַיִן ע
ſcio ſſ שִׁין ש	reſs R רֵישׁ ר	cof Q קוֹף ק
		tau T תָּיו ת

Præter has duas.& uigiti litteras.ſunt aliæ quinq;.quæ non ponuntur niſi in fine di ctionis. ut.

A ii

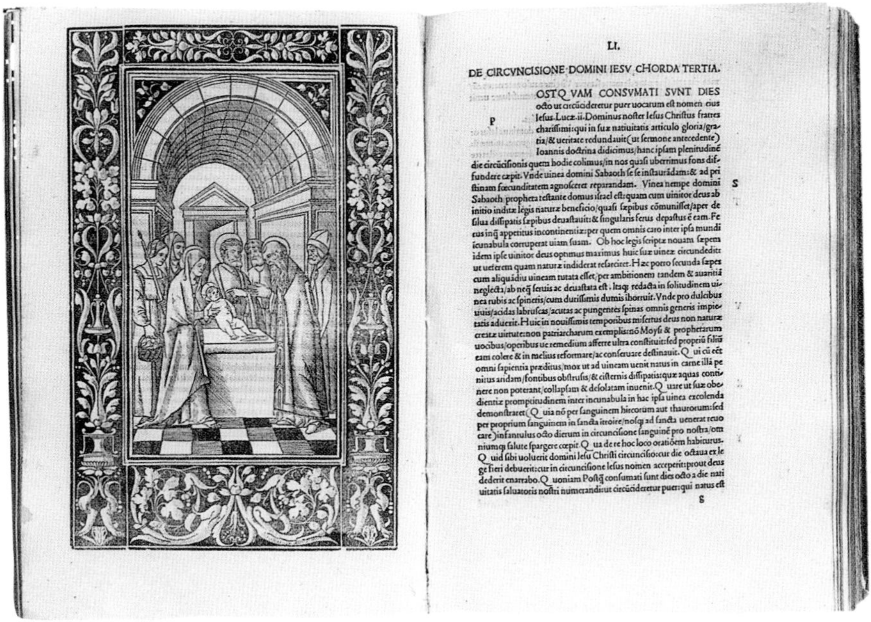
LI.

DE CIRCVNCISIONE DOMINI IESV CHORDA TERTIA.

POSTQVAM CONSVMATI SVNT DIES octo ut circũcideretur puer uocatum eſt nomen eius Ieſus.Lucæ.ii.Dominus noſter Ieſus Chriſtus fratres chariſſimi:qui in ſuæ natiuitatis articulo gloria/gra tia/& ueritate redundauit(ut ſermone antecedente) Ioannis doctrina didicimus/hanc ipſam plenitudinẽ die circũciſionis quem hodie colimus/in nos quaſi uberrimus fons dif fundere cæpit.Vnde uinea domini Sabaoth ſe ſe inſtaurãdam:& ad pri ſtinam fœcunditatem agnoſceret reparandam. Vinea nempe domini Sabaoth propheta teſtante domus iſrael eſt:quam cum uinitor deus ab initio inditæ legis naturæ beneficio/quaſi ſæpibus cõmuniſſet/aper de ſilua diſſipatis ſæpibus deuaſtauit:& ſingularis ferus depaſtus ẽ eam.Fe rus inq̃ appetitus incontinentiæ:per quem omnis caro inter ipſa mundi icunabula corruperat uiam ſuam. Ob hoc legis ſcriptæ nouam ſæpem idem ipſe uinitor deus optimus maximus huic ſuæ uineæ circundedit: ut ueterem quam naturæ indiderat reſarciret.Hæc porro ſecunda ſæpes cum aliquãdiu uineam tutata eſſet/per ambitionem tandem & auaritiã neglecta/ab neq̃ ſeruis ac deuaſtata eſt. Itaq; redacta in ſolitudinem ui nea rubis ac ſpinetis/cum duriſſimis dumis ĩhorruit.Vnde pro dulcibus uuis/acidas labruſcas/acutas ac pungentes ſpinas omnis generis impie tatis aduexit.Huic in nouiſſimis temporibus miſertus deus non naturæ creatæ uirtute:non patriarcharum exemplis:nõ Moyſi & prophetarum uocibus/operibus ue remedium afferre ultra conſtituit:ſed propriũ filiũ eam colere & in melius reformare/ac conſeruare deſtinauit.Qui cũ eẽt omni ſapientia præditus/mox ut ad uineam uenit natus in carne illã pe nitus aridam/fontibus obſtruſis/& ciſternis diſſipatis:quæ aquas conti nere non poterant/collapſam & deſolatam inuenit.Quare ut ſuæ obe dientiæ promptitudinem inter incunabula in hac ipſa uinea excolenda demonſtraret(Quia nõ per ſanguinem hircorum aut thaurorum:ſed per proprium ſanguinem in ſancta introire/noſq; ad ſancta uenerat reuo care)infantulus octo dierum in circunciſione ſanguinẽ pro noſtra/om niumq; ſalute ſpargere cœpit.Qua de re hoc loco oratiõem habiturus. Quid ſibi uoluerit domini Ieſu Chriſti circunciſio:cur die octaua ex le ge fieri debuerit:cur in circunciſione Ieſus nomen acceperit:prout deus dederit enarrabo.Quoniam Poſtq̃ conſumati ſunt dies octo a die nati uitatis ſaluatoris noſtri numerandi:ut circũcideretur puer:qui natus eſt

S

Jewish printers in Italy

Printing began to spread in Italy at the end of the 15th century. Movable characters invented in Germany in 1440 quickly took root, and by 1465 the first book had been printed. The art of printing soon made inroads into the Jewish world, in which scribes had copied the sacred texts for centuries. In 1475 the first two Hebrew books were printed in Italy: one came off Abraham ben Garton's press in Reggio Calabria, and the other was printed by the physician Meshullam Cusi at Piove di Sacco (near Padua). For over a century there was then an incredible output of printed books in the Jewish world. The physician Abraham Conat worked in Mantua from 1474 to 1476, and Abraham ben Chaim from Pesaro, a dyer, changed occupations to open a printing shop in Ferrara in 1477. When he moved to Bologna in 1482, there was already a Jewish printing works in the city. Books were printed in Rome from 1480. There was thus a very lively printing climate throughout Italy, when the Da Spira family arrived in Lombardy from Germany, and then settled at Soncino in 1483. Having worked in several Italian towns before eventually going abroad, this family greatly raised the standards of Jewish printing. But the printing of Hebrew books won international renown thanks to Daniele Bomberg, a Christian from Antwerp. A scholar of Judaism, he printed the first Hebrew books in Venice. For a long time he and his printing works had the last word on which books should be printed and which rejected. The Venetian Republic had actually banned the printing of Hebrew books in the city for some time. But after Bomberg made a particularly substantial offer, the cash-strapped Senate revoked the earlier ban. Printing of Hebrew books developed in Venice, thanks mainly to the great interest shown by some Venetian nobles in this new activity. In addition to Bomberg, there were other printers. In 1545 the nobleman Marcantonio Giustiniani was his first direct rival, followed five years later by another Venetian noble, Alvise Bragadini. The competition between the Giustiniani and Bragadini printing works soon turned out to be fierce: the two owners began to fight over who had the rights to print a book by Maimonides. But what should have been a straightforward commercial row had unexpected disastrous repercussions for Jewish life, when the ecclesiastical authorities in Rome were invited to pronounce on the question. At that time the leading figure was the Grand Inquisitor Carafa, the future Pope Paul IV, who proceeded to set up a trial to judge the Hebrew texts, and especially the Babylonian *Talmud* and the Palestinian *Talmud*. Accused of denigrating the most important Christian figures, they were placed on the Index for being blasphemous. In 1553 a bull issued by Pope Julius III ordered the destruction of every copy of the *Talmud* and any manuscript considered to be difficult to understand. All Hebrew writings obviously came into this category. For several years Hebrew books were burnt in the squares of Rome, Bologna, Venice, Ancona, Ferrara, Ravenna, and Mantua. In 1559 in Cremona alone 10,000 books were thrown to the flames. Only some localities in the Duchy of Milan and the Monferrato area were spared this violence. After a few years the printing of Hebrew texts started up again in Ferrara (with Abraham Usque), Sabbioneta (with Tobia Foà), Mantova, Cremona, and Riva di Trento (thanks to the good offices of Cardinal Cristoforo Mandruzzo). In Venice, however, Jewish printing did not begin again so soon. Each new publication was censored beforehand by the Church: the censors read the texts and cancelled with black lines any parts considered offensive to Christianity. This censorship continued throughout Italy for over 300 years. From the end of the 16th century and the beginning of the 17th century many of the burnt works were reprinted, except for the *Talmud*, which the popes expressly prohibited with specific papal bulls. Because of the bonfires and censorship, the Italian Jewish printers soon lost the preeminence they had enjoyed in Europe for around a century, and were superseded by Dutch printers. They continued, however, to print Hebrew books throughout the 18th century.

After emancipation, a passion for books led many Jews to open printing works and publishing houses — several still exist today.

סדר

הגדה של פסח

בלשון הקדש ופתרונו בלשון

איטליאנו

עם כמה צורות על כל האותות והמופתים אשר נעשו
לאבותינו במצרים ועל הים ובמדבר
וכל סדר קדש ורחץ צ' תרחק טמנו כיצורה קרובה וכן
מכות מצרים ואותיות כציורות מורות איכות הברכות
ודברים אחרים יפים עד מאד

המצאה חדשה ערוב' בכל עמוד ועמוד ולכל חנמצא בכתב נעשו צודי'
זו לזו בכל הכתוב בספר התור' ומחוכם יראו דברי נפלאים
לא שערם אבותיחם

הבינח וגם הקרח זה כמו עשרים שנה זקן שקנה חכמה חה חיששש
ונעלת בכור ישראל הזהרונו זל'

ואלח מוסיף על הראשונים פירוש צלי אש והוא קצור זבח פסח מהרב
הגרול השר דון יצחק אברבנאל זצל'

כדפס לתפארת שבמור היקר ומשכיל כמל' משה בן הנעלה לתהלה
כמל' גרשון פרינצו יצו'

בוינציאה

בבית ייואני קאליוני המדפיס
מנת שפט לפק'

Appresso gli Illustr. Sig. Pietro, Aluise, & Lorenzo Brag.

For centuries Genoa's own great mercantile ambition meant Jews were no allowed to reside in the city, since they were viewed as greatly feared rivals But in 1648, when a free port was established, Jews were given permission to settle in the city. Until then merchants and refugees had passed throug without being given permission to stay, and this was the case even in 1492 when masses of desperate people arrived from the Iberian peninsula. In 1660 the first ghetto was set up in the area of the old port along Via Pré. An adjoining area was used in 1674 for a second ghetto, when the first was too small for the fast growing group. Right from the outset, the Jewish presence was governed by *Capitoli* ("Chapters" — a kind of statute), which listed the rules the Jews had to obey to stay in the city. In 1675 when the *Capitoli* were renewed, the conditions were so harsh that many people chose to leave Around one hundred people stayed on. But given they were so few, there was no longer any need for a ghetto. Those who remained moved along the seafront to an area between Canneto and Malapaga. Here a synagogue wa created and continued to function until 1935 when the present synagogue was opened in the hilly area of the city center. Meantime the community had grown to 2,500 members. Today there are just over 400. The community was decimated by the Nazi-Fascist deportations: 300 people were deported, including Rabbi Riccardo Pacifici. A small square near the synagogue is named after him. Genoa was also the headquarters o Delasem, a Jewish organization that helped people to escape from the persecutions to America France, and Spain in 1939. At the end of the war i also helped survivors from the extermination camps to reach Palestine clandestinely, when the country was still under British rule.

Detail of a stained-glass synagogue window by Emanuele Luzzati. The synagogue was officially opened in 1935. The current windows were made in 1959 and depict the emblems of the twelve tribes and a seven-branched candelabrum.

Other localities in Liguria

Today the only large Ligurian community is in Genoa. La Spezia, however, has a modern oratory (at no. 165, Via 20 Settembre), which replaced an earlier prayer room in Piazza Garibaldi, destroyed during the Second World War. The Jews (there are now around fifty) arrived in La Spezia at the end of the 19th century. They had almost all come from Livorno (Leghorn), attracted by the development of the military shipyards and the opportunities for work they offered.

In some towns like San Remo there has been a continuous association between the place and the Jewish tradition: since antiquity Jews came to San Remo from Central Europe to buy citron (*etrog*) and palm leaves for the festivity of *Sukkoth*. In other localities place names record a former Jewish presence. This is the case in Lerici (Via del Ghetto), Monterosso (Via Zuecca), Noli (Quartiere della Giudaica), Recco (Salita della Giudea, in the village of Polanesi), and Savona (Vico Giudei, now Vico Crema).

The modern synagogue

Designed by the architect Francesco Morandi, the Sephardic synagogue a no. 6, Via Bertora, was opened in 1935. Having initially been rejected in 1924 by the city council building commission on the grounds it was "not artistic enough," after a few modifications, the design was then accepted in 1926 and eventually built. The synagogue exterior has a massive square rein forced-concrete structure, clad with Finale stone ashlars and surmounted by a central dome and four lowered calottes at the sides. The style may be described as vaguely Romanesque with Oriental touches. The long narrow windows are almost slits. On the entrance façade there is a rose window above the main door, decorated with a series of small arches and a Hebrew quotation from Isaiah; the lunette in the portal contains a reproduction o the Tablets of the Law. The slightly rising small square outside the syna gogue is closed by a gate and railings with a the seven-branched cande labrum pattern. Beside the door is a memorial stone dedicated to Rabbi Ric cardo Pacifici, who was deported in 1943. Inside, the ground-floor prayer room is shaped like an amphitheater with an apse at the rear. There are two focal points: the great *aron*, set in the apse, and the central *bimah*, opposite Raised from the floor by three steps, the ark is a large parallelepiped made of green Polcevera marble, crowned with the Tablets of the Law. Its doors are framed by two ochre marble colum

Ceramic Hanukkiah by
Emanuele Luzzati (detail).
The Genovese artist and stage
designer contributed to
the synagogue decoration
by designing the stained-glass
windows and ceramic tiles
on the bimah.

Synagogue interior. The room
is shaped like an amphitheater
with an apse at the rear
containing the holy ark.
Set in the middle of the room,
the bimah is like the crow's
nest of a ship. This polygonal
structure is decorated
by twelve ceramic tiles with
symbols of the Jewish months.

(the same material as the steps), bearing a Hebrew inscription. A recent construction designed by Emanuele Luzzati, the *bimah* is like the crow's nest of a ship. The polygonal wooden structure is decorated by twelve fine ceramic panels with the symbols for the Jewish months. The benches are arranged all round the prayer area. The stained-glass windows (1959) are also by Luzzati; two reproduce the emblems of the twelve tribes, whereas the third has the seven-branched candelabrum. The two-story women's gallery runs round three sides of the room. The first story has railings with stylized seven-branched candelabra. Below the railings are Hebrew inscriptions from Psalms. Reading only the letters with dots reveals the name of the community president: Tobia Cohen Pavia. Now equipped with an elevator, the second floor will eventually house a museum. Under the large dome is a room once used as a school. In the basement level are premises for lectures, the community offices, the *mikveh*, and a small prayer room for everyday use. The 18th-century furnishings of the small room are from the Malapaga synagogue, closed in 1935 when the new building was opened. The small prayer room is rectangular, and the lower sections of the walls are wainscoted. The ark is set against the long side, on the right, as you enter. Made of wood, it is divided into gold-decorated small panels with, on the four sides, ornamental false columns. An 18th-century silver *ner tamid* hangs from the ceiling. The small *bimah* is set in front of the ark, at the center of the first row of benches. The women's gallery has wooden railings.

The ghettos in the *carrugi*

The first ghetto, opened in 1660, was in Vico del Campo (later Vico Ebrei) and Vico Untoria, in the area called the *carrugi* ("alleys") round the old port. In the building where these two streets meet there was a Sephardic oratory. The second ghetto, opened in 1674, was in the area around Piazza dei Tessitori, near the church of Sant'Agostino, in Vico del Filo and Vico del Biscotto. In the piazza there was an oratory in the former building of the Weavers' Guild (hence the name of the piazza — *tessitori* means "weavers"). The area was razed during the Second World War. Although not a ghetto, the last Jewish quarter — where the Jews moved to of their own accord from 1675 on — was between Piazza dell'Olmo (now Piazza Tavarone) and

the walls of Malapaga. Here at no. 6 there was a synagogue that continued to function until 1935, when the new temple was opened with the furnishings from the old synagogue.

The cemeteries

The present cemetery (the third) is part of the city cemetery of Staglieno. There are two sections: one open since 1886, and the other more recent. The first Jewish cemetery (18th century) at Castelletto is mentioned on a plaque once on a building at Malapaga, now in the synagogue. A second cemetery (19th century) was situated near the sea at the Cave area (now Via Corsica). It was abandoned when the city expanded, and the headstones were moved to Staglieno. At the entrance to the cemetery, plaques commemorate the six million Jews who died in extermination camps and the 300 Jews deported from Genoa.

Spoken for more than 3,000 years, Hebrew is one of the oldest languages. At the time of Abraham the Jews spoke an early Aramaic dialect. Then in the land of Canaan, it was replaced with a language in the Canaanite group, like Phoenician, Moabite, or Ugaritic. These languages spread first from the River Tigris to the Mediterranean and from the mountains of Armenia and Southern Arabia to Northern Africa and as far as Ethiopia.

The oldest literary document written in Hebrew is the "Song of Deborah" (Judges 5) from the 12th century BC. Outside of biblical texts, Hebrew is also found in the Dead Sea Scrolls (1st century BC – 1st century AD), discovered at Qumran in 1947 and now highly guarded in the Israel Museum, Jerusalem.

Over 3,000 years of history, Hebrew has undergone changes and developments that the experts divide into three stages: Biblical, Post-Biblical and Modern Hebrew. The first was the language used in Palestine from the arrival of the Jews to the Babylonian exile and the destruction of the first Temple (BC 587). After this first Diaspora, the Jews continued to use Hebrew for prayers but began to speak Aramaic (in the East) and Greek (in the West). Hebrew as a spoken language (post-exile Hebrew) with the same structure, was used again by the Jews in Palestine after the return from Babylon (from BC 538).

Post-Biblical Hebrew was used in the literary Mishnaic and Rabbinical forms. The former (2nd century AD) used Hebrew in the sixty-three treatises of the *Mishnah*, the first collection of written rules from the Bible, previously handed down orally.

The Rabbinical form was strongly influenced by Aramaic. It then had a purer form in the Talmudic period (3rd-5th century AD) and remained unchanged throughout the Middle Ages up to the Jewish Enlightenment (*Haskalah*) at the end of the 18th and beginning of the 19th century, when it was used again as a spoken language. Modern Hebrew, incorrectly called Israeli, has the structure of the Biblical language but has been adapted, enriched by new words and given a simplified syntax. The return to Hebrew was proposed by the European exponents of the Jewish Enlightenment in the early 20th century in order to make it the shared language of the Jews of the Diaspora. The idea of reviving the language coincided with the birth of Zionism, the movement calling for the Jews to return to Palestine. The decision to make Biblical Hebrew the language for the national renascence had a symbolic and unifying force. The leading player in the revival was Eliezer Ben-Yehuda (1858–1922), a Lithuanian by birth, who moved to Palestine. He wrote the seventeen volumes of *The Complete Dictionary of Ancient and Modern Hebrew*. From a vocabulary of 8,000 words in the biblical texts, Hebrew now had 120,000 words.

Like all Semitic languages, Hebrew is written from right to left. Its structure is based on the trilitteral system of roots. With prefixes, suffixes, doubling, and vowel changes, the roots have a twofold – nominal and verbal – function. The nouns are not declined but there are some changes in endings. The vowel system was established from the 7th to the 9th century by the grammarians called the Tiberian *naqdanim*. The verbs only have two tenses, perfect and imperfect (or future), for complete or incomplete actions. The alphabet has twenty-two consonants. Originally the Hebrew alphabet was like the Phoenician alphabet but was then replaced during the Babylonian exile by the "square" alphabet of Aramaic origin, still used today. The archaic alphabet has not disappeared but is conserved by the Samaritans. Moreover, it was used by the Jews during the Judaic wars for coins and in the Dead Sea Scrolls to allude to the name of God.

Now, in addition to the "square" script for printed text, Italics is also used. Modern Hebrew is written without vowels, which are only added in the syllabaries, in publications meant for the new immigrants, verse, and liturgical texts. In the past the "square" Hebrew letters were used to write some Hebrew dialects spoken in the

Diaspora. These dialects interwove Hebrew expressions with local terms. The dialect spoken by some Italian Jews, such as Judeo-Venetian, Judeo-Piedmontese, and Judeo-Romanesque, would have been difficult to transcribe into Hebrew script. Italian Jews used the Hebrew alphabet, however, to write Italian when they did not want others to decipher their messages. Hebrew letters were commonly used in Judeo-Persian, Judeo-Arabic, Judeo-Spanish or Ladino, spoken by Jews of Spanish origin (Sephardim), and Judeo-German or Yiddish, widespread in central Europe among Jews of German origin (Ashkenazim). Much more than a dialect, Yiddish is now considered a full-blown literary language. The Academy for the Hebrew Language, which took over in 1948 from the Committee of the Hebrew Language, active under the British Mandate, now monitors the developments in the language. In fact modern Hebrew is continually evolving by absorbing expressions and words arriving in Israel with the new immigrants.

There have been many attempts to replace the "square" script by transliterating it in Latin letters, as happened for Turkish, but they have always been unsuccessful.

Door of a house in the ghetto, created in 1603 by the Venetians and liberated by the French in 1797. With the restoration of the monarchy, the Austrians returned to the city and forced the Jews to live segregated in this quarter with narrow alleys and unsanitary buildings.

Via San Martino e Solferino, originally two streets — Via Sirena and Via Urbana. They were the main streets in the ghetto, which was closed by four doors surmounted by plaques with a carved lion of San Marco.

Academies and universities

The Jewish community of Padua has a long uninterrupted history from the 11th century on. A number of features set it apart from the history of other communities: it has always been an important center for Talmudic studies and had a rabbinical academy as early as the mid-14th century and a rabbinical college from 1870. Padua was also the only university city in Europe to accept Jewish students in the faculty of medicine as early as the 15th century. These two aspects cast a fascinating light on the community of moneylenders and merchants, which in 1405 witnessed a change from the tolerant policy of the Da Carrara rulers to the discrimination practiced by the Venetian Republic, which had won control of the city. The community also had to suffer plundering by the troops of Maximilian of Austria in 1509 and then again a few months later by the counterattacking Venetians. In 1603 the Jews were forced to live in a ghetto. This quarter with narrow streets and insalubrious buildings was easy prey to the plague of 1631, which swept through the city killing 421 out of a total of 721 ghetto dwellers. The community had difficult relations with the rest of the population, which bullied and mocked the Jews, who also came under pressure from the Church to convert. In 1601 even the rabbi, Salomone Cattelan, converted and took the Catholic name of Prosdocimo. In 1797 the invading French pulled down the gates of the ghetto. But when the Austrians regained possession of the city, the populace accused the Jews of having supported the French. To placate the hostile demonstrations, the community had to organize a service of thanksgiving for the return of the Austrians in the synagogue. After the unity of Italy, the numbers in the community began to decrease, going from 1,378 in 1881 to 881 in 1911, 600 in 1938, 300 in 1943, and 200 today.

The Jewish quarter

The ghetto is situated in the heart of the historic center, near Piazza delle Erbe. The main artery is Via San Martino e Solferino (once called Via Sirena and Via Urbana): at the junction with Via Roma is the first of the four large doors, used to close off the quarter in the evenings. Above each door was by a marble plaque with a carved lion of San Marco (symbol of Venice) and the warning: "At night Jews and Christians must keep away from the enclosure walls. If the law does not stop them, enclosure will, and if not even this, then punishment." All of these plaques were removed in 1798 and subsequently lost. The first stretch of Via San Martino e Solferino still has buildings with the original Romanesque layout, albeit with overlapping styles (see, for example, the small Gothic portal adorning the house at no. 31). Via San Martino e Solferino crosses Via delle Piazze, where there was a second door at the end of the street near the church of San Canziano. In the corner block between Via delle Piazze and Via San Martino e Solferino there were two synagogues: the Italian synagogue of 1548 (the only one to survive) and the Spanish synagogue of 1617, now used as a lecture hall.

The synagogue today

The Italian synagogue is situated at no. 9, Via San Martino e Solferino (originally no. 1022, Via Sirena). The building also houses the community offices. The synagogue was built in 1548 thanks to the efforts of Rabbi Johannan

Treves, Aron Salom, Mordecai Ravà, and Moisè de Roman. Restored at various later dates (1581, 1631, 1830, and 1865), it was closed in 1892, when the large synagogue was inaugurated, but then reopened after the war (the large synagogue having been destroyed by fire). The exterior of the building is enhanced by a 16th-century loggia on the first floor, corresponding to one of the walls in the prayer room. Inside, plaques at the entrance and on the stairs up to the synagogue are dedicated to its foundation in 1548, and mention the names of the founders, the war dead and the deportees in the Second World War (forty-six, of whom only one returned). The prayer room is rectangular (18 × 7 m [59 × 23 ft.]) with two symmetric focal points: the holy ark and the *bimah*, opposite each other, thus dissecting the long side of the room. This is a rather unusual arrangement rarely found in Italian synagogues.

The historic furnishings

The holy ark is made of solid dark wood obtained from a plane tree struck down by lightning in the Padua botanical garden in the 16th century. Decorated with vegetal motifs, the gilded doors are framed by four Corinthian columns made of white-veined black marble, ending in a pediment holding up a rich baldachin. On the sides, two carved wooden chairs are meant for use by the rabbis. Opposite the ark is the majestic raised *bimah*, reached by two symmetrical flights of semicircular steps. The *bimah* is also made of solid wood and adorned by a baldachin supported by four columns ending in a decorated entablature.

The walls of the room are completely clad in dark wood, like the benches running all round the perimeter. The women's gallery rests on the entrance wall. Bronze lamps hang from the caissoned ceiling. The room receives daylight from the large windows of the loggia occupying the whole of the short wall opposite the entrance.

Rabbi Meir Katzenellenbogen's gravestone. Known as Ma ha-Ram da Padova, he is buried in the cemetery of San Leonardo, the earliest graveyard dating from the 14th century. His tomb is visited by pilgrims from Eastern Europe. Since 1384 the community has had seven cemeteries.

A pair of 19th-century silver rimmonim. They decorate the Scrolls of the Law together with crowns, medallions, and capes.

The destroyed synagogues

At no. 20, Via San Martino e Solferino is the entrance to a courtyard (Corte Lenguazza or Corte dei Lenguazzi), named after a Paduan family that owned the palaces there in the 16th century. The first German-rite synagogue was opened in these buildings in 1525 and remained in use until 1682, when it was replaced by the large synagogue, again a German-rite temple, in the premises upstairs, but with the main entrance in Via delle Piazze. The large synagogue was used until 1892, when the rites were unified and it was modified to meet the requirements of the Italian rite. The building was damaged by fire in 1927 and then a second fire, sparked off by a burning torch thrown onto the roof by Fascists, completely destroyed it in 1943. The ark was saved and taken to the synagogue at Yad Eliahu, Tel Aviv, in 1955. The same synagogue in Israel also has the grates from the women's gallery and some other furnishings that survived the fire. A plaque once above the ark is now in the Italian temple in Jerusalem. Having been exposed to the elements after the war, this plaque lost its black color and reverted to its original rough stone.

The lecture-hall synagogue

On the fifth floor of the synagogue building, the former Spanish synagogue is now a lecture hall. The entrance is at no. 14, Via delle Piazze. Beneath the roof you can make out the small arches of the windows that once admitted light to the synagogue and were preserved in recent restoration work. With a rectangular plan (14 × 4.9 m [46 × 16 ft.]), the synagogue was built in 1617 in the house of Michelino della Bella thanks to an initiative taken by the Marini family. The synagogue underwent a number of transformations in the 18th-century before being closed for good in 1892, when the large synagogue was opened. The furnishings were taken to Israel in 1955 to Jerusalem and the Heichal Shlomo synagogue, the seat of the chief rabbinate.

In the mid-14th century the rabbinical academy was at the corner of Via San Martino e Solferino and Via Arco, before being moved to Via Barbarigo. Throughout its long life, the Padua community was an important center for Talmud studies, attracting scholars from throughout the European Diaspora. Evidence of this tradition is also provided by the tombs of illustrious rabbis in the old Paduan cemeteries, some having even become the destination of pilgrimages. The academy building is now a hotel, but inside there is still a mantelpiece decorated with a dove, the crest of the Salom family, which once lived there. The third door to the ghetto was at the end of Via Arco, at the junction with Via Marsala (formerly Via Spirito Santo). Called Volto degli Ebrei, this area is one of the few nonporticoed streets in the historical center and has preserved its medieval layout. At numbers 19-21 and 16–22 there are some tower houses: higher than average for the city, they were the outcome of extending upwards to create more dwellings in the ghetto. Via San Martino e Solferino crosses Via dei Fabbri, and the fourth door was at the end of this street. On the corner house (built in the 16th century but remodeled in the 18th) is a Hebrew inscription.

Seven cemeteries

There have been seven Jewish cemeteries in Padua since 1384 and they contain the tombs of the illustrious figures and rabbis who lived and studied at some time in Padua. The 14th-century cemetery of San Leonardo contains the grave of Rabbi Meir Katzenellenbogen (1482–1565), known as Ma ha-Ram from Padua. His tomb — the headstone has an engraving of a crouching cat — attracts pilgrims from Eastern Europe. In the cemetery (1450) in Contrada Codalunga, near the Bastione della Gatta, is the tomb of Isaak ben Juda Abrabanel (1437–1508), chancellor to Alfonso V of Portugal. His son, who lived in Venice, buried him in Padua, and marked the tomb with a great obelisk adorned with the family emblem: two rampant lions and a blossoming branch. The cemetery was never used again after being devastated in 1509 by the troops of Maximilian of Habsburg. Some of the gravestones are now in the civic museum and Abrabanel's tomb was moved to the cemetery at no. 124, Via Sorio. Opened in 1862, this cemetery contains the graves of Samuel David Luzzatto (1800–1866), called Shadal, a Biblical exegetist who taught at the rabbinical college of Padua from 1829, and Rabbi Dante Lattes (1876–1965), one of the founders of the publications *Israel* and the *Rassegna Mensile di Israel*, which he edited from Padua from 1962 to 1965. There are other cemeteries in Via Zodio and Via del Campagnola (19th-century).

Grave of Samuel David Luzzatto, called Shadal. This biblical commentator taught at the Padua rabbinical college from 1829. For centuries the Padua community was a major center of Talmudic studies, attracting scholars from throughout the European Diaspora.

Old gravestones. Several are of illustrious rabbis who had come to Padua to study and discuss with the Jewish scholars in the community.

The city with the first ghetto

Venice was the first city in the world to force Jews to live in a "ghetto," a Venetian word that spread worldwide through the Diaspora. Ghetto came to stand for a separate quarter, gates and custodians, discrimination and poverty. The Venice ghetto was a very large quarter, and it is one of the few to have survived in its original urban form. For centuries there were groups of different Jews living side by side: Germans, Levantines, and Ponentines — the so-called "nations." These groups took a long time to mix and persisted with their own customs, rites, and synagogues. In some periods, "ghetto" also came to stand for a quarter with great economic activities and a very lively cultural and religious life. By the end of the 17th century — its golden age — the Venetian ghetto had attracted 4,000 to 5,000 people. In the 18th century increasing tax pressure put the community into such dire economic straits that in 1735 it declared itself bankrupt. In 1797 Napoleon's troops pulled down the gates of the ghetto, marking the beginning of emancipation. After the unity of Italy and with the economic decline of Venice, the community began to dwindle and became less influential. In 1931 there were 1,800 people but by the end of the Second World War there were 1,000 and today there are less than 500. The community still has a very lively cultural life, however, and attracts visitors from all over the world because of its unique artistic heritage.

Door of a house in the ghetto, created in 1516. Coined in Venice, the term "ghetto" spread throughout the Diaspora as a word for a quarter where Jews were forced to live.

The Scola Levantina (left) and the Scola Spagnola (to the right). Both were built in the 16th century, and are used in turns by the community for religious services.

Ghetto Novo

The first area used to enclose 700 Jews of German and Italian origin in 1516 was the so-called Ghetto Novo, an island surrounded by the canals Rio di San Girolamo, Rio di Ghetto Novo, and Rio del Battello. A *sottoportico* (typical Venetian passageway under houses) and a bridge closed by gates were the only way out to the rest of the city. Today Ghetto Novo is also joined to the squares called Ghetto Vecchio and Ghetto Novissimo by two bridges.

The heart of the ghetto was the trapezoid *campo*, a square enclosed by tall buildings ("16th-century skyscrapers"). This was where daily life took place: there were three wells, shops, loan-banks (at Sottoportico no. 2912, the sign for the Banco Rosso or "Red Bank" has survived) and synagogues. Today only some of the buildings and synagogues (Scola Tedesca, Scola Canton, and Scola Italiana) in the square have their original appearance. Part of the square was transformed in Napoleonic times: a number of buildings were demolished and replaced in 1844 by the Casa di Riposo (Rest Home — originally created as "a home for industry to give work to the poorer Jews" and then from 1890 a "Home for the Elderly"). Today in the Rest Home there is an oratory with the ark from the Scola Mesullamim, the Ashkenazi synagogue demolished in the 19th century. On a wall adjoining the Rest Home there is a Monument to the Holocaust (seven bronze panels with scenes of deportation by the sculptor Arbit Blatas, made in 1980). From 1943 to 1944, 246 Jews were deported from Venice. Only seven returned. The names of the deportees are commemorated in a plaque on the outside wall of the Rest Home.

The main point of interest in Ghetto Novo are the old synagogues (*scole*) and the museum. All the Venetian *scole* (including those in the Ghetto Vecchio) have a common feature: their rectangular plan with the holy ark and *bimah* opposite each other on the shorter sides of the room with rows of benches on

Campo del Ghetto Novo. This trapezoid-shaped campo is enclosed by tall buildings ("16th-century skyscrapers"), and is actually an island surrounded by canals (Rio San Girolamo, Rio di Ghetto Vecchio, and Rio del Battello). Chosen in 1516, it was the first quarter that Jews of German and Italian origin were forced to live in.

the longer sides. The center of the room is thus free. The walls have Hebrew biblical inscriptions, creating an additional decorative element. The richly embellished furnishings, a large number of brass and silver lights (called *sessandei* or "wandering fireflies" in Venetian), very fine fabrics, and curtains (mainly red) make these synagogues unique in the world.

The Scola Grande Tedesca

The Scola Grande Tedesca (German synagogue) was built by an Ashkenazi group in 1528. Remodeled from 1732 to 1733 and again in the 19th century, it was restored in the 20th century (1975–79). The plaques on the stairs inside document these changes and mention the names of the benefactors.

The prayer room (13.45 × 8.7 × 12.95 × 6.7 m [44 × 28.5 × 42 × 22 ft.]) was set up in the preexisting building. The *bimah* and ark are opposite each other on the shorter sides, while the 16th-century benches (with lion's claws and paws, and floral and zoomorphic decorations) are set along the long walls. At the center of the ceiling is a skylight, now covered with a pitched roof. The floor is Venetian style (*terrazzo*) with mosaics of multicolored marble chips. The lower part of the walls are clad with cherry-wood panels, while the upper sections are decorated with painted marble ending in a band with the Exodus version of the Ten Commandments. The women's gallery is elliptical and has carved wooden railings. Two windows frame the ark and three (originally five) surround the *bimah*. The holy ark (1672) is set inside a *liagò* (aedicule) — an addition to the original building. Raised from the floor by a few steps, the doors of the ark are decorated outside with a stylized Tree of Life and inside with the Ten Commandments in mother-of-pearl inlaid work. On the sides two Corinthian columns end in a broken-apex pediment, decorated with vases and horns of plenty. At each side is a candelabrum and a rabbi's seat, echoing the decorations of the ark. Originally under the central skylight, the *bimah* was

Façade of the Scola Italiana in Campo del Ghetto Novo. It was built in 1575 by Jews, mainly from Rome, as revealed by the Classical-style tempietto with four columns.

The Scola Canton was built in 1531–32. The exterior is characterized by the dome on the apse, providing lighting for the interior together with the five large windows overlooking the Rio Ghetto Novo.

moved opposite the ark in the 1860 restoration work. A polygonal structure, it is made up of gilded columns supporting an entablature with the same pattern as the ark.

The Museum of Jewish Art is also in the building of the Scola Grande Tedesca. On the ground floor is a bookshop and cafeteria. Opened in 1955, and reorganized in 1986, it has also been recently extended. The museum, synagogues and the cemetery on the Lido can be visited on guided tours. The museum proper has several rooms with collections of fabrics and silver ceremonial objects and furnishings, *ketuboth*, and other manuscripts. But the synagogues, and even the ghetto, may be considered as integral parts of one great museum.

The Scola Canton

Built from 1531 to 1532, and expanded and transformed over the following three centuries, the Scola Canton was restored and restructured from 1968 to 1989. Plaques both outside and inside the synagogue mention these works. The origin of the synagogue's name is not known with any certainty. It was possibly the surname of the donor's family or due to the position of the prayer room at the corner (*canton*) of the square. It may also be derived from the *canton des Juifs* as a reference to the Provençal Jews who used it. The exterior is almost completely hidden by the surrounding buildings. Only the calotte of the apse can be seen, since the front with the five large windows of the prayer room gives onto a canal — Rio Ghetto Novo. A stairway, extended in 1859, leads up to the first floor.

The prayer room is reached by a corridor (possibly once the women's gallery or a room used for mourning families or the poor). It is almost rectangular in shape (12.9 × 7.1 × 12.75 × 6.5 m [42 × 23 × 41 × 21 ft.]) and the entrance is half way down one of the long sides. The walls are clad in wooden paneling and decorated with geometrical patterns, landscapes, and biblical inscriptions. Restored in 1736, together with the women's gallery, the floor is Venetian style (*terrazzo*) and at the center has a large round shape with geometrical motifs. The grates of the women's gallery are set in the entrance wall. Five windows face the canal, while there are four more blind windows in a corridor. Made in 1672, the ark is raised by four steps. The gilded wooden doors with inlaid work have an inscription inside of the Ten Commandments. Two side columns end in a broken-apex pediment with at the center a small stained-glass window. At the top is an ornamental crown. The backrests of the chairs at either side echo the ornamental patterns of the ark. The *bimah* (1780) is set inside a niche, visible from the outside. Set high up, the pulpit is reached by five steps on each side. The *bimah* is richly decorated: a semielliptical arch on the balustrade is supported by two pairs of small columns decorated with interwoven branches. The walls inside the niche are paneled by the high wooden backrests of the officiants' seats.

The Scola Italiana

The Scola Italiana (Italian synagogue) was built in 1575 by Jews from central Italy, mostly from Rome, as also demonstrated by the style of the synagogue with its classical-like *tempietto* with four pillars in the façade. Since then the

The Scola Italiana interior has been altered several times since its construction.
The 19th-century holy ark and the 18th-century bimah, both made of dark wood, stand opposite each other.

The Scola Tedesca interior. It was built in 1528 but subsequently altered. The room is trapezoid-shaped with the bimah and ark on the shorter sides. The elliptical women's gallery has a carved wooden balustrade.

synagogue has undergone many changes, mentioned on some plaques. The first may have been only a few years after its construction and involved the whole building, including the entrance, which was moved to the side.

After going through a small hall, you come to the square-plan prayer room (10 × 9.3 m [32.75 × 30.5 ft.]). The lower sections of the walls are clad with dark wood panels, while above are gold inscriptions on stone, framed by stucco, added in 1810. Concealed by wooden grates, the women's gallery is in the upper section of the entrance wall. Reached by going up four steps, the early 19th-century holy ark is made of dark wood. The doors have an inscription of the Ten Commandments inside and are framed by Corinthian columns supporting an entablature decorated with a crown. The area is enclosed by a balustrade (donated in 1842), made of small wooden columns, while the gate has a crossed-arch pattern. The 18th-century *bimah* is raised from the floor of the room and reached by flights of steps on either side. It stands in the polygonal apse, covered by a domed skylight. Benches for the rabbis are set against the wood-paneled walls. The pulpit is flanked by pairs of Corinthian columns.

Ghetto Vecchio

A bridge — Ponte degli Agnudi — built in 1541 over the Rio Ghetto leads to the Ghetto Vecchio, once inhabited by the Levantine Jews. This area stretches out along a main street (Strada Maestra, later called Strada del Ghetto Vecchio) once full of shops and community services. There were two schools, which have recently been restored: the Leon da Modena midrash, with the rabbinical offices, and the Vivanti midrash (1853). Ghetto Vecchio was a maze of narrow streets (Calle Barucchi, Calle dell'Orto, Calle Sporca, and Calle del Fornaio), opening out into the small main square — Campiello delle Scuole (formerly Campiello del Pozzo). Little has changed since the days of the ghetto. The Scola Spagnola (Spanish synagogue) and Scola Levantina (Levantine synagogue) both sit on this square.

The Scola Spagnola

Built in the mid-16th century by Spanish Jews and Marranos who had fled the Iberian peninsula, the Spanish synagogue is the only temple that has been continuously used (except for the war years 1943–45). Today it is opened for everyday use and takes turns with the Scola Levantina. Said to have been designed by the famous Venetian Baroque architect Baldassarre Longhena (1598–1682), or his workshop, the building has a similar style to many contemporary Venetian monuments.

At the center of the façade are four round-arched windows with leaded panes, white stone frames, and a lintel above. Beneath the cornice are four small square windows. The windows on the lower floor are small and asymmetric. The entrance is at the corner of the building. The carved wooden door

is inscribed with a verse from Psalms. On the outside wall a plaque commemorates the deportees during the last war. The lower section of the rectangular hall is clad with the wooden paneling from the backs of benches. Some plaques higher up are dedicated to the benefactors, the deportees from Venice, and Marco Voghera, a young Venetian who died fighting in Israel. A large stair, rebuilt in 1894, leads up to the prayer room. The entrance is at the side of the *bimah*.

The prayer room is rectangular (22 × 13 m [72 × 42.5 ft.]). Clad at the base by wooden panels, the walls have several windows. The caisson ceiling is decorated with wooden panels and molds made of carved wood and stucco. Large Dutch lamps and brass and silver lanterns further enhance the room. The oval-shaped women's gallery stretches up very high. It is no longer in use and part of the benches in the prayer room are reserved for women. The floor is made of white and gray marble tiles forming a pattern of concentric squares.

Niche in the Scola Canton. The name "Canton" may derive from a donor family, the "corner" position in the square, or canton des Juifs, *a reference to the Provençal Jews who used it.*

The Scola Levantina interior. In this rectangular prayer room, the bimah *is opposite the ark. The black-stained wooden bimah has two semicircular stairs ending at twisting columns.*

Raised on a platform, the holy ark is enclosed by a semicircular wooden balustrade. The doors, made in 1755, are framed by four columns (two on each side) of white-flecked dark marble with Corinthian capitals ending in a pediment with double tympanums. The arch of the larger tympanum is decorated with gilded stars, and at the center are the Tablets of the Law surmounted by a crown. The raised *bimah* has two semicircular stairs at the sides and is made of two marble columns supporting a heavy, richly decorated wooden architrave. This piece of furniture has undergone various transformations, especially in 1900 when an organ was installed, depriving it of its real function. Now the organ has been set back and covered by some red curtains, thus restoring the *bimah* to its original use.

The Scola Levantina and the Scola Luzzatto

The Scola Levantina (Levantine synagogue) was built from 1538 to 1561 by Levantine Jews, and was possibly already rebuilt in 1680. An elegant building, its design is also attributed to Baldassarre Longhena or his workshop. Even some of the details in the façade are similar to the Collegio Flangini built in 1678 by the great Venetian architect: i.e., the small oval windows under the cornices, the large arched windows with iron grates alternating with projecting wall decorations, the base, and the windowsills. Two plaques on the façade allude to the destruction of the Temple of Jerusalem and list the Venetian Jews who died in the First World War. The entrance is now on the shorter side,

Old gravestones in the Lido cemetery, first used in 1386. In 1763 a second area, still in use, was added. The old section has 1,200 gravestones dating from the 16th to the 18th century.

whereas the doorway on the square gives access to the Scola Luzzatto. On the side of the building is a polygonal dormer window added later.

The main door leads to a rectangular hall (on the wooden walls there are plaques and *tzedakah* boxes). On the ground floor is the Scola Luzzatto, moved from Ghetto Novo in 1836, when the buildings on Rio di San Girolamo, including the synagogue, were demolished. Restored in 1950 and 1974–1981, this room is used for study and has no women's gallery. With a rectangular plan, the room's walls are decorated with inscriptions in praise of the Lord. The *aron* kept here is the oldest in the ghetto: it has Renaissance forms and gildings on a green background and is enclosed by small gates, added in the 19th century. Raised by four steps, the *bimah* has a 19th-century baldachin.

From the same entrance, stairs lead up to the Scola Levantina. The rectangular prayer room (14 × 9 m [46 × 29.5 ft.]) has two entrances from the women's gallery (a side gallery concealed by a moveable grate), one on the ark side and the other on the *bimah* side. The walls are decorated with Baroque gildings and red damask drapes. The women's gallery has a band of colorful stained glass with symbols. The prayer room is fitted with Dutch chandeliers, brass torch-holders, and silver lamps. The *bimah* is an imposing structure. Made of walnut wood painted black, it may have been the work of the Belluno craftsman Andrea Brustolon (1660–1732): two semicircular side stairs are flanked by two twisting black wood columns reaching to a stark architrave almost touching the ceiling. Under the parapet of the podium, a cupboard, with doors decorated by high reliefs, is used to store the sacred texts. The *bimah* is set inside the hexagonal niche, which projects in the exterior façade. The ark is enclosed by a balustrade with small marble columns and brass gates, made in 1786. On the inside the doors bear inscriptions of the Ten Commandments and the date 1782, documenting its construction. On the sides, four gray marble columns crowned by Corinthian capitals support an architrave, which has inscriptions from Psalms.

Ghetto Novissimo

A bridge built in 1633 joins up Ghetto Novo to Ghetto Novissimo, which was added to the other two areas in order to accommodate Ponentine Jews. Situated at the junction between the canals of Rio di San Girolamo and Rio del Ghetto Novo, it is the smallest of the three ghettos. The area is made up of three blocks of houses, with some fine buildings (such as the Palazzo Treves and the Palazzo Vivante), but with no shops or synagogues. At the end of Calle del Portòn there was a gate to lock up the area.

The Lido cemetery

First used in 1386, the old Venetian Jewish cemetery is situated along the busy seafront at San Nicolò on Lido. Over the centuries it underwent many alterations, mainly because of expropriations, and many of the gravestones were lost. In 1763 a new area was opened adjacent to the older cemetery. Entered from Via Cipro, this cemetery is still in use. In 1999 the old cemetery was restored and reordered and the 1,200 gravestones were catalogued. They date from the first half of the 16th century to the second half of the 18th century. Another 140 gravestones from the old cemetery are now in the new cemetery: some near the entrance and others in the nearby *Lapidario* (stone collection).

The community that celebrated the advent of the ghetto

The Verona community has gone down in history because of an unusual episode: in 1600, accompanied by singing and dancing, it celebrated the creation of the ghetto. This move was hailed as an act of liberation after the long months of furious wrangling over the distribution of dwellings and shops. The fact a solution had been found, even if it meant enclosure, seemed to be an achievement worth celebrating.

When the ghetto was eventually established in the streets round Piazza delle Erbe, Verona had been under Venetian rule for almost one hundred years and by then the Jews had been granted permission to stay and settle in the city. This had not been the case in previous centuries when short-term stay permits were often followed up by sudden expulsion orders.

The first Jews who came to Verona were of German origin. They were followed in 1638 by Sephardim from Venice and in 1655 by Marranos from Spain. The newcomers, however, remained in separate groups: they were concentrated in the Corte Spagnola, a street adjacent to the ghetto, where they built their own oratory. Only in 1675 did the two groups eventually come together to organize a single synagogue. At that time there were 900 people living in the quarter.

The doors to the ghetto were taken down in 1797 by the French and were not even put up again during the restoration of the monarchy and the return

Synagogue interior seen from the main entrance and women's gallery. Opened in 1864 in the heart of the old ghetto with a capacity for 1,000 people, the prayer room has a ceiling with Oriental-like decorations. The whole building was completely restored in 2003.

to Austrian rule. In 1864 the community numbered 1,400 members and began to build the present synagogue. Finally, in 1866, the annexation of the Veneto to the Kingdom of Italy brought complete emancipation. The community then began to dwindle in numbers: from 600 people in 1909 to 429 in 1931, 120 in the postwar period, and today just under 100. Thirty-one Veronese Jews were deported. They are commemorated in a plaque raised in 1957 on the synagogue façade.

A ghetto "under the roofs"

Via Portici (once called Contrà San Tomio) was the main street in the ghetto in 1600. Not far away is Corte Spagnola, a narrow alley where the Sephardim lived from 1638. The streets still have their original appearance: the buildings (now restored) have arcades with slightly projecting roofs, as described in the chronicles of the time, when the area was called "under the roofs." At the heart of the ghetto is the large German-rite synagogue, opened in 1864.

The present entrance is at no. 3, Via Portici, while the main façade gives onto the parallel street, Via Rita Rosani. This façade has three vertical parts: the central body flanked by two false towers. The portal is framed by two pillars, each made up of six panels with images of Jewish symbols. The two pillars reach up to form a broken-apex pediment, containing — at the center of the tympanum — the Tablets of the Law. The portal has a large arch decorated with vegetal motifs, while on either side there is a bronze globe. The Hebrew inscription on the architrave above the wooden door is from a psalm and alludes to the holy nature of the building.

The rectangular prayer room has a capacity of up to 1,000 people. Inside, the vaulted ceiling has Oriental-like decorations all round the room. The wall with the holy ark is particularly rich. At the top is a great arched window screened by a huge grate with inlaid stonework and a large *menorah* at the center. In the lower sections of the walls there are two Stars of David above the wooden seats on either side of the ark for use by the rabbis. The seats continue round the three walls of the prayer area. A small pulpit on the side wall is a reminder that the synagogue was built just after emancipation. The holy ark is decorated by two columns supporting a pediment: at the center the gilded doors have vegetal patterns. The *bimah* stands in front of the ark.

The prayer area is raised from the floor of the room and enclosed by a balustrade decorated with inlaid work between each baluster. Further down, in parallel rows, the benches face the prayer area. Large candle chandeliers light up the room, which also receives lighting from the large windows. The women's gallery is set in the entrance wall, and rests on columns.

Some of the furnishings in the synagogue come from the Spanish-rite oratory in the ghetto, now demolished. There are no longer any tangible traces of this or any of the other oratories once in the city.

The cemetery in Via Antonio Badile, at Borgo Venezia, dates from 1855. The earliest cemetery was at Campo Fiore, near Via San Francesco, while a second burial place, used for a century from 1755, was situated at Porta Nuova, in Orto Parolini.

Jewish life is governed by prescriptions and rules. Circumcision, or *Brit Milah*, eight days after birth, marks the entry into the Jewish religion. At ninety-nine years old Abraham circumcised himself, his son Ishmael, and all the males and slaves in his household. The following year Isaac was born, and he was circumcised on the eighth day. Through circumcision Jews leave behind the animal condition and become thinking men, capable of distinguishing between good and evil. There is also a symbolic significance: it is as if man assumed the responsibility of perfecting nature and the work of the Lord. During the ceremony, the newborn boy is placed for good luck on the chair of the prophet Elijah and is given a name. If the first-born is a male, then thirty days after his birth he must receive redemption (*pidyon*) from serving the Lord. Since everyone belongs to the Lord and comes from the Lord, in ancient times the first-born had to serve God. The ceremony consists in symbolically giving a descendant of Aaron (a priest or *kohein*) five silver coins, which were once given in charity or returned to the child's father. The ceremony still has the ancient symbolic significance.

According to Jewish law, at thirteen children come of age. They are thus responsible for observing the religious precepts and ready to enter the adult world. The celebration in the synagogue of the *Bar-Mitzvah* ("Son of the Law") is preceded by a period of study so that the law can be learned. For the *Bar-Mitzvah* the *tefillin* is worn for the first time. The *tefillin*, or *phylacteries*, are two leather pouches containing strips of parchment inscribed with passages of scriptures, worn on the left arm and the forehead during morning prayer on weekdays, as a commitment to observe the Law with mind and heart. On the day of the *Bar-Mitzvah* ceremony the boy goes up to the *bimah* in the synagogue and reads an excerpt from the *Torah*; this is public recognition he has come of age. From now on he will be included in the *minyan*, the quorum of ten males required before public prayers can be recited. The boy's father accompanies his son to the *bimah* and offers thanks to God for having allowed his son to reach the age in which he has become a Jew to all effects and purposes. Other members of the family also take turns in reading the *Torah*, thus stressing the union of the family and the commitment to hand on their faith. Girls have a similar ceremony at the age of thirteen (*Bat-Mitzvah*), often in groups and, in many communities, celebrated during *Shavuot*.

Marriage is a fundamental part in the scheme of creation. The duty to create a family is the first of the 613 precepts (*mitzvot*) in the *Torah*. Through children, their education, love and respect for their rights and personality, God gives man the chance to remedy his errors. Children are the "*Moshiach* [Messiah] of humanity," the perennial regenerating force leading men to justice and peace. Moreover, man and woman together, in love and mutual respect, reach physical, moral, and spiritual completion. Marriage can be celebrated in the synagogue, in the bride's house or in a garden. Before the ceremony the groom gives the bride's mother a *ketubah* or tra

Illuminated marriage contracts, or ketuboth, were usually written on parchment. One of the most important expressions of Italian Jewish art, marriage contracts have been used since the 1st century BC.

ditional marriage contract. It contains the names of the bride and groom and their fathers. It must be signed by the groom and two witnesses. In this document, the husband promises that in case of divorce or his own death, his wife will have the means for an independent and dignified life. The use of the *ketubah* dates back to the 1st century BC. Its purpose was to protect women both economically and socially. In Italy the *ketubah* was once an illuminated parchment and as such is one of the most important ancient expressions of Jewish art. The ceremony is carried out in two stages. In the *Kiddushin* (sanctification/betrothal), performed before two witnesses, the groom slips a ring on the right index finger of the bride and declares her to be his wife. Only divorce (repudiation) can separate them. In the *Nisuin* (marriage), watched by ten men, the couple pass under the nuptial canopy (*chuppah*) or the *tallith* (prayer shawl) — the symbol of cohabitation. The officiant recites seven blessings, and the bride and groom drink wine from a single cup, which the groom then smashes, signifying that even at the height of joy, human frailty must never be forgotten. It may also be an allusion to the destruction of the Temple of Jerusalem.

There are well-defined rites for the last stage of life: the corpse of the dead person is given a ritual washing, wrapped in a white shroud, as a symbol of spiritual purity, and then buried. The body cannot be removed unless it is to be taken to Israel. As the body is being buried, *Kaddish* is recited, an ancient Aramaic prayer of praise and resignation to the will of God. The graves are marked by simple stones, with minimal ornamentation and no photographs or images. After the dead person is buried, the relatives begin to mourn. This consists of three periods. The first lasting seven days is the most painful and intense mourning. The second ends after thirty-one days and marks an attenuation in the suffering. The third period lasts one year. These periods are rich in symbols. In the first stage, to stress their suffering, relatives tear off a strip of clothing and sit on low stools or on the floor. The men do not shave or cut their hair. Immediately after the burial, friends and relatives who are not in mourning serve the direct relatives their first meal. But the Jewish religion prescribes that despite the fact suffering for the loss of a dear person is indelible, those struck by mourning must return to normal life: "I have set before you life and death, blessing and cursing: therefore choose life" (Deuteronomy).

The community of Merano (once part of Austria) witnessed its greatest expansion under the Austro-Hungarian empire, when the town was renowned as a center for treating tuberculosis, and many of the hospitals and sanatoria were organized by Jewish doctors.

There had been many Jews either passing through or living in the Tyrol from the 13th century, but they only formed an official group in 1836 as a detached section of the community of Hohenems, a town in Vorarlberg (the western region of Austria, on the border with Switzerland and Liechtenstein). Despite being distant, Hohenems continued to be the main reference point. Indeed in 1901 its rabbi, Aron Tanzer, came to open the synagogue in Merano, the first allowed by Austria in the Tyrol. At the time the Merano group numbered 600–700 people, plus those staying in the town for health or work reasons. The community's guests included writers like Stefan Zweig and Franz Kafka, poets like Peretz Smolenskin (buried in Merano) and politicians like Chaim Weizmann, the first president of Israel. In 1918 Merano joined Italy and in 1930 the community became independent. Today it is still the only Jewish community in the region of Trentino-Alto Adige. The Jews assimilated the various political and cultural influences in the region: Italian in Trentino (the main towns being Trento and Riva del Garda) and Austrian in Alto Adige (with Bolzano and Merano).

The Merano group was badly hit by the Nazi deportations (eighty-one members were deported). It then became a reception center after the war for survivors from the Shoah. Today, although small, the community has a very active religious and cultural life.

Silver crown for the Torah. This is one of the ornaments decorating and honoring the Scrolls of the Law.

Synagogue interior. Officially opened in 1901, the rectangular prayer room is lit by colorful stained-glass windows depicting Jewish symbols and holidays. The bimah is set in front of the ark.

The synagogue in the trees

The only existing synagogue in the region, at no. 14, Via Schiller, was opened in 1901 after a year's construction. In 1900 eighty-one donations (a total of 5,200 crowns) had been collected from the Jews of Merano, thus making possible the construction of the synagogue. It then became the reference point for the whole area, especially during and after the war, when it was reopened despite a host of difficulties, such as the far from minor problem of recovering the assets plundered by the Fascists and Nazis. The lost items included a *Sefer Torah* for which the community paid the huge sum of 50,000 lire to ARAR, an organization that recovered assets abandoned after the war. The two-story building is situated in the middle of gardens with centuries-old trees. A plaque on the outside wall informs us that its inauguration took place during "Franz Josef's reign." Inside is a German-rite prayer room and a museum.

The rectangular prayer room is lit by large colorful stained-glass windows designed by Adele Friedenthal. The windows feature a number of Jewish symbols and festivities: the *menorah*, the Exodus, the Sabbath, *Yom Kippur*, Scrolls of the Law, and *Sukkoth*. The holy ark is set in a niche opposite the entrance wall. It is decorated with a series of stars and a Hebrew inscription from Exodus.

The *bimah* stands in front of the ark, with the benches lined up in parallel rows opposite. Wood paneling runs all the way round the base of the walls in the room, with the women's gallery overhead.

Opened in June 1998, the Jewish Museum of Merano is situated in the basement of the building. Divided into three main rooms, it is visited every year by over 3,000 people, mainly schoolchildren. The documents and items on show tell the story of the community, with a special focus on the 18th and 19th centuries, the Nazi-Fascist persecutions, and the deportations. After 1933, Germans fleeing Nazism sought refuge in Merano but in vain. Not far away in Bolzano, the Nazis set up a transit camp in 1944: over 11,000 prisoners passed through them before being loaded on trains bound for the extermination camps. Other documents and evidence reveal how at the end of the war, from 1946 to 1947, at least 15,000 survivors from the Shoah arrived in Merano. They were admitted to the sanatoria run by Jewish organizations. Many then went on to Palestine. In the 1950s, however, Merano was also a stage on the route used by Odessa, the organization that smuggled out Nazi criminals. Many Nazi bosses stopped off in Merano — including Eichmann and Mengele — and some stayed on incognito for years. Lastly, one section of the museum is dedicated to ceremonial objects and Jewish life.

The Anna Frank Cultural Center at no. 31, Via Leopardi has a specialized library with books on Jewish subjects in Italian and German.

The Jewish cemetery is a section of the town cemetery in Via San Giuseppe. Until the Second World War there had been an earlier cemetery in the Marconi Park since 1872, whereas before that date the Jews of Merano had used the Bolzano cemetery.

A community born under Austrian rule

Having settled in Habsburg-ruled Gorizia in the 16th century, the Jewish group in the town looked to Austria until 1918. After the ghetto was set up in 1696, the Jews purchased (rather than rented as happened in the rest of Italy) houses and shops in the ghetto area, where they engaged in traditional moneylending, but also silk spinning and wax production. In 1781 the Emperor Josef II issued a "tolerance charter" allowing them to work in any trade or job. In the meantime the Gorizia group had grown with the arrival of Jews from the territories of the Venetian Republic, which in 1777 introduced more restrictive legislation called the *Ricondotta* ("regulation"), limiting their activities and places of residence. In 1788 the community had 270 members, and their numbers rose to 314 in 1850. But then having gradually dwindled, it eventually died out.

Two interior views of the synagogue. Given its present form in 1984 after a preexisting room was remodeled, the interior has a rectangular plan. The high elliptical women's gallery, closed by moveable grates, is reminiscent of Venetian synagogues. The ark and bimah *are opposite each other. This synagogue is no longer used.*

A prosperous ghetto

In 1696 Via Ascoli was the main artery of the ghetto. A peripheral street in the town, it was closed by two large doors: one just before the church of San Giovanni and the other near the River Corno. On this side of the street there were eleven houses inside the ghetto and one outside. Halfway down the street was the house of Lazzaro Bolaffio with the synagogue. Opposite there were five houses with ground-floor shops. The buildings show signs of the flourishing economic life in the town and were embellished with fine balconies, wrought-iron railings, and stone frames round the windows. Even the door to the ghetto was replaced by a wrought-iron gate: it is thought to be the gate that still closes no. 1, Via Ascoli, once the house of the philologist and linguist Graziadio Isaia Ascoli (1829–1907), commemorated by a plaque on the wall.

The obligation to live in the ghetto was lifted at the beginning of the 19th century, and many Jews moved out. Their houses were then occupied by poor people. To create more room, they raised the buildings, thus changing the original structure of the quarter. In 1900 there were 865 people living in these cramped conditions, but only 52 were Jews. The urban decay became so bad that from 1955 to 1965 the whole area was redeveloped. It was at this time the buildings along the river beyond the synagogue were demolished. The remaining buildings, however, were gradually renovated.

The first (German rite) oratory was opened at no. 19, Via Ascoli in 1699. Extended in 1756, it was remodeled in 1894, when a courtyard was created in front of it by demolishing the house at no. 17. A plaque on the courtyard walls documents these changes.

The synagogue was devastated during the Second World War. Reopened in 1947 by Jewish American soldiers stationed in the town, it fell into disuse until recovered by Jews of Gorizian origin in 1969. The last restoration was in 1984. The exterior is dominated by a large rose window with a Star of David; at the side of the building an arcade overlooks the river. A plaque in the courtyard commemorates the forty-five Jews who were deported from Gorizia.

Inside, on the ground floor, is a small room, which until 1932 functioned as an oratory named after Abraham Vita Reggio. Today it houses the Gorizia Central European Institute of Hebrew Studies. Next to the institute is an exhibition space dedicated to the philosopher Carlo Michelstaedter (1887–1910). In the large hall is the museum — described as the "Little Jerusalem on the River Isonzo" — with showcases displaying objects, books, documents, booklets, and photographs. Seven plaques on the walls commemorate historical events and people from the community. A wide stair leads up to the first floor with the prayer room. The elliptical-shaped women's gallery has moveable grates. It is reached by a spiral stair in the hall. In the prayer room the holy ark and *bimah* are set opposite each other at the two ends of the room. The ark is adorned by four twisting black marble columns supporting a pediment with the Tablets of the Law. In front of the ark is a gilded wrought-iron gate made by Martino Geist, a German craftsman who worked in the town at the end of the 18th century. Four white marble candelabra stand on the floor in front of the ark.

Set against the entrance wall, the *bimah* is made of dark wood and is raised by five steps. On the platform an inscription records the date 1761, when a providential armistice put an end to a battle and saved the synagogue from destruction. This event is celebrated with a special Purim. The floor is made of black and white marble. Benches run along the walls, and behind them are twelve windows. Two wrought-iron chandeliers hang from the ceiling (only one is original). Today the room is used for cultural events.

The Gorizia Jewish cemetery, in use since 1371, remained outside Italian territory when the town passed from Austria to Italy in 1914. After the Second World War the cemetery became Slovenian territory. It is at Valdirose, not far from the border crossing at Casa Rossa.

The "Gateway to Zion"

The Trieste community reached the height of its splendor in the 19th century. In 1719 the Habsburgs rulers declared the city a free port and many Jews (including those from Corfu) came to trade in Trieste. Then in 1781 the Austrian rulers issued the "tolerance charter" granting the initial liberties to attend public schools up to the university, to buy and sell houses, and to engage in any manufacturing, commercial, or professional activities. Lastly, in 1785, the ghetto was abolished (the first had been opened in Corte Trauner in 1695, and the second at Riborgo in 1696). The Trieste community thus grew from a few hundred people in 1700 to as many as 6,500 by 1900. It was a very special group: some members had been decorated by the Austrian rulers with the highest noble titles. Playing an active part in the world of high finance, they founded the first insurance companies and were considered to be among the leading intellectuals in the city, especially in the field of psychoanalysis. The 19th century was thus a period of great vitality, paving the way, however, to a loss of religiousness and the gradual assimilation with the rest of the population. When Trieste became part of Italy and its port began to decline, the community was deeply affected and its numbers fell.

Jewish Trieste, however, played a key role in the clandestine emigration to Palestine, and was even dubbed the "Gateway to Zion." From the 1930s Jews fleeing the Nazis arrived in the city, while in the period immediately after the war, the survivors from the concentration camps were assisted and cared for by the community. Thanks to the efforts of Jewish organizations, hundreds of ships full of passengers left the port of Trieste, bound for the new homeland. Today the community numbers 600 people.

The synagogue entrance. Built in 1912, the building has a square structure with Oriental touches in the decorations of the biforate windows, columns, and carvings.

Detail of windows in the small oratory, used for daily prayers. The room has a rectangular plan with large arched windows. The walls have floral frescoes.

The area of the two ghettos

Via Trauner and Corte Trauner, behind Piazza San Silvestro, were the streets of the first ghetto, set up in 1695. Some tower buildings have survived from that period. The second ghetto was created in an area called Riborgo in 1696, between Piazza della Borsa and Via del Teatro Romano, and reached by going through Passaggio del Portizza. After decaying considerably from 1920 to 1930, most of the buildings in the area were demolished. Today only a few buildings still have their original appearance.

The quarter was circumscribed by Contrada Malcanton, Contrada Riborgo, and Contrada delle Beccherie (now Tor Bandena). Three large doors closed the ghetto: the first was in Piazza Vecchia (now Piazza del Rosario), the second in Via delle Beccherie, and the third in Contrada di Riborgo. At the center of the ghetto was the small square called Piazzetta delle Scuole Ebraiche and the Contrada delle Scuole Ebraiche, surrounded by a maze of small lanes (Contrada del Pane, Contrada delle Ombrelle, and Contrada del Ponte) and blind alleys, such as Contrada del Volto and Contrada Stretta. There were three functioning synagogues in this area.

The first, a German-rite temple called the Scola Piccola, was built in 1748 between Contrada delle Beccherie and Contrada delle Scuole. Destroyed by

Synagogue interior. Divided into a nave and two aisles, the rectangular interior ends in a large apse. Midway down the nave is a high starry dome. The ark has gilded doors surmounted by four dark marble columns supporting the Tablets of the Law, made of light-colored stone.

One of the three rose windows found on each of the façades. Although architecturally different, the façades all have the same motifs and friezes.

fire in 1822, the synagogue was built on a bigger scale in 1825 and continued to be used until 1935 as the oratory of the Jews from Corfu. In 1798 another two synagogues were opened in a single building situated on Piazzetta delle Scuole Ebraiche: the Scola Grande or Scola no. 2 (again a German-rite temple) on the second and third floor, and the Scola Spagnola, or Scola no. 3, a Sephardic temple on the ground and first floors. Lastly, in 1805, outside the ghetto, in Piazza Benco, yet another synagogue was built: the Scola Vivante, or no. 4, a Spanish-rite temple. None of these synagogues has survived. In 1928 Scola no. 3 was demolished and the ark taken to Abbazia (Opatija, now in Croatia); in 1934 Scola no. 2 was pulled down and the ark taken to Fiume (Rijeka, now in Croatia); in 1937 Scola no. 1 was demolished and, in 1956, the ark was shipped to Tel Aviv.

The modern synagogue

The present synagogue, at no. 19, Via San Francesco, was opened in 1912. Designed by the architects Ruggero and Arduino Berlam, with interior decorations by Piero Lucani, this synagogue has the typical size and structure of an emancipation temple.

The building has a square structure with Oriental-like elements in the decorations of the biforate windows, columns, and carvings. The three fronts give onto Via Donizetti, Via San Francesco, and Via Zanetti, respectively. They are architecturally different but have similar ornaments and decorations. The fourth side of the building backs onto a preexisting construction.

The main façade on Via Donizetti has a large rose window (also repeated on the other fronts) over a majestic portal decorated with floral patterns. The door leads directly into the large prayer room. This synagogue is only opened up for important occasions. Alongside is a small door decorated with an architrave, surmounted by a biforate window with a small column. Similar elements are repeated on the other fronts. The façade on Via San Francesco is enlivened by the projecting rectangular form of the loggia, providing access to the community offices in the building. Alongside there are another two portals on the street.

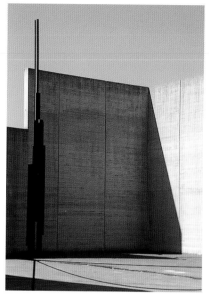

The most complex front is the third façade on Via Zanetti. At its center is a large apse with a domed roof. On either side two smaller projecting volumes are pierced at various heights by biforate windows, also covered by domes. There are three different-sized doors on the street. Inside is a large prayer room and a small oratory used for everyday purposes. The rectangular prayer room is divided into two aisles and a nave ending in a majestic apse. The nave is interrupted halfway down by a high dome with star decorations. The interior of the apse dome is covered by gold mosaics and framed by a vine-leaf and floral patterns adorned with colored studs. Pierced by two long symmetrical windows, the apse walls are clad in dark marble. At the center of the room is a monumental holy ark; its gilded doors are surmounted by four dark marble columns supporting the Tablets of the Law inscribed on light-colored stone. In front of the ark is a small *bimah* in the form of a lectern.

The prayer area is bounded by a marble railing embellished with flowers and corn ears (the symbol of the Trieste community). Standing in front of the *bimah* are two bronze seven-branched candelabra. The benches are lined up in two parallel rows. The two-story women's gallery runs round the room on three sides. The synagogue has a capacity of 1,500 people.

The same building also houses the community services, important historical archives, and a library.

The Jewish museum

The Carlo and Vera Wagner Museum was opened in 1993 in a building of great historical significance for the community at no. 5, Via Del Monte. Originally designed as a Jewish hospital, it became a primary school and in the 1930s a shelter for Jewish refugees fleeing the Nazis, before embarking for Palestine in the port of Trieste. Inside there was once a Polish Ashkenazi oratory.

The museum has two main rooms: the first is a lecture hall, while the second communicating room is organized for use as an oratory, thus recreating its original function. Here the *aron* (holy ark) is set in a niche in an eastern wall and is only opened during functions. The two rooms, however, are mainly used for exhibition purposes. Along the walls and in the middle of each room are glass cases containing religious furnishings and ceremonial objects belonging to the community. Some are very valuable and all survived the war and devastation by chance. They are used in rotation in the modern synagogue. The museum is thus a

Risiera di San Sabba: the monument to the victims, the façade of the old building, and the "room of crosses." From October 1943 to March 1944 San Sabba was first used as a transit camp and then as an extermination camp, the only one in Italy.

"strong box" keeping the community's furnishings safe. The rooms also host lectures and temporary exhibitions.

In the courtyard a covered *Lapidario* (stone collection) contains old headstones, some from the first Jewish cemetery in Trieste, which was at the top of Via del Monte, as is pointed out in the plaque at the beginning of the street. The plaque is also inscribed with verses on the subject by the Trieste Jewish poet, Umberto Saba. Used for over four centuries, this cemetery was replaced in the mid-19th century by the cemetery of Sant'Anna (no. 4, Via della Pace). Over 2,000 bodies were moved here, when the Via del Monte area was expropriated in 1909 to become the "Park of Remembrance."

The Risiera di San Sabba

Situated in the city outskirts, the Risiera di San Sabba (a former rice mill) was the only extermination camp in Italian territory. Today it has become a Museum of the Memory, designed by the architect Romano Boico. From October 1943 to March 1944 San Sabba was first used as a transit camp and then a place of extermination after the construction of cremation ovens. Thousands of people, including many Trieste Jews, were deported through or died in the Risiera di San Sabba.

Italian Jews and the Shoah

From 1938 to 1945 Fascist Italy was officially an anti-Semite country. The first practical move was the census on the Jewish religion and its followers, ordered on 14–15 February 1938 by the Ministry of the Interior. In July 1938 a theoretical document was distributed on "Fascism and the Problems of Race," later known as the "Manifesto of Racist Scientists." On August 22, a general census of Jews according to race was begun, and in October the Grand Council of Fascism approved the "Declaration on Race."

Authorized by the laws for the "defense of the race" and administrative measures, the suppression of Jews' rights began with the expulsion of students and teachers from schools (September 2) and employees from the public administration (November 10), including the army. Jewish employment was also limited in private commercial activities, and they could not register on unemployment lists. There were also limits on the right to own a house, land, and businesses, and marriages between Jews and non-Jews were banned (November 10). It is estimated that this set of discriminatory laws had already affected around 51,000 people in 1938, just over one per thousand of the Italian population. But then anti-Semitic hatred penetrated even more sectors of economic and social life in the country.

According to the Fascist plans, these initial discriminations should have led to all Italian and foreign Jews leaving the country within two years. But Italy's entry into the war on June 10, 1940, thwarted the implementation of these designs. That same month, however, the Fascists ordered the internment of Italian Jews judged to be dangerous and foreign Jews whose countries had an anti-Fascist policy. In May 1942 hard labor was imposed on some groups of Italian Jews (including women) and in May-June internment and hard labor camps were set up for Italian Jews. The Badoglio government then revoked some of the anti-Semite laws, but left the overall legislation in place.

With the armistice between Italy and the Allies on September 8, 1943, the physical persecution of Jews living in northern and central Italy began, i.e., in the area still occupied by the Germans and the new Fascist State, called the Italian Social Republic. The Allied troops had landed in southern Italy and on the islands, and so only the Jews in those areas (the minority) avoided the big round-ups.

In northern and central Italy the persecution was pursued jointly by Italians and Germans. Only the Operations Zones (*Alpenvorland* and *Adriatisches Künstenland*) were run by the Germans alone. Jews were arrested, interned in camps, and then deported to be physically eliminated. Their assets were confiscated. On September 15–16, 1943, twenty-two Jews from Merano were arrested and deported. At the same time at Meina, on Lake Maggiore, fifty people were killed. On October 16 the first systematic round-ups were carried out in Rome by special police divisions: 1,259 Jews were arrested, and 1,023 of them were deported two days later to Auschwitz. From December on, the Italian authorities also began to arrest Jews and intern them. They were first taken to provincial camps and then concentrated in the national camp at Fossoli, near Carpi, in the province of Modena. From March 1944 the Fossoli camp was run directly by the Germans who later moved the prisoners to Gries, Bolzano. From these camps the convoys left for Auschwitz.

A total of 8,500 people were deported from Italy. The identity of only 6,800 was reconstructed (almost 6,000 were killed), while it has not been possible to give a name to at least 1,000 people. Most of the deportees were taken to Auschwitz, and very few returned. During the war around 300 Jews were also killed in Italy. The Jewish group with the largest proportion of victims was that of the twenty-one chief rabbis of the communities: nine were taken to Auschwitz and none returned.

During the persecution there were some 45,000 Jews living in Italy: around 500 were in the south, 5,000 to 6,000 escaped to Switzerland, and the remaining

Monument to the Holocaust: seven bronze panels with scenes of deportation by the sculptor Arbit Blatas, in Campo del Ghetto Novo, Venice. The sculpture was unveiled in a wall of the square in 1980 to commemorate the victims of the Shoah.

29,000 survived by hiding in rural areas or in the cities. Around 1,000 Jews fought in the ranks of the Resistance, and one hundred died fighting or were arrested and executed.

At the end of the war the communities had to count their dead and many of the smaller ones no longer had enough members to continue with group life. Italy became a place of transit for refugees and camp survivors who embarked from Genoa or Trieste to Palestine (then under the British Mandate) and the Americas. The return to community life has not cancelled or diminished the memory of those years. The memory of the Shoah is also kept alive by living witnesses who feel a duty to inform young people about the horrors experienced so that they will not be repeated. Realizing the importance of educating young people about the Shoah, the Italian government created a "Memory Day" in 2000. This special day has been held annually since then in Italy and throughout Europe, on January 27, the date

Bolognese Jews and the Church

Jewish refugees from Rome and central and northern Italy arrived in Bologna in the 14th century. Many of them were merchants, especially cloth dealers. Significantly, in Bologna trading in used cloths was included in the "Guild of Drapers, Cloth Merchants, Pitch Workers, Titleless, and Jews."

The Jewish group always lived in precarious provisional conditions, especially after 1504, when the city passed from rule by the Bentivoglio to the Papal States. In 1566 the Church authorities set up the ghetto and three years later, in 1569, proclaimed the first expulsion decree. The cemetery in Via Orfeo was expropriated and the headstones destroyed. The Jews returned to the city in 1584, but only nine years later, in 1593, were expelled again, this time for good. The expelled people even took their dead with them to be buried in the cemetery at Pieve di Cento.

The Jews came back to live in Bologna two centuries later, in 1797, when Napoleon's army arrived. But their troubles were not over. The group was once more struck by a terrible episode of intolerance. In 1858, at the pope's orders, the six-year-old Edgardo Mortara was kidnapped under the pretext that the wet nurse had baptized the child when he was ill and apparently on death's door. The young Edgardo was locked up in a religious institute in Rome to be brought up according to Christian principles. The boy's parents fought with all their might to have their son returned. Sovereigns, leading personalities, and worthies at home and abroad lobbied the Church so that it would revoke the decision. But it was all in vain. The parents only met their son again many years later when he had become a priest. The "Mortara case" (not the only one of its kind) shocked the Italian Jewish community, and especially the Bolognese community, for a long time.

In 1864 the Bolognese community formed an association. Then, having rapidly grown in numbers, the association designed a large synagogue, inaugurated in 1877 in the 17th-century Palazzo Dei Gombruti, where it is still situated today. In 1943 the Bolognese Jews were also hit by the racial laws, and eighty-four were deported. The community was reconstituted after the liberation of Italy, but today only has 200 members.

A street in the ghetto, created in 1566 and closed by four gates. It was set up in an area around the Torre degli Asinelli and the Torre della Garisenda. The main streets were what are now Via Zamboni and Via Oberdan. The recently restored quarter has maintained its original appearance.

Palazzo Bocchi in Via Goito. The façade of this building has a Hebrew inscription from Psalms and a Latin inscription from Horace. In the 16th century the palazzo housed the Accademia Ermatena, a literary academy.

The ghetto under the two towers

The ghetto is in the historic center of Bologna, around the area of the two towers — Torre degli Asinelli and Torre della Garisenda. When created, it had two large arteries: Strada San Donato (now Via Zamboni) and Via Cavaliera (now Via Oberdan) and was to have four doors (only three were actually built). The first was situated at the beginning of Via dei Giudei; the second where Via del Carro meets Via Zamboni, and the third in Piazzetta San Simone, which leads into Via Oberdan. Today the only still recognizable access is the second entrance in a vaulted passage linking Palazzo Manzoli-Malvasia to the 18th-century church of San Donato.

In recent years the whole quarter has been carefully restored. To form an idea of what the ghetto was like, you only have to walk round Via dei

Giudei, Via Canonica, Vicolo del Mandria, Vicolo San Giobbe, Via dell'Inferno, Via del Carro, and Via Valdonica. Under the arcades in these Medieval streets, craft shops have been opened again (such as the shop specializing in Jewish prints, situated between Via dei Giudei and Via Canonica) and small stores (as in Via dell'Inferno), which have brought new life to the quarter.

At no. 16 (formerly no. 2638), Via dell'Inferno is the building with the only synagogue actually in the ghetto (only the exterior has survived). On the façade of the neighboring building is a stone plaque mentioning the creation of the ghetto and the persecution suffered by the Bolognese Jews.

The Jewish Museum
At no. 1, Via Valdonica is the Jewish Museum, the lively hub of the Jewish cultural revival in the quarter. The museum was officially opened in 1999.

Situated in the 15th-century Palazzo Pannolini, it is run by a foundation created jointly by the Region, Province, City Council, and Bolognese Jewish Community. The museum is used for educational purposes and is equipped with multimedia and other technological aids. A permanent exhibition with three different sections illustrates Jewish history from the origins to the present day at three levels: the general history of the Jewish people, Italian Jews, and the history of Jews in Emilia Romagna. Each section makes use of videos, descriptive panels, and CD-ROMs. There is also a small display of ceremonial objects in a glass case: the Scrolls of the Law with all its covers (mantle, crown, pointers, and plate). Another two cases contain everyday objects: a prayer mantle and prayer book, the seven-branched candelabrum, and a scroll containing the Book of Esther.

The museum promotes initiatives to spread knowledge about Jewish life and organizes seminars and courses on Jewish language and culture as well as lectures, exhibitions, shows, events, games for children, and trips in Italy and abroad to explore Jewish sites. There is also a specialist bookstore and shop with objects and kosher products.

To celebrate *Hanukkah* (held annually on varying dates in November and December), each year the great lamp with nine candles (*Hanukkiah*) is lit every evening for eight days in Piazza della Mercanzia, the heart of the ghetto.

The 19th-century synagogue

The 19th-century synagogue is situated at no. 9, Via dei Gombruti, and the main entrance is in a parallel street, Via Mario Finzi. The Art-Nouveau façade is dominated by a rose window with a Star of David. Next to the entrance door is a stone plaque commemorating the eighty-four Bolognese deportees.

The building was acquired in the mid-19th century by Jews who had come back to the city after over two centuries absence. They had already organized an oratory in a private house in Via dei Gombruti, but it had soon become too small for the needs of the new group. The remodeling work was entrusted to the engineer Guido Lisi. Opened in 1877, the new temple also soon turned out to be too small. The community thus decided to add an extension and commissioned the architect Attilio Muggia to design and build it. This new synagogue was completed in the extended building in 1928.

A room in the Jewish Museum opened in 1999 in a building in the old ghetto area. Equipped with the latest multimedia technology, the museum is used for educational purposes and hosts conferences, exhibitions, and debates.

Synagogue interior. Completed in 1928, the synagogue was destroyed by a bomb in 1943 and reconstructed in 1953. The room has a rectangular plan divided into a nave and two aisles with a barrel-vault ceiling. A large Star of David decorates the rose window.

The new room was the same size as its predecessor and had the same pavilion roof with exposed ribbing ending in a rectangle round an elliptical skylight. One of the walls was decorated by half-columns. The opposite wall was divided into two orders of strip pilasters and fascias. The two-story women's gallery ran along the side walls, supported by a double order of columns.

The synagogue was then destroyed by a bomb in 1943. After the war the community rebuilt it, having commissioned the design from the son of the first architect, the engineer Guido Muggia. He reelaborated his father's idea in a modern key. The new prayer room was opened in 1953 and is still in

use. In recent years it has been renovated, but the general restoration of the whole building is still in progress.

The prayer room

The rectangular prayer room is divided into a nave and two aisles. The barrel-vault ceiling has exposed ribbing. The perimeter wall has a rose window adorned by a large Star of David. On the opposite side, above the ark, is a cupboard framed by a wooden portal with an inscription of the Tablets of the Law. Further up is an elongated semicircular window with colorful stained glass and a painted seven-branched candelabrum. At the sides of the ark and the window are reproductions of psalms. The ark is enclosed by a marble balustrade. The *bimah* is set in front of the ark, while the benches are arranged round the prayer area. Resting on the two side walls, the women's gallery is reached by a stair situated outside one of the aisles.

The ground floor has a room used as a social center as well as for daily prayers. For this purpose, there is a small dark wooden ark set against the eastern wall. The building also houses a *mikveh*, the community offices, the rabbi's quarters and the premises of the kosher canteen, run by the community. Take-away meals may be ordered by booking in advance.

The cemetery

Part of the city cemetery, the Jewish cemetery is reached from Via della Certosa. It dates back to the second half of the 19th century, when Jews returned to the city. The old cemeteries dating from the period of the ghetto were destroyed. The only four surviving 16th-century gravestones from a cemetery once in Via Orfeo are in the Civic Medieval Museum at no. 4, Via Manzoni.

Judaica in the city

The city libraries and museums have some very interesting Judaica collections: in the University Library (Biblioteca Universitaria, no. 35, Via Zamboni) there are twenty-eight precious illuminated manuscripts, including a *machzor* with a 14th-century page from a Paschal *Haggadah* of Catalan provenance, and the *Avicenna Codex*, with 15th-century miniatures on medical themes. In the City Library (Biblioteca Comunale) at the Archiginnasio (Portico dell'Archiginnasio) there is a section of old Jewish texts, including 16th-century printed books.

Lastly, a curious item: a Hebrew inscription on the façade of the Palazzo Bocchi, at no. 16, Via Goito. It was raised by Achille Bocchi, who was a man of letters at Bologna University, a patron of 16th-century culture and founder of a literary academy (Accademia Ermatena), housed in this palace. On the base of the building are two inscriptions, one in Hebrew with Psalm 119 ("Deliver me O Lord from lying lips and from a deceitful tongue") and another in Latin, taken from Horace ("You will be king, it is said, if you act righteously").

The room for daily prayers is situated on the ground floor of the building. Also used as a social center and lecture hall, this room has a dark wood ark set against the eastern wall.

Silver and gold medallion for the Scrolls of the Law. With the crown and rimmonim, *the medallion honors the sacred nature of the scriptures.*

In the realm of a Renaissance court

The first Jews to arrive in Carpi in the 14th century were welcomed by the Pio — the local princes who created a splendid Renaissance court. From then to the beginning of the 20th century, an albeit small group continued to live in the town. In 1527, when Carpi was annexed to the Duchy of Este the group stayed on. The Jews then enjoyed two centuries of political tolerance until 1719, when under papal pressure the rulers agreed to create a ghetto. It was set up in a street where the Jews lived already, part of what is now Via Rovighi. Segregation was temporarily suspended in 1796 with the arrival of the French, and then ended definitively with the unity of Italy. To celebrate their newly won freedom, the group built a large synagogue to replace one already in use since 1722 in a building in the arcade of the corn market. Opened in 1861, the new synagogue was short-lived: the already small community dwindled further and by 1898 there were only thirty-one members, too few to warrant such a large prayer room, which was closed for good in 1922.

Entrance to the former synagogue in Via Rovighi. Completed in 1861, it was only used until 1922, when the community's numbers fell. The furnishings were then taken to Modena and Israel.

The Neoclassical room has a square plan with a niche, once used for the ark (now replaced by mirrors). The niche is decorated by two Corinthian columns, surmounted by an entablature containing a large shell. There are women's galleries on two sides of the room.

A one-street ghetto

Via Rovighi (at various time called first Via di Mezzo, then Contrada San Rocco and Contrada del Ghetto), was the only street in the ghetto, closed by two doors: the first was at the junction with Via Berengario, and the second half way down the street near the church of San Rocco (now demolished). The synagogue was at no. 57, in the Palazzo del Portico del Grano, and was the third built by the group in the town. Designed by Achille Sammarini, it was begun in 1858 and completed by 1861. After being closed in 1922, the synagogue was stripped of its furnishings: the *bimah* was taken to Modena, while in the 1950s the ark went to Israel, where it is still in the synagogue of the Ayanot Agricultural College. In recent years the synagogue has been restored, but is temporarily closed following recent earthquake damage. Neoclassical in style, it has a niche for the ark (now replaced by mirrors) decorated by two Corinthian columns surmounted by an entablature and, above it, a round arch containing a large decorative shell. There are two small women's galleries on the side walls, while a third larger women's gallery occupies the rear wall. The room was entirely decorated with stuccowork, scagliola, gilding, and friezes by Ferdinando Manzini, Gaetano Venturi, and Antonio Bernasconi.

The cemetery

Created in 1825 and used until 1922, the cemetery is in Via del Cimitero Israelitico. A square-shaped field, it contains only eleven gravestones. It was the fourth Jewish cemetery in the town. The first dated back to the first half of the 15th century but can no longer be found. The second was opened in 1624 near the Terragli (fortification works); the third in the village of Sant'Agostino (Via Sbrillaci) was moved outside the built-up area in 1816. The most recent cemetery is at Quartirolo. Acquired in 1823, it was used for a century.

A museum dedicated to the deportees

Situated in the Pio Castle in the middle of the town, the museum (also intended to be a monument) is dedicated to the political and racial deportees sent to

the extermination camps. It was opened in 1973, thanks to the efforts of the town council. The idea of creating a monument to commemorate the deportations arose in 1961 and that year an international competition was announced and won by the architects Belgiojoso, Peressutti, and Rogers. It took over ten years, however, to create the spaces in the castle and complete the project. The museum has thirteen rooms. Their walls are hung with graphic works and writings by famous artists — Guttuso, Cagli, Alberto Longoni, Picasso, and Léger. At eye level there are also engraved quotations from the book *Lettere dei condannati a morte della Resistenza.* ("Letters from Members of the Resistance Sentenced to Death"). There are also some glass cases displaying various items and documents from the extermination camps. The itinerary ends in a completely empty room with names of the thousands of Italian deportees on the bare walls. In the grounds of the building there are fifteen concrete slabs, six meters (20 feet) high, inscribed with the names of the Nazi extermination camps.

The Fossoli deportation camp

In 1942 a camp (at the time called the "old camp") was set up by the Fascist authorities for British prisoners of war at Fossoli, a village in the communal

AMMENDORF-AR
NSTADT-AUSSIG
-BAD-DURKHEIM
-BADEN-BADEN-
BAD-KLEINEN-
BAD-REHBURG

TREBLINKA-
TRZEBIONKA-
CZESTOCHOWA
-WADOWITZ-
WALDENBURG-
WALTERSDORF

Courtyard of the Museum and Monument to Political and Racial Deportees to the Extermination Camps. Opened in 1973, the museum consists of thirteen rooms on the ground floor in the Pio Castle. In the grounds there are fifteen concrete slabs inscribed with the names of the Nazi extermination camps.

Huts at Fossoli, used by the Nazis as a transit camp for political and racial deportees. Primo Levi also passed through this camp before being deported to Auschwitz. Today the huts are part of a museum.

area of Carpi. In 1943 the camp was then occupied by the Nazis, who initially only used a few huts. The camp had been chosen for Fossoli's excellent position as a junction on the main railway line north to the Brenner Pass. That year the camp was handed over to the Fascists of the Social Republic, who made it a provincial concentration camp (the "new camp") for Jews arrested in northern and central Italy. Until January 1944, the prison was run jointly by the Fascists and Nazis. But in February the "new camp" passed under the complete control of the German police, while the "old camp" continued to be run by the Fascists. As the deportations were stepped up, Fossoli began to be used as a transit camp for political and racial deportees being sent to the extermination camps. It continued to be used as such until August, when for security reasons it was abandoned and the logistic organization was transferred to the camp at Gries, Bolzano. In seven months around 5,000 deportees passed through the Fossoli camp, half of them were Jews (they included Primo Levi). At the end of November the "old camp" was also evacuated and received no more prisoners.

After the war, the huts were used from 1947 to 1952 by the Catholic community of Nomadelfia. From 1953 until the end of 1960s it hosted refugees from Dalmatia. It was then eventually completely abandoned. Today the huts still stand as mute witnesses to the Nazi-Fascist deportations. To perpetuate the memory of that period, in 1984 the Carpi Town Council announced an international competition for the redevelopment of the former concentration camp as a public park and national museum commemorating the victims of concentration and extermination camps. Of the 150 designs submitted for the competition, thirty-five were selected and published in a special book.

In 1991 the design by the Florentine architect Roberto Maestro was chosen from those in the competition. His design has transformed part of the park into a kind of Minotaur's labyrinth.

Good relations with enlightened rulers

Jews lived in Ferrara from the Middle Ages. Initially they settled in vario
areas in the city, but from the 15th century they were concentrated behi
the cathedral, where the ghetto was later to be established.

Under the Duchy of Este, the community enjoyed its finest years: t
dukes offered shelter to refugees from Spain and Portugal after 1492 a
from Eastern Europe when the Jews were expelled in 1532. After these tw
waves of immigration the Ferrara group became much larger and number
2,000 out of a total of 30,000 inhabitants. But the dukes also granted them t
right to practice several professions and various commercial activities
addition to the traditional moneylending. In this way the Jewish contrib
tion to the cultural development of the city was very important. Amo
leading Sephardic cultural figures were the university professors Abraha
Farissol (1431–1535) and Abraham Sarfati; the Abrabanel family fro
Naples; Doña Grazia Mendes and her brother Ariel de Luna, from Portug
Doña Grazia, who held a literary *salon* in the city, helped dozens
Sephardim to escape from the Iberian peninsula and many came to Ferra
Amato Lusitano, the printer Abramo Usque (who in 1555 printed two ed

Two streets in the ghetto, created in 1627. The Jewish quarter was behind the cathedral and closed by five gates. The present Via Mazzini was the main street, while other ghetto streets branched off. Now completely restored, the quarter still has its original structure.

tions of the Ferrara Bible, dedicating one to Ercole of Este a
the other to Doña Grazia Mendes).

The period of peace and well-being ended in 1597, whe
Duke Alfonso died with no male heirs and Ferrara was annexe
to the Papal States. Cesare of Este, in the minor branch, move
his court to Modena and many Jews followed him.

In 1627 the ghetto was established. The area chosen — on
after three years of discussion and a great deal of resistan
from the Jews — was an already mainly Jewish quarter ne
the cathedral. The area was closed by five gates: two at the end
of Via dei Sabbioni (now Via Mazzini); another two at the jun
tions of Via Vignatagliata with Via Contrari, at one end, ar
with Via del Travaglio (now Via San Romano) at the other. Th
fifth gate was at the junction of Via Gattamarcia (now Via Vi
toria) with Via Ragno. The perimeter of the ghetto was marke
in the map of the city made by Andrea Bolzoni in 1782, no
considered a very important historical document.

From the 18th to the 19th century various governments ruled Ferrara an
deeply influenced the life of the Jewish community. Twice — after the fa
and return of the Papal States — the gates were removed only to be put u
again. On 21 March 1848 they were finally destroyed for good. In 1859 the cit
became part of the Kingdom of Italy.

During and after the unity of Italy, the Ferrara Jews eagerly took part in cit
life, in which they felt deeply involved. Thus, many years later, in 1938 whe
they were classified as second-rate citizens by the racial laws, they wer
shocked and incredulous. Fascism inflicted deep wounds on the communit
in 1944 the German synagogue was devastated and ninety-six people wer
deported to extermination camps. Today there is only a small communit
(eighty people), but its members lead a regular and culturally very lively lif
as well as being fully integrated into the city.

A leap into the past

Few Italian cities have preserved the feel of the Jewish memory, both distan
and recent, as keenly as Ferrara. Going down the streets of the ghetto, sti

Filigree silver scent-holders. Scents are placed in the holders for the Sabbath blessing. The scents are used to alleviate the sadness felt at the end of the festivity.

The Scola Tedesca interior. It is one of the four synagogues in the historic community building used since 1481. Founded by German Jews in 1603, the Scola Tedesca is still opened for major festivities.

intact in their original layout, and entering the synagogues and museums, means exploring three centuries of history.

Via Mazzini (formerly Contrada Sabbioni) was the main street in the ghetto. At the beginning of the street, behind the cathedral, in the oratory of San Crispino, from 1695 the Jews were forced to attend sermons which, according to the Church, would convince them to convert. In earlier centuries the same kind of sermons had been given in the ducal chapel (now part of the Palazzo del Comune), near the castle. But they then had to be moved to avoid the Jews walking too far past the mocking populace. At the entrance to Via Mazzini you can still see the marks left by the hinges from one of the five ghetto gates and on the left-hand wall a plaque (difficult to read because it is so high up but reproduced in the museum) mentions the creation of the enforced isolation in this quarter. Now a pedestrian precinct, the street has a long backdrop of continuous buildings forming a single façade with ground-floor shops. Via Mazzini has always had — and continues to have — a commercial character. According to the chronicles, until the beginning of the 20th century this was where the main shops in the ghetto were, including Nuta Ascoli's delicatessen shop, famed for its Jewish specialties (goose salami, pastries, and caviar from sturgeon fished in the Po River). Despite the inevitable renovations and restorations, the buildings have preserved their original appearance. They were once linked by internal passages making it possible to reach the synagogue by going from one house to the other without having to enter the street. Mainly created for security reasons, some of these secret passages came to light again during recent restoration work.

Via Mazzini is cut vertically by two streets forming the backbone of the ghetto: Via Vignatagliata and Via Vittoria (formerly Via Gattamarcia, with the two appendices of the dead-end alleys Vicolo Torcicoda and Mozzo della Vittoria). By going down Via Vignatagliata you come out in Via Contrari (outside the ghetto), which is backed onto by the houses in Via Mazzini. These houses could have no windows facing the quarter and therefore many were bricked in. This is still the case with the building containing the synagogue at nos. 54 and 56. By returning to Via Vignatagliata, and then going on back to Via Mazzini, you come to Piazzetta Isacco Lampronti and the junction with Via Vittoria. The buildings on the street and in the internal squares have a more majestic look than those in Via Mazzini and have no ground-floor shops. Some buildings in this part of the ghetto were built in the 16th and 17th century by architects in the school of Biagio Rossetti, the leading designer of Renaissance Ferrara. The streets are all full of memories: at no. 39, Via Vittoria, there was a Rest Home named after Allegrina Cavalieri (she is mentioned in some plaques in the entrance hall beside others recording the names of benefactors). At no. 41 was the Scola Spagnola, the Spanish-rite synagogue destroyed by the Fascists in 1944 (as mentioned by a plaque on the façade). In the museum you can admire an accurate historical reconstruction of the prayer room. Some of the furnishings are now in the Lampronti oratory in Livorno.

No. 33 Via Vignatagliata was the house of the erudite rabbi Isacco Lampronti (here, too, commemorated by a plaque). At no. 79 there is a Jewish nursery and school, founded in the mid-19th century. A plaque raised in 2002 on the façade recalls that the teachers included the writer Giorgio Bassani.

At no. 95, still in Via Mazzini, is the historic community building: in 1481 (but possibly even in 1422) it housed the first synagogue, which was donated to the community by Shemuel Melli, who had come to Ferrara from Rome.

The former Scola Italiana is now a meeting room. The square-plan room contains three precious holy arks set against the walls. They came from the Scola Italiana and the Scola Spagnola (now demolished).

The 18th-century holy ark in the Scola Fanese, made of colored marble, is surmounted by the Tablets of the Law and decorated with floral motifs. At the sides are two black marble columns and two seats with colored marble inlaid work.

Here he acquired the building for 950 ducats from the Norzi family, which ran the Sabbioni loan-bank. At that time there were ten functioning synagogues in the city. On the façade, on either side of the entrance, two plaques commemorate the tragedy of the Shoah and list the names of the ninety-six Ferrarese Jews deported to the extermination camps from 1943 to 1945. Inside are two functioning synagogues (the Scola Fanese and the Scola Tedesca), a former Italian-rite synagogue now a meeting room (the Scola Italiana, described by Giorgio Bassani in the novel *The Garden of the Finzi-Continis*), the rabbinical tribunal, the Jewish Museum, and the community offices. By going up a steep stair on the left of the entrance hall you come to the first floor and the synagogue currently in use, the Scola Fanese. This small rectangular room is reached by going through a solid 19th-century door once in the synagogue at Cento. The door was accidentally mounted back to front, and so the Hebrew inscription "Let the Just come unto Me" greets the visitors on leaving instead of on entering the room.

The 18th-century ark, restored after being devastated during the last war, is made of polychrome marble and at the top has the traditional Tablets of the Law with floral ornaments and volutes. It is flanked by two black marble

The old cemetery in Via delle Vigne, used since 1626. The writer Giorgio Bassani, famed for the novel The Garden of the Finzi-Continis *is buried here.*

columns and two seats, adorned by colored marble inlaid work. The ark contains Scrolls of the Law once in Lugo. The *bimah* is in the center of the room, surrounded by two rows of benches, also from Cento. The walls are decorated with stuccowork.

Coming back to the entrance courtyard, you can visit the museum exhibition rooms, synagogues, and other rooms. On the right in the rectangular courtyard are two white marble columns used to construct the traditional tabernacle for the autumn festivity of *Sukkoth*. On the left, the stair leads up to the museum: in the entrance and along the ramp there are 17th-century *tzedakah* boxes and plaques dedicated to benefactors (one naturally mentions Shemuel Melli) and the war dead.

The Scola Tedesca (German synagogue) on the first floor is only opened for major festivities. It was founded in 1603 by German-origin Jews who, on settling in Ferrara, wanted to continue to pray according to their own rite. This temple was devastated in September 1941 by the Fascists. Since then it has had several restorations. The rectangular prayer room has a barrel-vaulted ceiling. The walls are embellished with stuccowork by Gaetano Davia, the artist responsible for the interior decoration of the Ferrara City Theatre (Teatro Comunale). The room is well lit by large windows. Concealed behind a closely knit grate, the women's gallery is set against the entrance wall. At its base, along the upper perimeter of the room, there are verses in Hebrew taken from Psalms. Some of the plaques mention the extension and restoration works. The furnishings are very spare: two parallel rows of wooden benches face the prayer area, set in a raised position. The *bimah* and wooden ark (17th century) are between white marble balusters, flanked by two rabbi's seats. The ark is decorated with the Tablets of the Law. Lamps and candelabra provide light for the synagogue while the *ner tamid* hangs in front of the ark. A stair leads up to the women's gallery, now part of the museum. In fact this small rectangular space contains glass cases with prayer books, and covers and capes for the *Torah*.

The door opposite the women's gallery door is the entrance to the museum. The six rooms of the museum provide an ideal reconstruction of a synagogue with ritual furnishings and objects, narrating the cycle of life (birth, circumcision, redemption of the first-born son or *pidyoin*, Bar-Mitzvah, marriage, and death) and the objects associated with each of these stages in life. The festivities are described with the ritual furnishings for each occasion. The museum illustrates the history of the community, beginning from the ghetto period (among the interesting items is a set of keys for the gates of the ghetto, previously in the Dioceses Historical Archives) with a description of daily life, and the lively literary output up to the French occupation and the unity of Italy. The museum also displays unique papers and correspondence on the birth of Zionism, experienced first-hand by some leading Ferrara figures, and has a section on the Shoah. This last theme will also be dealt with in a new museum soon to be built in the city.

The visit continues through the rooms of the rabbinical tribunal, reconstructed after the war in the atrium of the Italian synagogue, now only used for meetings. The rectangular prayer room in the synagogue has a number of historic plaques on the walls. It also boasts three valuable arks from the former Spanish synagogue and the Italian synagogue itself, when it functioned as the prayer room for the Italian rite.

Points of interest and curiosities

The Biblioteca Ariostea — a library in the Palazzo Paradisi in Via Scienze and Via Gioco del Pallone — houses a Judaica section with books printed by Abramo Usque and Gershom Soncino. In the historic center of the city, opposite the cathedral, the so-called Volto del Cavallo is embellished with two columns bearing statues. The equestrian statue of Borso of Este (1719) is set on a column partly made up of some old Hebrew headstones (brought to light during a recent restoration).

Not far away, in Corso Martiri della Libertà, four plaques on the Este castle walls commemorate those who died at the hands of the Fascists on 15 November 1943, when eleven anti-Fascists, including four Jews, were executed by a firing squad. This episode is recounted by Giorgio Bassani in a novel, *La lunga notte del '43* ("The Long Night of '43"), also a film by Florestano Vancini.

The Addizione Erculea cemetery

No visit to Ferrara is complete without going to the mysterious cemetery in Via delle Vigne, purchased in 1626 but possibly already in use in the 15th century. The entrance gateway (three granite slabs form the pillars and architrave) was built in 1911 by the architect Ciro Contini. The older part of this cemetery has sweeping lawns with only a few stones; many were destroyed at the time of the Inquisition (18th century). There are family tombstones with some artistic interest in the 19th- and 20th-century sections. The grave of the writer Giorgio Bassani, who died in 2000, is in an isolated position.

At the court of the Este

Having settled in Modena in the 15th century, the Jews enjoyed a long peri od of relative peace under the Dukes of Este, engaging in various activitie and professions. At the beginning of the 17th century, the existing grou (around a 1,000 people) was joined by the Ferrarese Jews after the Este cour had been forced to leave Ferrara. In 1638, however, under pressure from th Church, the Este had to capitulate and set up a ghetto in Modena. The ghet to had a long and complicated gestation period. The buildings in the are were redeveloped and 336 Christians had to leave thirty-five houses t make room for the new tenants. The buildings were divided up, and th doors and windows looking out of the ghetto had to be bricked up. Ther then ensued a difficult period of life in slums and poverty. But despite al this, three synagogues with different rites (Italian, German, and Spanish continued to function in addition to the oratories in private houses. Th ghetto also became a center for Hebrew and Cabalistic studies, attracting leading scholars from the Diaspora. The forced coexistence with the loca people of Modena led to the creation of a dialect, Modenese-Jewish, now extinct. Enclosure lasted until 1797, when the French pulled down the gates of the ghetto. They were then put up again during the restoration of th monarchy and finally abolished in 1859.

The large synagogue interior. Opened in 1873, it had a capacity of 1,000 people. The plan is rectangular with the area for the officiant slightly raised above the benches for the congregation. Framed by Neoclassical columns, the ark has leaf-decorated doors.

From the beginning of the 20th century the Modena community began to dwindle. In 1938, after the introduction of the racial laws, the publisher Angelo Fortunato Formiggini (1878–1938) committed suicide by throwing himself off the Tower of Ghirlandina to denounce the Fascist discrimina tion against Jews. This episode deeply shocked the community. Sixteen Jews were deported from Modena. Today the community, although small, is still a very lively center of Jewish culture.

Gates on the Via Aemilia

Piazza Mazzini, Via Coltellini, Via Blasia, Via Torre, and Vicolo Squallore were the main streets in the ghetto. This area was completely transformed in 1903 when the quarter was demolished: the heart of the ghetto was pulled down and its place was taken by Piazza della Libertà, now Piazza Mazzini.

When created, the ghetto was closed by four gates: the first was on the Via Emilia (the ancient Roman Via Aemilia) at the entrance to Vicolo Squallore (formerly Contrada Squaroa); the second was at the end of Via del Taglio; the third was in Contrada San Biagio (now Vicolo Blasia); and the fourth in Contrada San Domenico (today Via Cesare Battisti). Vicolo Squallore is the only street that has preserved its medieval structure of a continuous row of low houses. It ends at the church of San Giorgio. Via Blasia flanks the cur rent synagogue and joins Via del Taglio that still has the signs of the hinges of one of the ghetto gates on a curbstone. This brings you to Via Coltellini, known in the 17th century as Contrada degli Ebrei, but originally called Contrada dei Maccari, after Daniele Maccari, a German Jew who was stabbed here. The next street is called Via Torre, previously Contrada del Mezo Gheto ("Half Ghetto") because when the ghetto was extended in 1783 only the houses on one side of the street were included.

At the center of Piazza Mazzini, the synagogue (opened in 1873) replaced the previous ones that had functioned for over four centuries. All that is left of the two synagogues is a 15th-century ark, now in the Jewish Museum, Paris. Documents reveal that there was once a German school or *yeshivah* in

use from 1620 to 1630 in the square near the present synagogue and a Span ish-rite oratory at no. 25, Via Coltellini, where the internal courtyard sti has a Spanish feel.

The emancipation synagogue

Begun in 1869, the construction of the large synagogue was preceded by the demolition of some adjoining buildings to create the space required. The design was by Ludovico Maglietta, an architect who had built the provincia railway buildings in Modena, while some of the decoration was by Ferdi nando Manzini, who had worked in the church of Sant'Agostino. The new building was opened in 1873. The exterior is Neoclassical, with tympanum: and short flights of stairs. The façades, one overlooking Piazza Mazzini and the other Via Coltellini (originally the main entrance), are identical. Each is formed by a central doorway, two side doors and arched windows, with fou brick half-columns clad in marble-painted *scagliola*. The whole building has recently been restored.

A hall with large sliding glass doors (an original solution for the taberna cle of *Sukkoth*) leads to the synagogue antechamber, where there are five walled plaques: they commemorate the creation and opening of the syna gogue, the names of the benefactors, King Victor Emmanuel II, and the deportees. Designed to hold up to 1,000 people, the prayer room is rectan gular in shape. At the center of the ceiling is an elliptical dome, decorated with a star-studded sky. From the center hangs a large chandelier, original ly oil, now electric. The women's gallery follows the elliptical shape of the dome. The structure is made of brick and painted marble. It is enclosed by a balustrade and supported by twelve columns (possibly an allusion to the twelve tribes of Israel).

The prayer area is raised above the rest of the room and closed by the gates and railings. At the center is the holy ark with the *bimah* in front it. The ark is framed by Neoclassical columns and its doors have a leaf decoration: the overall effect is rather Oriental. Lower down, at the center of the room, are two rows of wooden benches for the congregation.

This Italian-rite synagogue is only used for major festivities, marriages, and public ceremonies. Everyday prayers are held in the German-rite oratory, which is in the same building, but entered from no. 10, Via Coltellini. Originally this was the private oratory of the Donati family. The rectangular interior has a decorated ceiling. On the eastern wall is a Neoclassical *aron* with at the top an opaque glass pane concealing a window. Two rows of benches run along the walls. The building also contains a *mikveh* (ritual bath), the community offices, and archives of documents dating from the 17th century to the present day, as well as material from the communities of Carpi and Reggio Emilia.

Judaica in the city archives

The Este Library (Biblioteca Estense) contains illuminated Hebrew manuscripts (forty-three from the Modena archives and nineteen from the Campori archives). Eleven of these manuscripts were acquired by the Duke of Este in 1573. The library also owns *La Bibbia di Borso d'Este* — a Bible with 15th-century miniatures by Taddeo Crivelli. Lastly, there is also a collection of illuminated *ketuboth*, scrolls of the Book of Esther, and particularly interesting and culturally important antique books.

The cemetery

The elliptical dome has a starry sky decoration. At the center hangs a large lamp, once oil-fired, now electric. The large Italian-rite synagogue is only used for major festivities. Everyday prayers are held in the German-rite oratory.

Since the early 20th century the cemetery in Strada Cimitero San Cataldo has been part of the city cemetery. The graves, arranged in several rows, have inscriptions in both Italian and Hebrew. Worth noting is the grave of Pio Donati, near the wall dividing the Jewish section from the Catholic section. In the Catholic section, on the other side of the same wall, is the tomb of Francesco Ferrari, Donati's anti-Fascist friend. They were forced to go into exile together to escape from the Fascists. Their bodies were returned to Italy to mark the twentieth anniversary of the liberation and were buried in the same place, albeit in different sectors. A number of bricks were then removed from the wall and replaced by glass bricks so that the two tombs can be seen from both sections.

The San Cataldo cemetery is not the first Modena community cemetery. The earliest was situated at Fosse, along the historic city walls. A second, in use until the end of the 19th century, was located between Via Pelusia and Via Emilia. Some of its headstones, many with Hebrew inscriptions, are now in the present cemetery.

Jews lived in Parma from the 15th to the 16th century and then from the 19th century right up to the present. Having settled in the city in the second half of the 15th century, they lived under the Visconti and the Sforza, when the initial climate was tolerant. Then in 1555 Duke Ottavio Farnese forced them to leave Parma (and Piacenza in 1570) but in 1562 allowed them to resettle in sixteen localities in the area. In 1574 their residence permit was renewed but only for a few localities. At the end of the 19th century the Jews returned to Parma, and they gradually abandoned rural areas. In 1881 the community numbered 70 people. The Parma Jewish community was very active culturally: from 1845 to 1848 it published a magazine called *La Rivista Israelitica*. By the beginning of the 20th century the group's numbers had fallen. Eighteen Parma Jews were deported by the Nazi Fascists. Today Parma has the only community (around twenty members) in the provinces of Parma and Piacenza.

The synagogue in the historic center

The synagogue is at no. 4, Vicolo Cervi. It was opened in 1866, a few years

Synagogue interior and women's gallery.
Officially opened in 1866, the small synagogue has a rectangular plan with a skylight in the middle. The 18th-century Neoclassical ark came from the Colorno synagogue, now demolished. Opposite the ark is a 19th-century bimah.

after the Jews returned to Parma, following an absence of two centuries. On the anonymous façade there is a plaque with an engraving of the Ten Commandments and the year the building was purchased (1822). The prayer room is on the first floor. It has a rectangular plan with at the center a large skylight. The walls are decorated with marble-painted stucco and broken up by thin gray pilaster strips ending in capitals. A gray skirting board runs round the perimeter of the room. The ark, originally from Colorno, is raised by three steps and set against the wall opposite the entrance. The 18th-century Neoclassical ark is embellished by a semicircular tympanum with a Hebrew inscription in the middle. In front of the ark is a 19th-century wooden *bimah*. Over the entrance wall, the women's gallery is supported by slender Corinthian columns forming five arches with an oil lamp hanging at the center of each arch. On the railings there is a Hebrew inscription commemorating the day the room was officially opened: July 27, 1866. During the Second World War, the furnishings were hidden in the Biblioteca Palatina. Some were brought back to the synagogue. Others are preserved in the Jewish Museum of Soragna.

The De Rossi Collection in the Biblioteca Palatina

The Biblioteca Palatina, a library in the Palazzo Pilotta, owns the most important and largest collection of Hebrew manuscripts (1,612 items) in Italy, and is second only to the Bodleian Library, Oxford, in the world. The collection is named after Giovan Battista De Rossi (1742–1831), a collector and scholar of Hebrew manuscripts. The Duchess Maria Luigia purchased the collection (1,432 items) for 100,000 gold ducats and then presented it to the Biblioteca Palatina.

The 19th-century cemetery

The 19th-century cemetery is a section of the city cemetery at La Villetta. At the entrance a plaque recalls the Nazi-Fascist persecutions. Among the graves is that of the Garibaldian Eugenio Ravà (1901). The inscriptions on his headstone include a copy of a letter to him from Garibaldi. Not far from this grave are the tombs of two soldiers who died in the First World War, an Italian and an Austro-Hungarian.

From 1669 to 1670, at the behest of the regent Duchess Laura Martinozzi, a ghetto was set up for 900 people in Reggio Emilia. Small groups of Jews had already settled in the city in the 15th century.

The period of segregation was culturally very lively, especially for the school of Jewish studies attended by celebrated rabbis who had come from all over Italy. Here Rabbi Anania Coen (1757–1834) printed Hebrew school texts and set up a printing works. Some of the books he printed are now in the A. Panizzi City Library (Biblioteca Comunale).

From the second half of the 19th century to the Second World War, the community gradually waned and the synagogue was closed for good in the 1950s. Its furnishings were taken to the synagogue of Kiryat Shmuel, in Haifa, Israel, and are still there.

The ghetto in the historic center

The ghetto stretched from Via Cagiati to Via della Volta, Via dell'Aquila, Via Monzermone, and Via San Rocco. All these streets bordered (and still border) on the Via Emilia, on one side, and Via San Rocco, on the other. The quarter was closed by six doors: two on Via Emilia, two near San Rocco, and two near the church of Sant'Egidio. During the day, moving from one street to another meant going onto Via Emilia, while at night people had to go by Via San Rocco, which was inside the ghetto, and cut through the four streets perpendicularly. As in other Jewish quarters, the inhabitants had created passages inside the buildings to enable them to move from one house to another without going out into the street.

The area has been restored, but preserves its original appearance. Only two of the four churches have survived: Sant'Egidio and San Silvestro.

Silver crown and rimmonim for the Scrolls of the Law. These refined objects were made by craftsmen, usually non-Jews, who were provided with models by their patrons.

A street in the ghetto, created in 1669–70 and closed by six doors. The area was large enough to accommodate 900 people. Remodeled in its present form in 1858, the synagogue is no longer used. The ark (1756), made of colored Carrara marble, was taken to Israel in the 1950s.

In 1672 a large synagogue, at no. 4, Via Dell'Aquila, was opened and replaced the oratories used before the creation of the ghetto. The synagogue was extended in 1858, when it was given its present form. The community spared no expense and commissioned the design from Pietro Marchelli, a leading architect of the day.

The prayer room is dominated by a cross-domed vault closed by a skylight. The walls are given a lively rhythm by columns and pilasters, while the women's galleries rise up over three floors.

The original ark, dated 1756 and made of colored Carrara marble, was in a raised position, reached by going up four steps. In the 1950s it was taken to Israel. The synagogue façade has a plaque commemorating the Jews deported from Reggio Emilia. The interior has been restored, but is no longer used for its original function. It is usually closed to the public but can be visited by applying to the Modena community.

The 19th-century cemetery

The present cemetery, opened in 1808 and extended in 1850, consists of two sections. As indicated by a red Verona marble plaque, the earlier section is dedicated to Beniamino Foà (1808). The second section, still in use

today, has gravestones fixed on the cemetery walls and a number of family tombs, like the Cantoni family tomb with eleven identical headstones.

This is the community's sixth burial place. The earliest (15th century) was situated in Via dell'Orto, now Via San Rocco; there was a second (16th century) cemetery at no. 13, Borgo Emilio in the parish of Santi Giacomo e Filippo; a third and fourth were at no. 5, Contrada Bellaria. The fifth and largest was in Via della Veza. All that remains of these cemeteries are archive documents.

Jews arrived in Soragna after being expelled from Parma (1555) and Piacenza (1570), and when Duke Ottavio Farnese allowed them to open loan-banks in sixteen rural localities in 1562. Soragna was among these towns and remained the seat of a Jewish bank even when the number of localities where Jews were allowed to reside was reduced in 1574. Always small, the group basically had a relatively trouble-free life thanks to the tolerant policies of the local princes — the Meli Lupi. There were, however, some episodes of discrimination on the part of the local populace. In 1803 the Jews greeted Napoleon's troops as liberators and won their first freedoms. After the restoration and the Unity of Italy, the group lived in the shadow of the larger Parma community, of which the Soragna community is now a section.

The synagogue museum

Synagogue interior. Remodeled in 1855 in the Neoclassical style, it has a rectangular plan. The walls are decorated with floral motifs and enhanced by half-columns made of shiny stucco ending in Corinthian capitals. Round the perimeter walls are Hebrew inscriptions from Psalms and the Book of Kings.

The synagogue is situated in the town center (no. 43, Via Cavour), opposite the Rocca, the castle still inhabited by the Meli Lupi family. The building was already used as a Jewish oratory in 1584. The interior was remodeled, however, in 1855, while the original façade was left intact. The renovation cost 40,000 lire. The original holy ark was replaced by a niche in the wall, while the 17th-century wooden ark, designed by Petitot, was not used for a century. Then, in 1967, it was taken to Jerusalem and placed in the oratory of the Knesset (Israeli parliament), where it still is today. In 1939, as a consequence of the racial laws, the building was confiscated and used as the Casa del Fascio and the Opera Nazionale Balilla — two Fascist institutions. Abandoned after the Second World War, it was restored in 1979 (but the works continued until 1982) thanks to the efforts of Fausto Levi, at the time president of the Parma community. The building now hosts a museum with the synagogue room as an integral part. On show in the two floors of the museum are furnishings, ceremonial objects, and various items from the former Jewish communities in the Parma and Piacenza area.

On the ground floor the video room screens films providing an historical introduction to the life of the local Jews. The next section displays objects of everyday use for educational purposes, and is followed by a section dedicated to the Shoah, with documents on the persecutions and deportations of Italian Jews, with a special focus on Parma and Piacenza. The first-floor exhibition consists of objects from the various former communities in the area (such as the wrought-iron gate at the entrance to the floor, once in Fiorenzuola d'Arda) and original documents and copies reconstructing three centuries of history (1555–1803). In the corridor leading to the prayer room there are showcases with liturgical objects (the Scrolls of the Law, complete with covers; pointer, silver plates and crowns for the *Torah*, a *yad*, and scrolls containing the Book of Esther). Alongside is a prayer mantle, prayer books, and *phylacteries*, the ritual ram's horn (*shofar*), the lamps for *Hanukkah* and the Sabbath, and a cup for the Sabbath benediction. In the passageway to the synagogue there are two plaques, one in Hebrew and the other in Italian, recording the date of the inauguration (22 October 1855) with the names of the benefactors.

The rectangular prayer room is Neoclassical in style. The barrel-vault ceiling is decorated with floral motifs — the work of the painter Giuseppe Levi from Busseto. The walls are embellished by half-columns with splendid stuccowork ending in Corinthian-style capitals and entablatures. Running round the perimeter is a cornice with verses in Hebrew from Psalms and the Book of Kings. The holy ark is set opposite the entrance and raised by three steps: it is lit by windows on either side and three lunettes just under the ceil-

ing. The two repoussé gold leaf doors are framed by two columns. In front of the doors the *ner tamid* hangs from the ceiling, while on either side are large candelabra. The *bimah* has been replaced by a large lectern standing in front of the ark. Two rows of benches are lined up towards the prayer area.

The women's gallery looks down from the entrance walls and is adorned by a closely knit wrought-iron grate with an arabesque pattern. It is reached from an outside stair. Embellished *ketuboth* are exhibited on the walls in the area in front of the women's gallery. Today this room is used by the town for concerts and cultural activities.

A rural cemetery

At a locality called Argine, the small Jewish cemetery dating from 1839 is still in use. The graves are arranged in parallel rows. The oldest grave is that of Elia Sforni (1854). This was the second burial place for Soragna Jews. There was an earlier cemetery, used in 1750, near an inn called the Locanda del Lupo.

Dance was born as a prayer and praise of God, as can be read in Ecclesiastes. "For everything there is a time... a time to weep and a time to laugh, a time to mourn and a time to dance." There is no mention of dancing in general terms in the Bible but seven individual dances are described with their various gestures, movements, occasions for being performed, and meanings: you could dance by "turning and circling," or "hopping and rotating," or "hopping, jumping with two feet, and limping." Dancing accompanied the Ark of the Alliance in processions. Some dances were performed round the altar of the temple, while others could become ecstatic. Military victories were accompanied only by women's dances. But both men and women jigged for the harvests, and the dances became full-blown country feasts. In the biblical age, highly symbolic dances marked the stages in the life cycle – birth, cir-

cumcision, and marriage. Originally the dances were distinguished between those for men and those for women and were performed in a circle to a rhythm. The circle is a symbol representing the circle of life, with no beginning or end. Dancing in a circle means expressing chorality, a sense of belonging to a group, to a people, and is a form of communication: inside the circle the dancers look at each other and communicate with gestures and glances. The dance leader can mix in with those who follow and imitate his or her movements. After the destruction of the Temple of Jerusalem (AD 70) and the dispersal of the Jews in the Diaspora, dancing underwent deep changes. With the loss of the Sanctuary, music and singing, conceived as expressions of joy and praise of the Lord, were not only inappropriate but often prohibited by the rabbis. The ancient dances, however, remained part of the Jewish cultural heritage and varied from place to place, especially during the age of the ghettos. At that time dancing in public was prohibited for security reasons, whereas the ritual dances – for the Sabbath, birth, circumcision, and marriages – continued and developed. Dancing at a wedding was considered to be a religious duty (*mitzvah*) and there were various dances with different movements before, during, and after the celebration of the rite.

In the age of the ghettos, dance developed greatly in Italy. Sicilian Jewish dancers accompanied the nuptial procession of Ferdinand II of Aragon and Isabella of Castile in 1469. In Jewish families, dancing was an important part of education. In the mid 15th century, public dance and music schools were opened in Venice and Parma by Jews and also attended by Christians. It comes as no surprise that a Jew called Guglielmo from Pesaro wrote a key treatise on the art of dancing in 1463. In the 17th and later centuries dance continued to develop and was enriched in various European countries with large Jewish communities, especially in Eastern Europe (Ukraine and Podolia) where the mystical Hasidic movement developed.

There was then a revival of traditional Jewish dance in the late 19th century when groups of European Jews began to settle in Israel. And with the birth of the Jewish State (1948), new popular dances came into being. The most famous is the *hora*, from Romania, which soon became the symbol of the kibbutz. In addition to dances from the Hasidic group are the equally suggestive dances of the Yemenite Jews – faithful custodians of the ancient traditions. Today there is a renewed interest in Jewish dance even outside the communities.

Music has always accompanied the most important moments in Jewish religious life: from birth to death, in all the happy or sad occasions. In the various celebrations, the liturgy has always been sung but with no instrumental accompaniment. Transmitted orally from generation to generation, the songs vary from place to place and reflect the history of individual communities, the stratification of the elements composing them and their relations with the non-Jewish musical context.

Singing in the Italian synagogues originally followed the Roman tradition, with elements derived from the interpretation of the ancient Hebrew Bible. Then the liturgy began to be differentiated, due to the influence of the cultural contribution of new groups of Jews in the community. Jews from the Sephardic world (Iberian Peninsula and the Mediterranean) or with Ashkenazi traditions (Central Europe) deeply changed the original music, giving rise to new blends. In this context, culturally and musically very different traditions existed side by side and began to exercise mutual influences.

Over the centuries, Jewish music has absorbed non-Jewish Italian melodies. Always well integrated into the life of the country, the Italian Jews enhanced their liturgical repertory with popular songs in dialect, operatic arias, or Risorgimento marches and hymns, thus creating a curious mixture of styles. Their musical taste was always ultimately modeled on that of Italian music. From the late 16th century, Baroque-style polyphonic music was composed in the ghettos. Written for special occasions in Venice, Siena, and Casale Monferrato, Jewish cantatas became an integral part of the musical heritage of the time. This was the case with Salomone Rossi (Mantua, 1570–1630), a conductor at the court of the Gonzaga at the time of Monteverdi and one of the main interpreters of 17th-century violin music. Rossi wrote sonatas for two violins and *chitarrone* and vocal music (madrigals and twenty-eight Psalms and Jewish songs for religious services). At the court of the Gonzaga, more-

over, in addition to Salomone Rossi there was a large group of Jewish artists and scholars. Mantua was no exception. In Venice, a great musical center throughout the 17th century, a collection of synagogue polyphonic settings of Psalms, all in Hebrew, was published in 1622–23, arousing a great deal of interest on the grounds of its novelty.

Much of the rich musical heritage of the Italian communities has been lost over the centuries. Around a thousand melodies were saved from being lost forever, however, by the musicologist Leo Levi (1912–1982). From 1954 to 1959 with the collaboration of the RAI and the National Music Academy of Santa Cecilia and the indispensable help of the cantors who remembered the old songs, Levi recorded synagogue songs in around twenty by then almost extinct Italian Jewish communities. The Levi collection is now divided between Rome (Ethno-musicological Archives, National Music Academy of Santa Cecilia) and Jerusalem (National Sound Archives, National and University Library). It has been the subject of intense cataloguing and research work, which has culminated in an anthology CD. This very special heritage is relatively unknown to the wide public and often even in the Jewish world. In recent years there has been a good deal of interest in *Klezmer* music, Jewish folk melodies from Eastern Europe, which, however, historically never actually took root in Italian Jewish culture.

Jews in Medicean Florence

The Florence community enjoyed a golden age from the late 19th century to the early 20th century: in 1882 a large temple was opened, symbolizing their new-found freedom, and the old ghetto was razed, thus wiping out almost three centuries of segregation. In 1899 the renewed community, by then 2,700 strong, witnessed the opening of a Rabbinical College by Rabbi Samuel Zvi Margulies, the life and soul of Florentine Jewish life for thirty-two years, and the driving force in publishing the reviews entitled *Rivista Israelitica* (1904–15), *Settimana Israelitica* (1910–15), *Israel* (from 1916 and later transferred to Rome), and the *Rassegna Mensile d'Israel* (from 1925, then in Padua and lastly Rome). The history of the Jewish group goes back a very long way (some scholars even claim it dates from ancient Roman times). The Florentine Jews were subject to the changing policies of the local rulers over the centuries, especially the Medici, who invited Jewish moneylenders to the city as early as 1430. At that time they lived on the other side of the Arno River from the city center, in what is now Via dei Ramaglianti (formerly Via dei Giudei), in Borgo San Jacopo, where they had a prayer room and cemetery. The oratory building was blown up by the Germans in August 1944.

In 1570 Cosimo I de' Medici — desperate to obtain the title of grand duke from Pope Pius V — agreed to create ghettos in Florence and Siena. He continued, however, to pursue a liberal policy in Livorno (Leghorn) and Pisa. Jews

The Moorish-style synagogue, built in 1882. The building was clad in alternating blocks of white and pink stone. The central dome sits on a drum with windows. At the corners of the main façade are two small domed towers.

Detail of windows in the façade. The building has long arched windows and a rose window filtering light into the large Moorish-style prayer room.

came to the Florence ghetto from the rural areas where they had been living near San Miniato, San Gimignano, Volterra, and Monte San Savino. The opening of the ghetto marked a period of confinement that ended 278 years later in 1848. In the meantime, in 1738, the House of Lorraine had taken over from the Medici as the rulers of Florence.

The community went through terrible ordeals in the 20th century. In addition to the devastation of the deportations, its temple was occupied by the Nazis and used as a garage for military vehicles. When forced to flee, the Germans mined the building: the columns on the left-hand side were blown to smithereens by the explosion but the women's gallery above did not collapse. During the restoration work the columns were replaced by identical cement columns, while the surviving old capitals are now in the garden. On November 4, 1966, the terrible flood that hit the city, when the river burst its banks, was another terrible blow for the building and its furnishings. The waters of the Arno were three meters (10 ft.) high outside and two meters (6.5 ft.) high inside: 90 of the 120 Scrolls of the Law and 15,000 books in the historical library were badly damaged. Today the community numbers 600 people.

The architect Buontalenti and the ghetto

The Florence ghetto, imposed on the Jews by the Medici in 1570, was redesigned from the urban-planning and architectural point of view by the engineer of the Grand Duchy of Tuscany, Bernardo Buontalenti. The area chosen stretched from Via Roma (formerly Via dei Succhiellinai), to Piazza della Repubblica (formerly Piazza del Mercato Vecchio), Via Brunelleschi (formerly Via dei Rigattieri) and Via Tosinghi (formerly Via Chiasso di Malacucina). It was closed by two gates: one in Piazza della Repubblica and the other in Via Roma. The central square in the quarter was Piazza della Fonte, where a well

supplied water for the whole area. In this square there were two synagogues, one Italian rite and one Spanish or Levantine rite. The holy ark from the Spanish synagogue was taken to Israel in 1956, and placed in the synagogue of the Yavne kibbutz. From 1705 to 1721 the ghetto was extended as far as Via de' Pecori and a third gate was added in Piazza dell'Olio. In 1848, after 278 years, the Jews were finally allowed to leave the ghetto for good. By then the area was a terrible slum. It was reoccupied by a new army of poverty-stricken people, who transformed the area into a den of crime. The sanitary situation reached such dangerous levels that the city council had to intervene and "reclaim" the area by carrying out slum clearance work from 1881 to 1898. The operation was part of a redevelopment program for the whole city, begun when Florence was capital of Italy (1864–71). Today, therefore, the old ghetto is unrecognizable. A plaque on the arch on the eastern side of Piazza della Repubblica asserts that: "The old center of the city was restored to new life after centuries of squalor."

A new temple for the emancipated Jews

Watercolor by Ottavio Levi depicting the interior of the former oratory in Via delle Oche, closed for good in 1962, when the furnishings were taken to Israel.

Silver amulet placed on a cradle to protect from Lilith, Eve's rival, who might send evil spirits to kidnap a baby. This is a lucky charm with the words "the Almighty" in Hebrew at the center.

In 1872 a project was approved for the construction of a new temple in the quarter of Mattonaia, near the church of Sant'Ambrogio, but far from the Jewish quarter. Some Jews, called "Centralists" (because they wanted a temple in the city center), rejected this decision and in 1882 opened two oratories in a Jewish-owned building at no. 4, Via delle Oche, a crossing of Via dei Calzaiuoli: one was an Italian-rite synagogue and the other was used by the Mattir Assurim Confraternity. In 1962 both were closed and their furnishings taken to Israel; today they are commemorated in an inscription.

On the wall of the corner building in Via dei Calzaiuoli there is a plaque commemorating the Florentine sojourn of the poet Salomone Fiorentino. Not far away, on Via de' Lamberti, in the second niche on the side of the building, there is a shrine to the Virgin Mary, connected to an act of intolerance in 1493: a Jew was accused of having disfigured the face of a 14th-century image of the Virgin Mary, and for this crime was executed. On the plaque on the shrine are the following words: "Hanc ferro effigiem petiit judeus et index, ipse sui vulgo dilaniatus obiit. MCCCLXXXXIII."

Florentine museums and libraries are full of items linked to Jewish culture and have Judaica sections. For example, the Biblioteca Medicea Laurenziana has a large section of Medieval and Renaissance illuminated manuscripts.

Eight years to build the Moorish-style temple

Situated at no. 4, Via Farini, the large new synagogue was designed by the architects Marco Treves, Mariano Falcini, and Vincenzo Micheli. Begun in 1874, the work was completed eight years later in 1882. The building cost one million lire, an exorbitant sum at the time, made possible thanks to a legacy from a former community president — David Levi. The Moorish-style building is surrounded by grounds originally planted with exotic trees and enclosed on the street front by cast-iron railings decorated with volutes, made by Pasquale Franci from Siena. A wide path leads up to the entrance of the temple. It is flanked on one side by a low building constructed in the 1960s, housing the community offices and the school, while on the other side are the surrounding walls with two plaques: the first is dedicated to the Florentine Jews who died in the First World War (1915–18), and the second commemorates the Jews deported from Florence (248 people). Behind the apse of the temple is the Settimio Saadun Rest Home, entered from no. 11, Via Carducci.

The temple's exterior is clad with alternated white and pink stone blocks (travertine from Colle Val d'Elsa and pink *pomato* from Assisi). The domes are covered with green copper sheets. The large central dome is set on a drum with windows, while the two small domes sit on top of two towers at the corners of the main façade. Crowned by a semicircular tympanum, the façade is divided into three parts both vertically (the central body and the two small towers) and horizontally (with three arches in the entrance lodge, three groups of biforate windows in the center, and inside the tympanum, a triforate window, two single windows, and a rose window). The side elevations each have a projecting body, surmounted by a semicircular tympanum. The fourth side, opposite the main façade, is the apse. The windows and arches are all horseshoe-shaped.

There are five entrances (three at the front and two at the side). The main entrance leads to a rectangular hall running the length of the building. Plaques on the walls in this room record the First World War dead and Rabbi Margulies; opposite, above the ornate stone laver (wash basin), another plaque celebrates the visit to the synagogue by Victor Emmanuel III in 1911, while three subsequent medallions mention the donor, other benefactors, and the architects who designed the temple. The last plaque records the visit to the synagogue of King Umberto I and Queen Margherita in 1887. A few years ago an elevator was installed in the right-hand tower, entered from the hall, to take people up to the base of the dome. The left-hand tower has a bookshop and a temporary exhibition space.

Floor decoration in the Margulies Oratory, used for everyday functions. It is named after Samuel Zvi Margulies, who ran the rabbinical college in Florence from 1899 to 1922.

Oratory interior. This room is in a wing of the large synagogue. The light blue ark came from Monte San Savino, while a second Neoclassical ark was once in Arezzo.

At the two side entrances, the floor has marble mosaics indicating the dates for the beginning and completion of the building work (1874–82). The walnut doors are carved with geometrical motifs and arabesques. The same patterns are also found in the frescoes on the walls. Large windows look through to the quadrangular prayer room, divided into a nave and two aisles. The nave has a barrel-vaulted ceiling and is apsed at the rear. The women's gallery rests on granite columns painted like brown marble, ending in perforated capitals painted with lively colors. The gallery runs on three sides and is screened by wrought-iron railings (made by Francesco Morini), interrupted by stylized seven-branched candelabra. At the base of the women's gallery there is an ornamental band with gold inscriptions from Psalms on a blue background. All the decorations in the room, with its dominant colors of red and ocher, were by Giovanni Panti. The recurrent motif in the inlaid work on the marble floor is the Star of David.

The prayer room ends in the apse, where the floor is raised by three steps from the rest of the room. Inside the apse at the center is the *bimah*, consisting of a lectern made of carved wood with floral decorations on a gold background and enclosed by railings echoing the motifs and inlaid work, and embellished by three candelabra. Set behind the *bimah*, the ark is a single compact structure: the two gilded wooden doors by Ferdinando Romanelli are adorned with the symbols of the Temple and the Great Priest. At the sides,

six dark marble columns support a double Moorish arch. At the center of the arch is a medallion with verses from Ezekiel. Also clad with mosaics, the baldachin stretches up to form the Tablets of the Law. In front of the ark is the *ner tamid*, made by Francesco Morini.

Along the apse walls are seats embellished with marquetry. To the sides, two rooms meant for use by the choir and organ, respectively, are no longer in use. The right-hand aisle leads to the oratory dedicated to Samuel Zvi Margulies (1858–1922), the rabbi who was in charge of the Florentine Rabbinical College and raised its standards considerably from 1899 until his death.

Used for everyday functions, the oratory has a light blue ark, once in Monte San Savino, and a Neoclassical ark from Arezzo. The black and yellow marble star decoration at the center of the floor was once in the oratory of the Mattir Assurim Confraternity at no. 4, Via delle Oche (the building was sold in 1962). The museum is installed in some rooms of the women's gallery on the first and second floor. It is reached by going up a flight of stairs or by elevator.

At the bottom of the stair is a plaster copy of the monument to the deportees modeled on the original bronze work by Nathan Rapaport, now in the Martyrs' Forest at Kesalon, Jerusalem, Israel. Plaques and chandeliers from the two oratories in Via delle Oche are lined up along the walls of the stairs.

In the entrance to the museum there are two models reconstructing the old ghetto of Florence and the present temple. Designed by the architect Alberto Boralevi, the museum is divided into two sections: the first is a series of photographs telling the story of the Florentine Jews and their temple; the second consists of several showcases with liturgical objects, marriage contracts, and precious fabrics. One of the most interesting items is a large late-17th-century fabric, called the Curtain of the Ten Commandments, possibly made in Venice, using the embroidery technique of the Hungarian stitch.

The ark in the prayer room is from the old Lippiano synagogue (made of green wood with a round decoration at the center of the doors, and framed at the sides and above by columns, cornices and friezes); there is also a 19th-century Elijah's Chair, used for circumcision.

The Florentine cemeteries

At present there are two Jewish cemeteries in Florence, but only one is used — the cemetery at no. 13, Via di Caciolle in the quarter of Rifredi. Opened in 1871, the cemetery was reorganized from 1881 to 1884 by Marco Treves, the same architect who had designed the temple at that time. It is closed by large wrought-iron gates between two wings of rusticated stone surmounted by pediments. Inside there are many chapels and funerary monuments, including the tomb of Rabbi Margulies, who died in 1922. But the Jewish group in Florence had many other burial places over the centuries. The oldest was at what is now Lungarno della Zecca, at the corner between Via Tripoli and Via dei Malcontenti. There were also others, all in the San Frediano area: the first was at Fondaco la Piazzetta; there was another at Porta Romana, used from 1645 to 1777 when a new cemetery, which still exists, was opened at no. 14, Viale Ariosto. This cemetery is of interest because many of the funerary monuments were designed by architects and artists: for example, the chapel in the form of a pyramid made for the Levi family, the small temple for the Franchetti family and the neo-Egyptian tomb of Chiara Rafael Sanguinetti (1846).

The modern synagogue interior, officially opened in 1962. The design of the room alludes to the image of the great tent used to preserve the holy ark. The elliptical floor plan is like that of an amphitheater. Dated 1708, the ark came from Pesaro and is made of gilded carved wood, surmounted by a crown formed by garlands.

Borsa dei Massari, detail of gold and silver embroidery. This 18th-century "administrators' bag" is in the small Jewish museum installed in the Marini Oratory. The oratory served as a prayer room when the old synagogue was unfit for use and the new one not yet ready.

The city with no ghetto

The community of Livorno (Leghorn) was founded after Ferdinando I de' Medici had sent letters patent (called the *Livornina*) to invite mainly Portuguese Marranos to settle in Livorno and Pisa in 1593. He offered them the freedom to trade and worship as well as protection from the Inquisition, and naturally no ghetto. The Medici wished to develop the port of Livorno, already declared a free port in 1548, and to make nearby Pisa a trading center. The gamble on Livorno went beyond their wildest imaginings: from an initial 114 Iberians in 1601 the Jewish population rose to 3,000 in 1689, 4,300 in 1784, and 5,000 in 1800 — an eighth of the population. Spanish soon became the language of the community, which naturally practiced the Spanish rite; in the city, *Bagitto* (a mixture of Italian, Spanish and Jewish) became the *lingua franca* and Jewish cooking blended with Livorno cuisine. The Livorno community grew so large that by 1614 it was independent from the Pisa community. The Jews mainly lived round the port, in the main street, Via Grande or Via Ferdinando, and the adjoining streets of Via Pratese (later Via dei Materassi and Via Tazza), Via Saponiera (with its soap factories), and Via Balbiana (later Via Reale). The synagogue was at Trivio della Bertolla (the building was demolished in 1908). This area was then redeveloped after slum clearances in the historic center. From the 16th to 18th century, due to its prosperity and vitality, the Livorno group was a cultural reference point for the whole Western Diaspora. But after being damaged by the Napoleonic blockade and having lost its status as a free port, Livorno went into decline and with it the Jewish community. From 4,500 members in 1852, its numbers dropped to 2,500 at the beginning of the 20th century. After the Second World War and the deportation of ninety people, the community numbers fell to the present 600 members.

A modern temple like a great tent

The synagogue at no. 1, Via Benamozegh (formerly Via del Tempio) was opened in 1962. Designed by the Roman architect Angelo Di Castro, it was built on the site of the previous synagogue, which had been badly damaged during Second World War bombing. Built in 1591 and embellished and extended over three centuries, the earlier synagogue was considered one of the most splendid religious monuments of the European Diaspora. Indeed it was used as a model for the contemporary synagogue in Amsterdam, which still exists today. When the synagogue was to be rebuilt in the postwar period, the community was divided between those in favor of reconstructing the previous temple and those who wanted a modern building. The second idea won the day: the work cost 180 million lire, and a further 35 million was required for the building next door.

Made of a reinforced concrete, the exterior was formed by a series of molded flying buttresses that broaden upwards, pierced by two orders of hexagonal stained-glass windows, with dark blue as the main color. At the top is a long window with red panes. The entrance portal is embellished with stylized Ten Commandments. Alongside is a sculpture and a plaque commemorating the 200th anniversary of the birth of Moses Montefiore (1985). The two side doors are adorned with seven-branched candelabra. In the small vestibule two plaques celebrate the inauguration of the temple (Spanish-rite), and those responsible for its construction. The monumental prayer room alludes to the

image of the great tent used to preserve the holy ark. The elliptical floor plan is like that of an amphitheater. The *bimah* stands at the center, raised on a small podium with steps and a marble balustrade, both from the previous synagogue. The ark is set opposite and cleverly highlighted at the point where the pitched roof and pilasters form an ideal tabernacle. Dated 1708, this Baroque ark was made by the cabinetmaker Angelo Scoccianti from Cupramontana in the Marches. It was brought to Livorno in 1970 from the Spanish synagogue in Pesaro, to replace the original. Made of gilded wood, the ark's doors are framed by two columns resting on a base and surmounted by a crown made of gilded carved wooden garlands. At the side the two 17th-century wooden seats are for use by the rabbi. Behind them hang two *parocheth* (curtains for the ark) dated 1784 and 1814. They hang against the balustrades of the two flights of steps, behind the ark, leading to the Lampronti oratory on the lower floor. The whole area is circumscribed by wrought-iron railings. The benches and the women's gallery stretch around three sides of the room. The floor has various colors: walnut and blue in the central area with the *bimah* and benches; white and blue round the ark. The synagogue is used for major festivities, while everyday services are held in the Lampronti oratory. The Spanish-rite Lampronti oratory has a rectangular plan, with the ark and *bimah* opposite each other on the long sides of the room. The 17th-century furnishings came from the Spanish temple in Via Vittoria, Ferrara. The polychrome marble ark has two doors decorated with stylized motifs between two dark columns set on a base and supporting a curved architrave. The *bimah* is also made of polychrome marble and is enclosed by railings with small columns bearing six white ornamental amphorae. In the same architectural style, the building annexed to the synagogue hosts the community offices, a library, and archives.

The small museum

In 1992 the Jewish Museum was opened at no. 21, Via Micali. This Neoclassical building outside the historic center once housed the family oratory of the Marini, who owned the building. It was then used until 1867 as the offices for a charity confraternity and then a prayer room, when the old synagogue was damaged and the new one not yet ready. The building is surrounded by a garden with some marble fragments of the ark from the old synagogue. Today on the ground floor there is a primary school while the first floor accommodates the museum, installed in the prayer room and the small women's gallery of the old oratory. The prayer room has a square plan with windows on all four sides. Showcases in the middle of the room contain liturgical and other objects, some very valuable, such as the so-called *Borsa dei Massari* (an 18th-century "administrators' bag"), covered in embroidered repoussé gold and silver. The 17th-century ark is set against the east wall. This ark is shrouded in legend: it was said to have been brought in pieces to Livorno by Portuguese immigrants. A similar ark was taken to Israel in 1956 and placed in the central Sephardic synagogue in the old city of Jerusalem. This gilded wooden ark has inlaid work with Oriental-like floral patterns. The doors and panels at the center become wider to hold the Scrolls of the Law. Above the doors is a stylized decorative balustrade under three miniature domes culminating in pinnacles.

Burial places

The cemetery in Via Fabio Filzi, used since 1898, is the fourth in chronological order. Of the others, only the third, at no. 134, Via Ippolito Nievo, has survived.

Freedom and tolerance in the period of the ghettos

Like Livorno (Leghorn), Pisa had no ghetto. With the letters patent, known as *Livornina*, in 1593 Ferdinando I de' Medici invited the Marranos from Portugal to settle in the two cities, offering them economic advantages, the greatest commercial and religious freedom, and protection from the Inquisition. The Medici had plans to make Pisa a commercial emporium and Livorno its sea outlet. Things turned out rather differently, however: Livorno experienced an unexpected independent growth and the Jewish community broke away from the mother community of Pisa in 1614.

After the *Livornina* another 500 Portuguese Marranos arrived in Pisa. They were joined by Ashkenazi groups who had been expelled from the Duchy of Milan, thus further accentuating the mixed composition typical of the Pisan group since its foundation earlier than the 11th century.

The community had always been concentrated in a single quarter: in the 14th century it was at Chiasso dei Giudei, near Piazza dei Cavalieri; then until the 16th century near the Torre del Campano, the market area of Vettovaglie around the house of the Da Pisa (a family of powerful bankers) at no. 36, Via Fra' Domenico Calavalca, still called the "Jews' House" today. Lastly, having grown in numbers, the group moved to the other side of the Arno River, and opened a prayer room in the Palazzo Da Scorno, along what is now Lungarno Gambacorti. In 1594 the synagogue was transferred to the present building in Via Palestro, near the church of San Pierino, while Jews also settled in the surrounding area.

The interior of the synagogue, remodeled in its present form in 1863 by the architect Marco Treves. The Neoclassical room has a square plan. The broad windows draped with red curtains run around three sides. The walls are decorated with stuccowork and the ceiling with large rosettes.

The community's modern history is bound up with the economic history of the city, since Jews played an active part in its growth. In the 19th century, for example, they played a leading role in some textile firms, which were particularly important for the city's economy.

In 1881 the community numbered 700 people. It was then devastated by war and persecutions: on 1 August 1944 the Nazis broke into the house of the president, Giuseppe Pardo Roques, at no. 22, Via Sant'Andrea, and murdered him together with another eleven people, both Jews and Catholics, who had been hiding there. A plaque on the façade of the house commemorates the massacre.

After the war the community began to dwindle, and today there are less than 200 members.

The Neoclassical synagogue

The synagogue at no. 24, Via Palestro was built in 1594. At the time the building belonged to the Serravallino family who first rented it and then sold it to the community in 1647. The original idea was to build the prayer room in the internal kitchen garden (now the area used for the *Sukkoth* tabernacle). It was then decided to install the prayer room on the second floor, where it still is today. The synagogue was remodeled in 1785 and then definitively restructured in 1863 by Marco Treves, the architect who also designed synagogues in Florence and Vercelli.

The façade has a portal with two side columns surmounted by a pediment. Above the round-arched windows are two eyelike *tondi*. This pattern is repeated in the upper section of the building, above the string-course. The corners are clad with fake rustication. The entrance is at the side of the building, where the street widens into a small square.

Inside, the ground floor contains the premises once used by the confraternities and the oven for unleavened bread. Now there are some 18th-century furnishings from other oratories and a laver (wash basin), with a dedication, and the date 1806; an 19th-century *aron* was taken to Israel from here in 1956 and placed in the Machon Gold synagogue, Jerusalem, where it still is today.

A flight of stairs leads up to the second floor landing, embellished by a lacunar ceiling with a large central rose decoration. A hall then provides access to the prayer room. On the walls of the hall are plaques commemorating the dead from Pisa in the First World War and Rabbi Augusto Hasdà and his wife Bettina Segre, who were deported together with another twelve Pisan Jews in the Second World War. A third plaque records the details of the new ceiling. Next to the entrance are some slits in the wall for the charity, or *tzedakah*, boxes.

The square-plan prayer room is Neoclassical in style. Two rows of windows with red curtains run round three sides of the room. The walls are decorated with imitation stucco, also adorning the ceiling with large rosette decorations.

The ark is set opposite the entrance. The carved wooden doors are framed by four marble columns with Corinthian capitals surmounted by a pediment with vegetal motifs. The area in front is bounded by a Carrara marble balustrade, reached by going up a few steps. Three lamps hang from the ceiling supported by a wrought-iron tendril with volutes.

Raised from the floor by three steps, the round-shaped walnut *bimah* is situated opposite the ark. The benches, also made of carved walnut, are arranged in two parallel rows and along the walls. The women's gallery is set in the entrance wall on four columns and closed in the upper section by balusters ending in round arches. The gallery is reached by an external stair leading to the second floor, where a library and archives are also located.

The plaques in Piazza dei Miracoli

Not far from the synagogue, Piazza dei Miracoli is also worth a visit. Situated along the eastern walls of the city, just outside Porta Nuova, the piazza has some Hebrew inscriptions carved in the stones. The oldest is dated 1274. According to the historian Michele Luzzati, this was the site of a cemetery in which the poorest Jews in the city were buried along the city walls. Unable to afford gravestones, the names of the dead were simply inscribed on the stones in the walls. Nearby, in Via Cammeo, is the cemetery used since 1674. The earlier burial sites disappeared under the urban growth of the city.

Little Jerusalem

Pitigliano became a haven for Tuscan Jews who did not wish to be enclosed in the ghettos of Florence and Siena in 1570, as well as many others who arrived later from the Papal States. The latter mainly came from small towns in Lazio and chose to settle in Pitigliano rather than be enclosed in the Rome ghetto, in the misguided belief they would soon be able to return to their old homes. Pitigliano is in fact situated on what was once the southern border of the Grand Duchy of Tuscany, but is nearer to Rome than Florence. A ghetto was eventually also set up in the town by the Medici in 1622, thus taking by surprise the many Jews who had sought refuge in this remote town of the Maremma area in the hope of avoiding segregation. Enclosure in the ghetto, however, did not stop relations and trading with the local population. The quarter became the liveliest rural Jewish center in Italy. Indeed it was known as "Little Jerusalem." Jewish life in Pitigliano was very intense until the mid-19th century and emancipation. At that time there were around 500 Jews in the town, accounting for thirty percent of the whole population. After emancipation many left Pitigliano to go and live in the cities. The result was that the community eventually died out altogether. Recently an association called "The Friends of Little Jerusalem" has been working to reconstruct the local Jewish presence by restoring the historic monuments and organizing events to inject the culture with new life.

Synagogue interior. The building had to be reconstructed in 1905 when some of the town collapsed down the hill. The furnishings, decorations and inscriptions all had to be remade, but the women's gallery and grate survived. The synagogue is now a popular tourist attraction.

The very old cemetery at the foot of the town is still in use. Near some locular tombs gouged out of the tufa rock are 19th-century graves, adorned with statues.

The synagogue on the edge of a cliff

The synagogue is in the heart of medieval Pitigliano, an area embracing three streets lengthwise: the central Via Roma, Via Zuccarelli, and Via Vignali. They are crisscrossed by a dense network of alleys stretching the whole length of the town. The synagogue in Via Zuccarelli is exactly where the ghetto (going from Via Zuccarelli to Vicolo Marghera and Vicolo Goito) was set up in 1622. Built in 1598 by Leone di Sabato, for centuries the prayer room was the center of Jewish life. It won fame in 1773 when visited by the Grand Duke Peter Leopold on his way through Pitigliano. In his travel diary, the duke gave a glowing description of the synagogue — "all gilded stuccowork and well designed." In fact it had been restored in 1756 and was to remain open for another two centuries. Then when the community numbers fell, it was closed. In 1956 the 18th-century ark was sent to Israel and is now in the Carmiel synagogue.

At the beginning of the 1960s the building shared the same fate as many of the houses in Pitigliano built on a cliff: the walls collapsed down the hill and the furnishings and archives were lost. According to the historical chronicles, for *Shavuot* or Pentecost — in Italy called "The *Pesach* of Roses" — rose petals were scattered on the synagogue floor. In 1995 the Pitigliano town council decided to restore the synagogue as it had been, maintaining the original parts (the women's gallery, enclosed by a gilded wooden rail carved with leaves, and some side walls with decorative capitals) and rebuilding the rest of the room with the old structures and decorations. They include a large cartouche with the inscription "If I forget thee, O Jerusalem, let my right hand wither," on the west wall, alongside two inscriptions commemorating the visits to the synagogue by the Grand Dukes of Tuscany Ferdinand III in 1823 and Leopold II in 1829. Opposite the entrance a false oval window is symmetric with the real

window situated over the door. Here another cartouche celebrates the visit of the Grand Duke Peter Leopold in 1773. Inside, the original part has been left in exposed brick and the rest is clad with white plaster. The furnishings, benches, *bimah*, and ark are stylized reproductions of the originals. Alongside the synagogue, the old unleavened bread oven was recovered together with the *mikveh* (ritual bath) and the room where meat was butchered according to kosher methods. There is also a small museum with objects and documents.

In the shops of the old ghetto local kosher wine is sold and the bakers' windows are laden with *sfratti* (honey and walnut biscuits) and *bolli* (large doughnuts with aniseed and sultanas). These delicacies are so much part of the local tradition that many people are unaware of their Jewish origin.

The cemetery at the foot of the town

At the foot of a hill on the road to Marciano, the cemetery stretches over terraced slopes. This very old burial site has tombs in niches gouged out of the tufa rock. Alongside are some monuments unusual for the Jewish tradition, such as a 19th-century tomb with a supine child and another with an angel.

The Siena community was famed for its bankers, like Ismaele (Laudadio) da Rieti in the 16th century, scholars, and rabbis. Initially made up of Italian Jews, the group's ranks swelled with the arrival first of Spaniards in 1492 and then Ashkenazim some time later. Forced to live in the ghetto from 1571, they organized it as a city within the city, with as many as five Rabbinical schools earning Siena the name of "Little Jerusalem." The community always had to defend against anti-Semite attacks, begun by Bernardino da Siena, who from

1405 lashed out at the Jews for over forty years. Then in 1799 the Viva Maria sacked the ghetto and killed nineteen inhabitants. The Viva Maria was a gang of peasants and thugs that had formed in nearby Arezzo. They supported the House of Lorraine against Napoleon and were backed by the Austro-Russian army. This massacre, commemorated every year with fasting, signaled the beginning of the end for the community. Its members fell from 500 in the 18th century to 300 in the 19th century, 200 in the 20th century, and less than 100 today.

The ghetto near Piazza del Campo

The ghetto, which lasted 288 years (from 1571 to 1859), was situated near the most famous square in Siena — Piazza del Campo. It originally stretched from Via del Salicotto (with the first gate) to Via San Martino. These two streets were crossed by a number of smaller parallel streets: Via delle Scotte (once Piazzetta del Tempio, due to the presence of the "temple"), Vicolo del Luparello (with the second gate, school

Synagogue interior. Officially opened in 1786, the Neoclassical synagogue room has a rectangular plan and barrel-vault ceilings. The bimah is in the middle of the room opposite the ark, with the benches set against the walls. On the walls are inscriptions of verses from Psalms, framed by stuccowork.

Inlaid work crowning the backrest of Elijah's Chair, used for circumcision. Gifted in 1860 by Rabbi Nissim, the inlaid work includes inscriptions of Biblical verses on the importance of this religious practice.

and various confraternities), and Vicolo del Realto. In the middle of the ghetto Via degli Archi had the community fountain, which was decorated with a statue of Moses in the 16th century. Possibly made by Jacopo della Quercia, the statue was removed in 1875 and is now in the Museo del Comune. The other central streets were Vicolo della Fortuna, Vicolo Manna, Vicolo della Coda, and Vicolo Vannello. The quarter was radically altered in 1935 and redeveloped. Some corners, however, have survived intact (such as Via delle Scotte), along with the old place names. The Italian-rite synagogue, at no. 14, Via delle Scotte, was opened in 1786 in a building used for an earlier synagogue. The Italian synagogue was designed by the Florentine Giuseppe del Rosso, while the internal wood decorations were made by the cabinetmakers Nicolò Lande and Pietro Rossi.

Like all the synagogues built before emancipation (1848), the building's façade is anonymous. Next to the entrance a plaque commemorates the fourteen Sienese Jews deported during the Second World War. In the ground-floor hall another plaque records the Jews who died fighting for Italy in the First World War; on the first floor, in the hall leading to the prayer room there are two plaques dedicated to the restoration of the synagogue in 1902 and the visit by the Grand Duke of Tuscany Leopold II in 1829. The 17th-century *tzedakah* (charity) boxes on the wall only came to light during recent restoration work. The Elijah's Chair, a gift presented by Rabbi Nissim in 1860, is made of wood with inlaid inscriptions of Biblical verses on the importance of circumcision. The Neoclassical prayer room reveals the influence of Domenico Vanvitelli, who also worked on other buildings in Siena. The room is rectangular with a barrel-vault ceiling. The benches run along the walls, broken up by pilasters with Ionic capitals, interwoven with garlands. The arched entablature reaches up to the ceiling, decorated with stuccoes containing colored inscriptions of the Ten Commandments. In the arches of the vault are some windows adorned with friezes and festoons in late Baroque style. On the walls are four-teen verses from Psalms, framed by Baroque stuccoes.

The holy ark stands on the short wall opposite the entrance. The women's gallery over the entrance is screened by close-knit wooden grates. The structure of the gallery consists of four marble columns with Corinthian capitals ending in a round tympanum. At the pediment apex is the Hebrew inscription "Know before Whom you stand," surmounted by a crown. In the middle are the finely carved gilded wooden doors with, below, the inauguration date (1786) and the donor's surname — Gallichi. The ark is raised by six steps and separated from the rest of the room by a marble balustrade with small columns and a central wrought-iron gate. In front of it are six candelabra and some lamps. The roundish walnut *bimah* (1756) is at the center of the room.

The cemetery, at no. 17, Via del Lanaiolo, has tombs from the 16th century.

Marranos burned at the stake

A bridge between Europe and the East, the port of Ancona was always a hub of economic activities for the local Jewish community. Over the centuries these activities attracted thousands of merchants, especially Levantines and Marranos, who, however, never fully integrated with the Italian Jews.

Local Jewish life from the 16th century was conditioned by the rule of the Papal States, which had annexed Ancona in 1532. The popes decreed the creation of the ghetto, imposed the wearing of the badge, and persecuted the Marranos. In fact, in 1556 twenty-five Marranos were burned at the stake in Campo della Mostra (today Piazza Malatesta, where a plaque was raised in 1992 to record the event) after an auto-da-fé. The news of the burnings spread far and wide. Even Suleiman I the Magnificent intervened: the port of Ancona was boycotted and for two years all cargoes went to Pesaro.

The Ancona community was so large that it inevitably played a vital part in the city's economy: from 1,400 in 1618 (around 13.9 percent of the whole population), its numbers rose to 1,900 in 1877 (around 6 percent). This was when the decline set in: the Napoleonic continental blockade, the abolition of the free port and a subsequent period of famine and epidemics drove many Jews away from the city. Today the community, the only one in the Marches, has 200 members with sections in Senigallia and Urbino.

Plan of the Levantine-rite synagogue. In use from 1549, the old Levantine synagogue was demolished in 1860 during the redevelopment of the whole old ghetto area. In 1876 it was then reconstructed in the building it still shares with the Italian synagogue.

The old cemetery on Mount Cardeto was used from 1428. Situated on a cliff, many gravestones have fallen into the sea. In recent years reinforcement work was carried out and some stones were moved to a safer position.

One building with several synagogues

From 1569 there were only two ghettos in the Papal States — in Rome and Ancona. The Ancona ghetto soon spread over a vast area of the city, and its population grew to over 1,000. The inhabitants were not only Ancona Jews but also those forced to abandon rural areas and live in the ghetto. Except for Via Astagno and Via del Bagno, the whole area was altered in the 20th century.

The main artery of the ghetto was Via Lata, now Via Astagno, the backbone for a whole maze of alleys and narrow streets: Via del Traffico, Via del Bagno, Via lo Speziale, Via dei Banchieri, Via Stalle, Vicolo del Gozzo, Vicolo Strettore, Via del Gallo, Via delle Azzimelle, Via del Macello, and Via delle Prostitute. There were two gates: one at the junction between Via lo Speziale and Via Calamo (later Corso Mazzini), and the other where Via del Traffico joins Via Calamo. Two successive slum clearances cut the ghetto area in two. In 1860 Corso Vittorio Emanuele II (later Corso Garibaldi) was opened up and then in 1930 Corso Stamira was created. These two new streets radically changed the area, sweeping away the old urban structure, including the synagogues.

The building at no. 14, Via Astagno, now housing two synagogues, was built from 1873 to 1876. In 1860 a building that had served as the Levantine-rite synagogue since 1549, in the former Via de' Levantini, was demolished. In fact the redevelopment scheme to provide access to the port from Piazza della Repubblica (formerly Piazza dei Cavalli) had not spared this very old *scola*, whose plan was based on the Safed synagogue, with a raised *bimah* reached by two

stairs set against the walls, as in the surviving Pesaro synagogue. The 19th-century building in Via Astagno also hosted the Italian-rite synagogue, which had been transferred there from a house at the beginning of the street. This house was then pulled down in 1930–35, when demolition work began on the ghetto area (its place was taken by a cinema).

Opened in 1597, the Italian synagogue had once been in Via Gozzo, but had to be moved a few years later to Via Astagno after the confraternity of Santi Rocco e Sebastiano protested because it was too near their church. Thus the prayer rooms for the various rites were eventually concentrated in the same building. The Italian-rite synagogue (now rarely used) was reconstructed in 1932 on the raised ground floor of the building, below the Levantine-rite room, which already occupied the first and second floors.

With a rectangular plan (18 × 10 m [59 × 32.75 ft.]), the Italian synagogue has

the "bipolar" arrangement, with the ark and *bimah* opposite each other on the short sides of the room. The *bimah* is situated between the entrance doors: it stands between two columns under a baldachin that in the previous synagogue was in front of the ark. Here the holy ark is monumental: the upper half of the repoussé silver doors depict the Tablets of the Law with below two vases of flowers, while at the sides are two twisted columns carved with gilded leaves. The whole complex is made of wood and gilded stucco and is enhanced by a series of side columns surmounted by an equally finely decorated entablature. At the sides are two windows. Wooden benches run round the perimeter of the room; at the front, another two rows of double benches leave a narrow passage at the center, while brass candelabra hang from the ceiling. At the

same height as the room, the recesses of the women's gallery are on one of the long sides.

Still used today, the Levantine synagogue is situated on the first floor. Based on a rectangular plan (like the Italian room beneath), it is organized on two stories. The present arrangement of the furnishings dates from the 1940s. When the furnishings were moved in 1876, the original bipolar structure was preserved, with the ark and *bimah* opposite each other on the short sides. But today the ark is set against the wall opposite the entrance with the *bimah* in front of it. The whole area is raised from the floor and enclosed by a wooden balustrade. The ark has 17th-century repoussé silver doors, decorated inside and out with Jewish symbols and adorned on the sides by ten wooden columns with Pompeian-red painted marble, Corinthian capitals and, in the upper sections, deep grooves. The entablature supports a large crown, surmounted by a baldachin. The wooden structure is Baroque. The two arched windows flanking the ark provide daylight. There is a row of windows on the long walls; some are blind and screened by the old women's gallery. In the bay of one of these blind windows is the small carved gilded wooden balcony originally from Pesaro, with, concealed inside, the organ. A second row of rectangular windows is set high up, just under the ceiling. Here on three sides is the new women's gallery. The building has a typical ritual bath (*mikveh*) and an internal balcony used for the *sukkah* (the tabernacle for *Sukkoth*).

Gold-embroidered cape for the Scrolls of the Law, detail. Together with the silver objects, this is one of the ornaments used to honor the scriptures.

The Levantine-rite synagogue has two floors and a rectangular plan. The 17th-century ark is the most original feature. Its doors are decorated with symbols and red-painted wooden columns ending in Corinthian capitals. The entablature is surmounted by a large crown.

In an adjacent building (no. 12), the community premises house some fine furnishings and unusual objects (an Elijah's Chair used for circumcision, drawings, and some painted marble panels for the *sukkah*).

The cemetery at Tavernelle is part of the city cemetery and replaced the old Jewish graveyard at Monte Cardeto (also known as Monte delle Cavorchie) in 1863. Part of the land was ceded to the army engineers corps. The cemetery at Monte Cardeto had been used since 1428. Set on a sheer cliff, many of the gravestones have fallen into the sea. The cemetery is now being shored up and some stones have been moved to a safer position.

Short-lived splendor

The Jews of Pesaro and Urbino have a similar story. Their fate depended on the Dukes of Urbino (first the Montefeltro and then the Della Rovere). When Guidobaldo II Della Rovere (1538–1574) moved his court from Urbino to Pesaro, many Jews followed him, and the community enjoyed a period of great splendor. Illustrious figures came to the city, like the printer Gershom Soncino. Moreover, the Ancona Jews also came to Pesaro after twenty-five Marranos had been burned at the stake in 1556. As a protest against the killings, the Jews saw to it that all the maritime traffic with the Levant was moved from the port of Ancona to the port of Pesaro. In 1569 the Pesaro Jewish community was the largest in the Duchy of Urbino. This period of splendor came to an end with the Duchy's annexation to the Papal States in 1632 and the creation of the ghetto in 1634, which lasted until Napoleon's troops arrived in 1797. When the French left Pesaro, as happened in Urbino and Senigallia, the ghetto and synagogues were sacked by the Sanfedisti (an antiliberal clerical association). This marked the beginning of the end and by 1870 the Pesaro community numbered 145 people. By 1901, there were 93. Today it no longer exists.

A synagogue with scenic effects

Created in 1632, the old ghetto was right in the middle of the historic center, from Via Castelfidardo to Via Sara Levi Nathan (formerly Via del Ghetto Grande), Via delle Scuole, and Via delle Botteghe (formerly Via del Ghetto Piccolo). This area, however, has been radically transformed. The quarter was originally closed by three gates: the first was at the end of Via delle Botteghe at the junction with Via Tortora; the second at the entrance to Via Sara Levi Nathan and the Salita della Ginevra; and the third between Via Castelfidardo and Via del Corso. The ghetto was made up of small streets and alleys, like Via dei Mulattieri and Via delle Stalle, which stretched as far as Via Tortora, and what is now Via Almerico da Ventura. In the 1940s many buildings in the area were demolished to make room for Piazzale Primo Maggio. There were originally two synagogues in Via delle Scuole, one Italian rite and the other Sephardic rite (still present today). There was a third synagogue (another Italian-rite temple), in Via delle Zucchette (once Piazza Giudea), but being outside the ghetto, it was closed down.

The building of the Italian-rite synagogue was on the corner of Via delle Scuole (the entrance was at no. 26) with Via Sara Levi Nathan. A second entrance and the women's door were in the parallel Via delle Botteghe. Damaged by an earthquake in 1930, the building was sold in 1938 (for 1,000 lire). The furnishings were removed: part of the ark is in Milan (in the central synagogue at no. 19, Via Guastalla); the ark's columns and dome, together with the *bimah*, were taken to Israel in the 1950s and are now in the synagogue of Kyriat Tsans, Netanya, and in the Italian synagogue in Jerusalem.

The Sephardic-rite synagogue has been closed for many years for structural restoration work. Situated at no. 25, Via delle Scuole, it has an anonymous façade with a large doorway reserved for the men and a smaller door for the women. The women's door leads directly up a steep staircase to the two rooms of the women's gallery. The main entrance has a large glazed door that opens onto the internal courtyard, where the tabernacle was built for *Sukkoth*. Some of the rooms were used for the unleavened bread oven, the well, and ritual bath (*mikveh*).

A flight of stairs leads up to the prayer room on the first floor. It has a rectangular plan with the ark and *bimah* opposite each other on the short sides.

The entrance is under an internal gallery, used as the area of the *bimah*, reached by going up a flight of stairs set against the two side walls. The gallery has three arches, each supported by four marble-painted columns and capitals decorated with floral festoons. On the side walls there were once two 19th-century tempera paintings: *The Walls of Jerusalem* (with local Urbino landscapes in the background) and *The Camp at Mount Sinai*. The room is lit by large windows in the rear walls of the gallery and two rows of windows on the long sides (to the right on entering). On the opposite side is the two-story women's gallery. The room has a high barrel-vault ceiling, divided into caissons decorated by large rose-shaped pateras and oak leaves. Before being restored, the ceiling was bright yellow and cobalt blue. According to the scholar Maria Luisa Moscati, this was an allusion to the sun yellow and sea blue of the Iberian peninsula — a *saudade* that the nostalgic Sephardim remembered from their new homeland. In the restoration, however, the ceiling was painted white. The prayer room is now empty. The monumental ark, once positioned opposite the *bimah*, has been used since 1970 in the Livorno synagogue; a small 18th-century carved gilded wooden balcony is now in the Levantine synagogue, Ancona. The wooden grates carved with shapes like small Stars of David are in the Talpioth synagogue, Jerusalem.

Situated on a panoramic road on the hill of San Bartolo, the cemetery has recently been reordered and its headstones restored by a private sponsor.

The former synagogue interior. This Sephardic-rite temple is the only survivor of three synagogues (the other two were Italian-rite). Currently being restored, it has an original architectural structure. The high barrel-vaulted ceiling is divided into caissons decorated by large rose-shaped panels and oak leaves.

The largest fair in 14th-century Europe

As early as the 14th century the coastal town of Senigallia held one of the largest fairs in Europe: up to 500 ships moored in the port, while 50,000 merchants came to do business worth 10 million *scudi*. The Jews also attended this great Mediterranean bazaar and gradually began to settle in the town and organize in a group. They always lived in precarious conditions and had to face popular prejudice against them, fueled by the preaching of the Minor Friars.

Having first passed from the Malatesta to Della Rovere family, Senigallia became part of the Papal States in 1632. A ghetto was immediately created (1633) and wearing the badge was made obligatory (1691). Despite the restrictions, by the beginning of the 18th century over 500 Jews lived in the town. Their number fell in Napoleonic times, when the fairs gradually lost their importance. After the French left in 1799, a gang of Sanfedisti, aided by the local rabble, sacked the ghetto, devastated the synagogue, and destroyed or stole the furnishings. Thirteen people were killed and around one hun-

dred wounded. Having fled by sea, 600 sought refuge in Ancona. They came back after a few months, but by then the community was completely drained of its vitality. Today there are only a few Jewish families left, and the Senigallia community has become a section of the Ancona community.

A completely redeveloped area

Created in 1633, the ghetto embraced a vast area from Piazza del Duca to Piazza del Comune, Via dell'Ospedale Vecchio, and Via della Sinagoga Vecchia. At the entrances there were four gates. The whole area has been radically transformed and only Via dei Commercianti, the street with the synagogue (no. 20), still gives some idea of the original appearance of the quarter. In 1892 some buildings in Via dei Commercianti opposite the Palazzo Comunale were set further back. After the 1930 earthquake, the houses were lowered to two stories, only for most of the quarter then to be demolished to create Piazza Simoncelli. A plaque on the wall at no. 34 in this square records the existence of the ghetto.

The Italian-rite synagogue dates from 1634. It replaced an existing temple in Via Arsilli (previously Via della Sinagoga Vecchia), just outside the walls of the ghetto. The building originally had three floors and the synagogue was on the top floor. It was then moved to the first floor (where it is situated today) after the 1930 earthquake, which undermined the stability of most buildings in the town.

The entrance is divided into five doors, each framed by an Istrian stone portal. The number five is no random choice. According to the *Cabbala* we should "Remember that your hand has five fingers not four," and therefore is made to give not to take. The entrance leads to a wide staircase going up to the community offices and prayer room on the first floor. The 18th-century door to the prayer room is divided into panels embellished by large rosettes. The room is rectangular with some asymmetric points (12 × 7 m [39 × 23 ft.]). Between two windows on the right-hand side, the holy ark is

Some gravestones from the old cemetery were moved to the entrance of the new cemetery in 1871.

The Italian-rite synagogue interior was given its present form after the 1930 earthquake, when it was moved from the first floor to the ground floor for safety reasons. It has a rectangular plan and large windows on two sides providing the room with light.

decorated with gold patterns. Set in front of it, the lectern-type *bimah* is enclosed by a balustrade like a semicircular balcony made of gilded carved wood. The balustrade in the original synagogue was supported by six Corinthian columns and there were pincerlike flights of steps on either side up to the *bimah*. This structure was dismantled after the earthquake. A second *bimah*, on the left-hand wall, is made of poorer-quality wood and has gilded motifs. The furnishings are 19th-century. When the ghetto and synagogue were sacked in 1799, most of the furnishings were lost.

The walls have six windows, four on the long side opposite the entrance and two on one of the short sides. Wooden paneling round the walls acts as a backrest for some of the benches, arranged in two parallel rows. Between the rows are long tables once in the community rooms. They give the room the appearance of a place of study. A cupboard in the women's gallery contains the Scrolls of the Law. The community archives, however, are in Rome, in the Bibliographic Center of the Italian Jewish Communities' Union (UCEI).

The Senigallia cemetery at no. 2, Via delle Grazie has been used since 1878. It also preserves eighty-five stones from the earlier cemetery at Portone, recovered when the area was redeveloped in 1977. A small area in the cemetery has been made into a park, named after Anne Frank.

The Jews of Urbino enjoyed long periods of serenity under the Dukes of Montefeltro until 1508. They were followed by uncertain times under Francesco Maria II Della Rovere, who died in 1631, up to the end of all illusions of freedom, when the city came under the direct political influence of the Church with the annexation to the Papal States. The following year the Jews were forced to live in the ghetto (1633) and attend obligatory sermons. This marked the beginning of greater discrimination against them. There had evidently also been anti-Jewish prejudice in earlier centuries, however, as suggested by the *predella* (part of an altarpiece) by Paolo Uccello, now in the National Gallery of the Marches (Palazzo Ducale, Urbino). Dedicated to the theme of the *Profanation of the Host*, the painting was executed some time between 1467 and 1468 for the confraternity of Corpus Domini. Having originated in Paris in 1290, this story was readily used as a way of spreading anti-Jewish sentiment. Indeed, basically the same story is found later in Trani,

Apulia, where it is still the subject of a popular festivity.

The creation of the ghetto ushered in two centuries of poverty and destitution. By 1718 the population had fallen to 200 inhabitants compared to 369 a century earlier. With the arrival of Napoleon's troops in 1797 the doors were removed from the ghetto. But after the French left it was sacked. The Jews did not return to the ghetto with the restoration of the monarchy. In fact, they had already begun to move pending future emancipation, which they enthusiastically took part in. From then on the Urbino group dwindled. In 1944 ten Jews were deported, and today there is no community.

The synagogue with the towers of the Ducal Palace in the background. Created in 1633, the ghetto was at the foot of the Ducal Palace and closed by three doors. The present synagogue was built in the same year and then remodeled several times. The last remodeling was after the earthquake of 1848.

The synagogue room is rectangular with an apse and vaulted ceiling. Set in the middle of the apse, the walnut-root ark is circular in form and crowned by a dome. The doors are decorated by six gilded carved columns ending in Corinthian capitals.

At the foot of the Ducal Palace

The streets where the ghetto was established in 1633 are under the characteristic two towers of the Ducal Palace, near the gate called Porta Valdona, in the area between Via Stretta and Via delle Stallacce. Originally the area was very different from today. In addition to Via Stretta and Via delle Stallacce, which have remained intact, there was a small alley and a square linked by steps to the street above. The monks of the monastery of San Francesco raised a building in the square, now no. 27, Via Stretta, in 1789. A house (once next door to the synagogue at no. 24) that collapsed at the beginning of the 20th century is now only a widening in the street. Due to changes in the urban layout, the steps in Via delle Stallacce only lead to a dead-end courtyard.

The ghetto was closed by three doors: the first at the corner of Via Stretta, where the synagogue stood, and the other two at either end of Via delle Stallacce. Today, at one end, this street leads up some steps to Via Garibaldi (not yet built at the time of the ghetto) and at the other end to a bridge street built after the creation of the ghetto.

The well at no. 11, Via Stretta was used by all the inhabitants of the ghetto (369 people; many had come from Cagli, San Lorenzo in Campo, Fossombrone, Pergola, Sant'Angelo, Mondolfo, Orciano, and Mondavio), while the butcher's shop was at no. 15 and the synagogue at no. 24. There was also a number of other shops in the street. The synagogue building, dating from 1633, has been altered several times, the last reconstruction being after the earthquake of 1848.

When the ghetto was created, the Italian-rite synagogue had inherited the furnishings from an earlier temple at no. 12, Via Veterani; the Jews had to abandon this building because it was too far from the area they had been assigned. These furnishings were used until the renovation of 1859. The 15th-century ark was kept in the schoolroom until 1906, when the community sold it to help pay for the expense of the restoration. After being on the antiques market, it is now in the Jewish Museum, New York.

Curtain for the holy ark, embroidered with the "Rose of Pesaro" and woven with gold thread. Precious embroidered fabrics were gifted to the synagogues to mark major family ceremonies, such as births and marriages.

The synagogue was restored from 1970 to 1973. Like all places of worship in ghettos, the façade is anonymous. There are three doors: a main door leading to the vestibule; a second door going down to the basement, containing the unleavened bread oven and the well; and the third, leading up four flights of stairs to the women's gallery. In the vestibule are two Hebrew plaques: one offers thanks for the hospitality given to the Jews by the Dukes of Urbino, and the other records names of two donors, Mordechai and Pinchas Coen, who made possible the restoration of 1859. Lower down are six walled charity (*tzedakah*) boxes.

The rectangular room (11.7 × 6.4 m [38 × 21 ft.]) is apsed with a vaulted ceiling. The entrance door is situated at the center of one of the long sides. Opposite is a second door leading to a courtyard in the rear, where the tabernacle for *Sukkoth* was prepared. The walls are richly decorated: large rosettes on the apse ceiling (similar in number and workmanship to those in Urbino cathedral), columns with Ionic capitals right round the perimeter of the room, crowned by a fascia of floral stuccoes. On the walls are some cartouches with Biblical writings and framed fine damask fabrics. The arrangement is "bipolar" with the ark and *bimah* opposite each other on the short sides. Raised from the floor of the room by two steps, the veneered walnut-root ark stands in the middle of the apse. Shaped like a *tempietto*, it has a circular plan and is crowned by a dome. The two doors are embellished on either sides by six carved gilded wooden columns ending in Corinthian capitals. The entablature has floral motifs echoing the pattern of the stuccoes. The area is circumscribed by a wrought-iron balustrade in front of which hangs the *ner tamid*.

The *bimah* is now set on the opposite wall, whereas until the 19th-century restoration it had been in the middle of the room. In a raised position, it is reached by going up pincer-shaped stairs and is enclosed by a small decorated walnut-root balcony, embellished at the base by a frieze of gilded acanthus leaves. The wooden banisters of the two side stairs have cornices and brass fittings for eleven candleholders. The *bimah* is so majestic that it is more like a pulpit. Behind is an arched window replacing the original three windows. This new opening and the four large lunettes preserved in the side wall provide lighting. Three brass chandeliers (with candles) hang from the ceiling. Benches run round the perimeter walls, while at the center there are five walnut benches. All the wooden furnishings were made by famous craftsmen, including Francesco Pucci, a cabinetmaker, and Crescentino Pieretti, a gilder, both from Cagli. The women's gallery (9.5 × 6 m [31 × 19.5 ft.]) overlooks the prayer room protected by a wooden balustrade with inlaid work. The gallery is reached from an outside door. The room next to the synagogue on the first floor was once used as a school. Today it is furnished with a long table and cupboard for liturgical objects and books.

The Urbino Jewish cemetery is at Monte degli Ebrei, in the village of Gadana. The first grave dates from 1874. There was an earlier cemetery in the same area but it had to be abandoned because of land subsidence. The old headstones were recovered and lined up in the new cemetery.

The Jewish calendar is mainly lunar but also solar: the holidays, days, months, and years are based on the time taken by the Moon to complete its orbit round the Sun, while the seasons are based on the time taken for the Earth to orbit the Sun. The lunar year and the solar year differ by around ten days. To make up the difference, in ancient times some embolistic years were added with thirteen months instead of twelve. The year 2003–2004, for example, is 5764 in the Jewish calendar. As the calendar is "mobile," the holidays fall on different days every year.

The calendar begins with the month of *Tishri* ("the beginning"), corresponding to September and October. The first and second days of *Tishri* are *Rosh Hashanah*, the New Year — the day of creation. This is a festivity for reflection, introspection and self-scrutiny. According to tradition, the Lord examined men and their behavior in the year just finished. Therefore it is also called *Yom ha Din*, the Day of Judgment, which will only become definitive, however, at *Yom Kippur*, the Day of Atonement, when the Lord writes in the book of life only the names of those who will live in the year that is about to begin. Between these two holidays are the "ten days of repentance."

Rosh Hashanah is also known as *Yom Teruah*, the day when the *shofar* (ram's horn) is sounded during the ceremony in the synagogue to call the people to repent. But the horn is also blown to remind people of the sacrifice of Isaac, when the ram was sacrificed in his place. It is therefore also the "Day of Remembering": on this day the Lord completed the creation of Adam, the first man. *Rosh Hashanah* is characterized by several customs. One is *tashlikh* ("casting off"), when people must go to the banks of a river or the sea and recite a prayer and empty their pockets. Symbolically, this act represents throwing away sins before promising to avoid all bad behavior. Another custom practiced at this time by the Ashkenazim is that of dressing in white, a sign of purity and spiritual renewal. The synagogue is also all draped in white. At *Rosh Hashanah* the food must be sweet (e.g., apples dipped in honey), bread has a round form, like the crown of the Lord, reminding of the cyclical nature of the year, and wheat and maize seeds are planted as a wish for prosperity.

Yom Kippur falls on the 10th of *Tishri*. The holiest and most solemn day in the whole calendar, it is a day of total fasting dedicated to prayer and repentance. On this day the Lord completes his judgment of the individual. Before *Yom Kippur*, both spiritual and material debts towards others must be paid off and pardon must be asked of those who have been offended. Only in this way can the Day of Atonement begin. It is the most deeply felt of all the festivities and also respected by even less devout Jews. The liturgy begins with *Kol Nidre*, a prayer asking that the vows and promises unfulfilled during the past year be annulled. The festivity ends after twenty-five hours with the sound of the *shofar* calling people to prayer for the last time.

On the 15th of *Tishri*, *Sukkoth*, the so-called "festival of the tabernacles," is celebrated. This is an allusion to the temporary dwellings used by the Jews who lived in the wilderness for forty years after leaving Egypt and before reaching the promised land. In farming it marks the last harvest before winter. Like most Jewish festivities, it combines a historical meaning and a significance associated with the natural cycle and farming. *Sukkoth* is also called the "harvest festival" because it coincides with the end of the harvest. Most of the day is spent in the tabernacles (kinds of booths) made of branches with fruit, flowers, drawings, and a roof of thinly laid branches so that there is more shade than light but the stars can still be seen. The last day of *Sukkoth* is called *Hoshanah Rabba* (an invocation meaning "Please save us"). On this day the long period of repentance begun at *Rosh Hashanah* comes to an end. Pardon is asked by beating the *lulav*, a bouquet made of one palm branch, two willow branches, three myrtle branches and one *etrog* (citron) branch. Symbolically, the different species are reunited for the occasion: the palm has no scent but tasty fruit; the willow has neither taste nor scent; the myrtle has scent but no taste; and, last, the

etrog has both taste and scent. According to another interpretation, the *l*⸗
⸗or man: the palm is his backbone, the willow his mouth, the myrtle his ey⸗
etrog his heart. In this way the whole body is reunited in prayer to God.

The *Shemini Atzeret* (the assembly of the eighth [day]) is the conti⸗
Sukkoth and is the last day everyone goes into the *sukkah*. The next day
Torah, or the "rejoicing in the Law." It marks the end and the beginning
the weekly *Torah* readings. In this way the reading is continuous over time
⸗ul festival and one of the three (with *Pesach* and *Shavuot*) "pilgrimage"
⸗because in ancient times the Jews had to go to the Temple of Jerusalem.

On the 25th of *Kislev* (November-December), *Hanukkah* (the festival ⸗
⸗celebrated. Of all the ancient festivities this is the only one not grounded i
⸗and scriptures. Established by the Masters of the *Talmud*, it records an eve
⸗n 168 BC, when Antiochus IV of Syria wished to impose paganism on Juda
⸗opposed by Mattathias the Hasmonean, a priest from Modi'in, who with
⸗sons began a rebellion that lasted three years until they reconquered the
⸗this point the Temple had to be rededicated but there was only enough
⸗one day. Miraculously, the oil lasted for eight days, thus allowing priests
⸗more pure oil. To record this miraculous event, for eight days candles are

joyful festivity, when children receive spinning tops (*dreidels*) with the initials of the words "a great miracle took place here." In recent years in some Italian cities nine branch candelabra have been set in large squares, and the candles lit publicly every evening. At home the candelabrum is placed on the window shelf so that the flame can be seen from outside. The celebration takes place near the winter solstice, when the hours of darkness are longer. The light of the candelabrum thus serves to contrast the surrounding darkness. On the 15th of *Shevat* (January-February), *Rosh Hashanah La'Ilanot,* the New Year of Trees, is celebrated. It marks the end of winter and the reawakening of nature. Although the weather is still cold, in Israel this is traditionally the day when the almond trees begin to flower. In the past it was used to calculate the tithes to be paid to the sanctuary during the year: the fruit that ripened before the 15th of *Shevat* belonged to one year, and the rest to the following year. It was also used to establish when the first three years of life of a tree were over: i.e. the initial period when its fruit could not be gathered. The family reunited to celebrate this festivity by eating a meal based on fruit from seven species: wheat, barley, grape, fig, pomegranate, olive, and dates.

On the 14th of *Adar* (February-March) *Purim*, "the festivity of lots," is celebrated. It refers to the story of Esther, the wife of King Ahasuerus of Persia, who saved her people from destruction. The date for the extermination (13th of *Adar*) had been fixed by "casting lots," hence the name of the festivity. This story is told in the Book of Esther, which for the occasion is read in the synagogue. *Purim* is a kind of carnival when children dress up, play, and swap sweets or biscuits — in Italy called "Haman's ears" — and gifts. It is preceded by a day of fasting — a reminder of when Esther fasted to invoke the help of God. *Pesach* or Passover, the festivity of unleavened bread, falls on the 14th of *Nissan* (March-April). It commemorates the exodus from Egypt and the end of slavery. In farming it marks the first reaping and the period for the spring births of domestic animals. *Pesach* lasts seven days and no leavened foods can be eaten or even kept in the house for this period. On the first two evenings of solemn festivity, there is a ritual meal called *seder*, when the family reads the *Haggadah* of Passover, which narrates the liberation from the slavery of Egypt. The dinner is an important time of family reunion when everyone takes part in reading the scriptures, asking questions, and performing highly symbolic rites. On the 6th of *Sivan* (May-June) *Shavuot* (Pentecost) or "the gift of the *Torah*" is celebrated. This festivity commemorates the Ten Commandments given to Moses on Mount Sinai. In farming it marks the first harvest of fruit and vegetables. For the occasion, the synagogue is adorned with sweet smelling flowers as a reminder of the place where the commandments were given to the Jews. The family meets on the eve to eat a light meal based on milk. After dinner, many people study the *Torah* all night.

The most important festivity of all is the *Shabbat* or the Sabbath, because it is celebrated every week and sets the rhythm for the year in individual, family, and community life. The Lord completed the creation on Saturday and then rested. In Hebrew *Shabbat* means "to cease." Jews thus celebrated the Sabbath by giving up all working activity and dedicating the day to the family, study, and meditation. On this day all men and women are equal and no one can make use of the work of another. Even the animals must rest. It begins with the rising of the first star on Friday and ends with the appearance of the first stars on Saturday. Before the Sabbath begins, food is prepared and cooked for the dinner, and the ritual candles are lit. The meals on Friday evening and Saturday lunch begin with the blessing of wine. The end of the Sabbath is marked by *Havdalah*, the ceremony of separation, signaling the end of the festivity and the beginning of a new week. The head of the family recites four blessings, fills a glass of wine, picks up a sweet smelling branch, and with a *Havdalah* candle shows the contrast between light (the Sabbath) and darkness (all the other days).

The oldest community of the Diaspora

The Roman community has a very special, fascinating history: its ancient origins, rich historical and artistic heritage, and monuments that have survived to the present day make it a unique example not only in Italy but in the whole Diaspora. This long continuous presence has left traces stratified with those of the other inhabitants with whom through good and bad the Jews have lived for over two millennia. Thus many ancient Roman monuments bear signs or memories of their presence. One great example is the Arch of Titus, in the Roman Forum, with scenes showing the deportation of Jews from Palestine, including, arguably, the most emblematic image of all: prisoners carrying a seven-branched candelabrum to Rome after the destruction of the Temple of Jerusalem.

A constant factor in the Jewish history of Rome was papal policy. For centuries it meant persecution and discrimination. Having left the initial Jewish quarter (the earliest synagogue has been identified as being at no. 14, Vicolo dell'Atleta in the Trastevere area), they settled in what was to become the most miserable fetid area in the city. Here in 1555, all the Jews in Rome were

forced to live and, from 1569, also all the very many Jews who had previously lived in villages and towns in the surrounding territory of Lazio. Many assumed the names of these localities (Di Segni, Di Veroli, Piperno, Alatri, Sermoneta, to mention but a few). The order to live in the ghettos (in the Papal States there were two: one in Rome and the other in Ancona) forced lots of other groups to move. Many came up from Sicily and southern Italy after 1492, when they were expelled from the territories under Bourbon rule. At the same time, to avoid being enclosed in the ghetto, many Roman Jews sought refuge in other places such as Pitigliano in Tuscany, hoping they would soon be able to return home. The ghetto was only finally abolished in 1870, after three centuries of poverty and humiliation. Once emancipation eventually came, the history of the Roman community reflected that of the whole of Italy. The demolition of the ghetto and the construction of a large new temple were greeted as signs of refound freedom. The Roman Jews took part in the strug-

The Portico of Ottavia is still the center of Jewish life in Rome. Set up in 1555 at the behest of Pope Paul IV, the ghetto stretched from the island in the Tiber River to the Ponte Quattro Capi, the Portico of Ottavia, Via Ottavia, and Piazza delle Cinque Scole.

The Tempio Maggiore was officially opened in 1904 after the ghetto had been demolished. Built in Neo-Baroque Oriental style, it is a large cube surmounted by a sail-vault dome resting on a quadrangular drum.

gle for the unity of Italy, and eagerly embraced libertarian ideas. Thus one of the most honest and able mayors of Rome (1907–13) was the Jew Ernesto Nathan, who had been raised on the liberal ideals of Giuseppe Mazzini. But there was still to be more mass mourning. The Nazi occupation of Rome in 1943 was one of the most tragic chapters in the history of the long-standing community: 2,091 Jews were captured and deported on October 16, 1943. The Museum of the Liberation at no. 145, Via Tasso has many documents and testimonies to those terrible days.

Another tragedy struck the city in March 1944: as retaliation for a bomb attack on German soldiers in Via Rasella, 335 people were massacred in a quarry called the Fosse Ardeatine, including 75 Jews. In Via Ardeatina, at the site of the massacre, a statue by Francesco Coccia entitled *The Martyrs* (1950), commemorates the dead in the entrance square. On the walls of the quarry there are commemorative plaques. In the ditches where the bodies were thrown, a *Sacrarium* (shrine) was raised in 1949: the individual graves were arranged under a massive reinforced block resting on six pillars.

In 1948 the creation of the State of Israel was also a turning point for the

The interior of the Tempio Maggiore has an elongated Greek-cross plan with a colonnade on three sides. The ark and bimah are set in a raised position. The apse containing the ark has six columns in Assyrian style. They are surmounted by an architrave and a pediment ending in the Tablets of the Law, adorned by a crown.

Street sign in the old ghetto for the piazza where there were once five synagogues (scole) housed in the same building: Scola Castigliana, Scola Tempio, Scola Siciliana, Scola Nova, and Scola Catalana. The building was demolished between 1908 to 1910 during the slum clearances of the whole ghetto.

Roman Jews: for the first time in 2,000 years they walked again under the Arch of Titus (fulfilling the promise never to do so until Israel was free). But the Middle Eastern crisis also struck the Roman community in 1982, when a terrorist group shot at members of the congregation as they were leaving the synagogue: the young Stefano Gaj Taché died and forty people were wounded. Lastly, in 1986 there was a definitive turning point in relations between Jews and the Catholic Church: John Paul II visited the synagogue, and for the first time a pope described the Jews as "elder brothers."

Today the community of around 10,000 people is the largest in Italy.

Jewish life round the Portico of Ottavia

The ghetto was created in 1555 by Pope Paul IV. It was situated in the area that today stretches from the Tiber River at the Tiber Island to the Ponte Quattro Capi (or Fabricio), Via Portico d'Ottavia, Via Ottavia, and Piazza delle Cinque Scole: around 30,000 square meters (only 23,000 are built up). The area underwent sweeping changes over the centuries. The most recent large-scale demolition works in 1886–1904 completely altered the urban layout. Today only some streets (Via del Portico d'Ottavia, Via della Reginella, and Piazza delle Cinque Scole) can give an idea of the original appearance of the quarter.

The ghetto was a web of insalubrious alleys often flooded by the waters of the Tiber, which flows along the side of the quarter. The houses were raised up to six or seven floors to accommodate the increasingly large numbers of inhabitants: 1,750 in 1555, and 5,000 in 1870, when the gates of the ghetto were removed for good. The ghetto had five gates: the first at the Portico d'Ottavia, the second in Piazza Giudea, a third opposite the church of San Gregorio at Quattro Capi; and the last two along Via della Fiumara.

For over three centuries the quarter was the heart of Roman Jewish life and today its piazza is still a meeting point. In 1989 an urban conservation scheme was begun by Rome City Council to preserve the last areas.

The building containing five synagogues at no. 37, Piazza delle Cinque Scole was demolished from 1908 to 1910, by which date the rest of the ghetto had already been pulled down. The new square was called Via del Progresso and only in the early 1980s was the old name restored. In the late 16th century, at the orders of the papacy, all the synagogues had to be brought together. They belonged to the various groups of exiles who had sought refuge in Rome after the expulsion from the Iberian peninsula and southern Italy, begun in 1492 and subsequently continued in France and Germany. The building in Piazza delle Cinque Scole housed the Scola Castigliana (Castilian synagogue) and the Scola Tempio (Temple synagogue) in the right wing, towards Via della Fiumara, whereas the left wing, ending in a clock tower, accommodated the Scola Siciliana (Sicilian synagogue), the Scola Nova (New synagogue), and the Scola Catalana (Catalan synagogue). From 1834 to 1835 a Neoclassical aedicule, attributed to Giuseppe Valadier, was added to the façade.

Three views of the old ghetto. The quarter has been completely transformed and only a few corners recall the old unsanitary ghetto, liberated definitively in 1870.

This building began to go into decline after a fire in 1893, which destroyed the wood-clad Scola Tempio, and damaged the Scola Castigliana. In the end it was decided to pull the building down; the furnishings were saved, however, and are now in the Tempio Maggiore, the Spanish temple, and the Di Castro oratory in Via Balbo.

A temple in Oriental Neo-Baroque style

The large new temple (Tempio Maggiore) was built from 1901 to 1904 on an area of 3,373 square meters (36,306 sq. feet) in the center of the ghetto. The building was designed by the architects Vincenzo Costa and Osvaldo Armanni, while the interior decorations were by Annibale Brugnoli and Domenico Bruschi. This imposing building in an eclectic Oriental Neo-Baroque style has the form of a great cube surmounted by a sail-vault dome (46 meters [151 ft.] high) clad in aluminum, resting on a quadrangular drum with three windows on each side. The entrance is in a portico, bounded by four columns with Doric capitals. The small garden (which continues round the back of the building) is enclosed by iron railings with pillars, and contains the entrance steps decorated at the sides by period lamps. Inside the portico there are three entrances only used for certain occasions. The usual entrance to the temple is through a side door.

A crenellated frieze divides the first and second floors. Here, behind four half-columns with Ionic capitals, is a window providing daylight for the central women's gallery. The side walls are strikingly decorated by two bas reliefs with palm branches. The pediment crowning the façade contains the Tablets of the Law at the center with, above, a seven-branched candelabrum. The façade on the Tiber River side is tripartite in both directions with a rusticated base. On the walls near the entrance four stone plaques commemorate the First World War dead, those deported on October 16, 1943, the Martyrs of the Fosse Ardeatine and Stefano Gaj Taché, the boy who was killed in the attack on the synagogue in 1982.

Inside, the prayer room has an elongated Greek-cross plan with a colon-

nade on three sides; in the central area benches face the apse where the ark and *bimah* are set in a raised position. The two aisles and entrance vestibule, which support the women's gallery, serve as ambulatories. At the center of the hexagonal apse, the ark has six columns in Assyrian style, with gilded friezes and volutes, surmounted by an architrave and pediment ending in the Tablets of the Law, adorned by a crown. The *bimah* stands in front of the ark. Reached by side stairs, the prayer area is raised and separated from the room by a wrought-iron balustrade. The rear walls of the apse are divided into panels containing eight-branched candelabra and medallions. Hebrew inscriptions contribute to the already rich ornamentation on the walls.

The drum of the dome over the middle of the room is supported by four fluted pillars, enhanced by columns and capitals. The windows behind the central women's gallery have very lively colors. The area reserved for women is closed on three sides by iron railings. The aisles have two holy arks, originally in the building of the five *scole:* the first from the Scola Siciliana, dated 1586, was subsequently modified; the second from the Scola Catalana, was rebuilt with elements of various provenances. Other furnishings from the building of the five synagogues are also kept here. They will be placed in the basement, the future museum, after refurbishing work has been completed. There has already been a museum in the building since 1960. Extended in 1995, it occupies two rooms on the first and second floors of the building, while the bookshop is at the entrance. The museum is divided into three sections: the first is dedicated to the history of major events in Jewish life in Rome, reconstructed through copies of old plaques, printed texts, manuscripts, illustrations and drawings; the second section focuses on silver ceremonial objects: seven-branched candelabra and *Hanukkah menorahs*, *Kiddush* cups, jugs and basins, book bindings and decorations for the Scrolls of the Law (crowns, pointers, and medallions), *yadim*, scrolls with the Book of Esther, manuscripts, and miniatures. The third section consists of a display of

sumptuous fabrics, many once in the building of the Cinque Scole: capes for the *Torah*, curtains for the ark and cloths to cover the *bimah*. If in good enough condition these objects are used in turn in the synagogues. The museum has in fact maintained its function as the "wardrobe of the temple."

In the upper floors, the building houses the community and rabbinical offices. The Spanish temple is in the basement, next to the Tempio Maggiore. In 1932 it was moved here from the synagogue building on Lungotevere Sanzio, where it had been installed in 1910 by the architects Costa and Armanni (they had already designed the Tempio Maggiore) after the demolition of the Cinque Scole. Unlike the Tempio Maggiore, which follows the Italian rite (*Bené Roma*, directly descended from the Jerusalem rite), this smaller temple is a Spanish-rite synagogue. In the rectangular prayer room, the ark and *bimah* are opposite each other on the long sides, with benches arranged on the short sides in parallel rows. The furnishings came from the Cinque Scole, while the colored marble ark was once in the Scola Nova. Divided into panels of finely worked gilded wood, the doors are framed by two carved fluted marble columns. The original pediment could not be reassembled because the new room was not high enough, but is on show in the corridor. On the sides of the ark are two marble seats, made from 1622 to 1628 and once in the Scola Catalana. The white marble *bimah* of 1851 was in the Scola Castigliana. In the vestibule of the Spanish temple is a door leading to the back of the building and the garden that has some inscribed marble stones, fragments, and furnishings once in the Cinque Scole and confraternities. Other furnishings, again from the Cinque Scole, are now in the Di Castro oratory, at no. 33, Via Cesare Balbo. The Ashkenazi-rite oratory was built in 1914 for people who had moved to live outside the area of the ghetto. It has a square room, with the ark and *bimah* opposite the entrance wall and the women's gallery above. The walls and ceiling are divided into panels with Oriental-style decorations. The colored windows were made in 1991 by Aldo Di Castro. The candelabra over the *bimah* and the *ner tamid* in front of the ark came from the Scola Castigliana, as did the gilded wooden ark and the candelabra adorning the oratory. Designed by the architect Angelo Di Castro, it was installed in the basement level of the oratory building in 1972.

The synagogue at Ostia Antica

In 1961 the remains of a synagogue were found in the archaeological area of Ostia Antica (an ancient Roman site, 15 km [9.3 miles] to the southwest of Rome). Situated at the end of the *decumanus maximus* (main street) near a river bank, the complex was built in the first half of the 1st century AD, and then modified and extended in the 3rd–4th century. Consisting of several rooms occupying a rectangular area of 860 square meters (9,250 sq. feet), oriented east-west, it was a complex building with a prayer room, study room, oven, and ritual bath (*mikveh*), and had been transformed over time by subsequent building over and additions. This is proved by the various techniques used to build the walls: the earliest building was made in *opus reticulatum*, and the more recent in *opus vittatum*, i.e., blocks of tufa arranged in horizontal rows. Similarly, a lower layer of flooring is made of mosaics and an upper layer of marble.

A vestibule with three entrances (for men, women, and to the *mikveh*), bounded by four Corinthian columns, leads to the rectangular prayer room (25 × 12.5 m [80 × 41 ft.]): the *bimah* was set against the short side and opposite is a niche used for the ark, preceded by a baluster with corbels (the originals

*The Fosse Ardeatine.
In March 1944, as retaliation
for a bomb attack in Via
Rasella, the Nazis massacred
335 people in a quarry called
the Fosse Ardeatine, including
75 Jews. Today the former
quarry is a museum of
remembrance with a monument
to the dead and commemorative
plaques on the walls.*

*The entrance gate like a tangle
of thorns was made by Mirko
Basaldella, who also
constructed some of the grates
placed at the entrance to the
quarry, where the massacre had
been perpetrated.*

are in the Ostia museum) surmounted by the entablature with Jewish symbols (*menorah, shofar,* and *lulav*). The vestibule, where there was once a water cistern, leads to the first room, probably a kitchen with an oven and receptacles for preserving food. A second room with counters along the walls may have been used to offer hospitality to travelers.

The Jewish catacombs

The earliest burial places used by Roman Jews were the catacombs. Five have survived to the present day: Villa Torlonia on Via Nomentana, Vigna Apolloni on Via Labicana, Vigna Cimarra and Vigna Randanini on Via Appia, and Monteverde on Via Portuense. Today, however, only the catacombs in Villa Torlonia and Vigna Randanini can — with some difficulty — be visited. Vigna Randanini is officially opened once a month. Since 1984 the catacombs have been run by the Archaeology Department of Rome City Council, which took over from the Pontifical Commission for the Archaeology of Sacred Sites. The Villa Torlonia catacombs are being restored and consolidated. After the period of the catacombs, the Roman Jews used many burial places, but the plots were often expropriated and the headstones lost. This happened to the cemetery of Porta Portese and the Aventine cemetery, which was demolished to make way for the Circus Maximus and the rose garden on its slopes. In 1895 the community had a field at the Verano cemetery. In 1922, 372 graves and some monuments were moved to Verano, but they were only a part of those in the old cemetery. In 1916 the community acquired another area adjacent to the Verano cemetery, thus guaranteeing the Jews a permanent burial place for their dead for the first time in Rome.

Inside the Verano cemetery a monument commemorates the Jews who died in Libya, while a second is dedicated to the 2,728 Roman Jews deported to the Nazi extermination camps.

Jewish cuisine

No other people has made cooking and food such a meaningful part of their history, religion, and daily life as the Jews. In no other religion does food and the way it is prepared have such great significance as evidence of faith, identity, and memory. This holds true in the various historical periods and independently of the civilizations the Jews came into contact with. Although each civilization obviously influenced Jews in terms of raw materials and recipes, they always continued to respect their own rules and symbolic meanings.

The basic recipes for Jewish cooking come from two books of the *Torah*: Leviticus and Deuteronomy. In these books, kosher food, i.e., "proper" or permitted food is listed as well as food that is not allowed. They also contain rules about butchering animals and the preparation of dishes.

Permitted animals are quadrupeds with a cloven hoof and ruminants (cud chewing). Nonruminants, such as pigs, wild boar, donkeys, rabbits, hares, and carnivores are prohibited, as are birds of prey. Among the permitted fish are those with fins and scales, while mollusks, crustaceans, and sea mammals are prohibited. Reptiles and all kinds of slithering animals are prohibited.

One fundamental rule is that meat cannot be combined with any dairy products or even placed beside them. The meal must be either of meat or milk. Over the years Jewish gastronomy, therefore, has adapted, elaborating all possible variations to prepare tasty dishes without violating these laws. It leaves out, for example, all preparations of meat that include the addition of pork sausages, and cooking or condiment with milk, cheese, or butter, which are replaced by goose salami and fat. Moreover this has led to the invention of some remarkable dishes like the Venetian *sarde in saor* (sweet and sour sardines), the Roman *carciofi alla giudia* (Jewish-style artichokes), or *cuscussù* from Livorno.

Sweets at the end of a meat-based meal cannot include milk or butter, which are replaced by whipped egg whites. The sweets are often full of aromas, redolent of the Promised Land: honey, dates, dried fruit, almond, pine nuts, candied fruit, vanilla, aniseed, and cinnamon.

For Jews, the house and the family are just as important places of worship as the synagogue, if not more so. The family gathers round the table to begin Sabbath celebrations on Friday evening as well as for the main festivities and birth, marriage, and death. Each of these occasions involves preparing dishes dictated by tradition. On the Sabbath table, decked with lamps and wine cups for the blessing to be recited by the head of the family, there are always two loaves of *challah*, slightly sweet white-flour homemade bread in the form of a braid (like a nuptial garland, recalling the foundation of the family). The meal is rich with meat and fish dishes (*gefilte fish* for Ashkenazi tables) and there is always a sweet to mark the festivity, for example, the Italian *dolce* made of almonds and spinach. Since absolutely no work can be done on Saturday, the meals must be prepared beforehand. Thus "self-preparing" dishes, such as eggs cooked for twenty-five hours, were invented: at times together with vegetable and coffee aromas, they were placed whole in a pan of water and left to cook slowly until the following evening, thus absorbing the flavors and aromas of the condiments.

At *Rosh Hashanah* (the New Year), the tables are laden with pomegranate, honey, and apples, and dinner begins with slices of apple dipped in honey as a way of wishing well. *Yom Kippur* has a very special menu. The last meal before the beginning of the twenty-five hours of fasting is very substantial, but with no spices. They

could make you thirsty and the fasting must be complete, i.e., without even a drop of water. At the end of the fast, donuts, biscuits with coffee, tea, or consommé are taken before the main meal, which is light.

Fresh fruit or fruit with sweet fillings dominates for the seven days of *Sukkoth*. Meals are eaten in the *sukkath* (tabernacle dwelling) and always include the *bollo* a filled donut. For *Simchat Torah*, meat roulades and rice in vine leaves are prepared (to recall the vineyards of Judaea) and in the absence of vine leaves, cabbage leaves are used.

For *Hanukkah*, fried foods are prescribed with flour or apple fritters (called *prec cipizi* in Italy) or potatoes, called *latkes* by Ashkenazim and *pampuches* by Sephardim.

For the *Rosh Hashanah La'Ilanot* (New Year of Trees) seven plant species are eaten: wheat, barley, grape, fig, pomegranate, olive, and date. At *Purim*, the festivity of "lots," the typical desserts are "Hamantaschen" and almond-based sweets.

At *Pesach* all leavened food must disappear from the home and is substituted by unleavened food. All the *seder* dishes have a very special symbolic significance: the unleavened bread stands for the hasty flight with no time to let the bread rise, the bitter herbs recall the harshness of slavery, the boiled egg is a reminder of the animals sacrificed in the Temple, celery and lettuce soaked in vinegar are a sign of renewal but also the tears of slaves, the sheep's foot is the sacrifice before departure, *charoset* (a mixture of fruit pulp, spices, and dried fruit) is a reminder of the mortar used by the Jewish slaves to build the pyramids.

For *Shavuot* food made from milk, cheese, and sugar are eaten as symbols of purity, fertility, and happiness. The last festivity, *Tisha B'Av* in August, just before the New Year, commemorates the destruction of the Temple of Jerusalem: the meal before fasting begins with an unsalted boiled egg and lentils, symbols of mourning

Baron Rothschild and the Neapolitan community

The Jews of Naples are fairly representative of the Jewish history of southern Italy, where the changes in rulers directly affected the life of the many groups who had lived from ancient times in the south of the peninsula. Especially along the coasts there was a widespread Jewish presence as early as Roman times, as revealed by archaeological finds, gravestones, and catacombs. The city of Naples and the region of Campania differ, however, from the rest of the south of Italy because they were the only areas where a community re-formed in the 19th century after several expulsions (the first was in 1541; the Jews returned in 1740 and 1830).

The Neapolitan Jews were mentioned in the chronicles as early as 536 for supporting the Goths in the defense of Naples besieged by the Byzantine general Belisarius. Their numbers varied considerably in the different historical periods. In 1159, one visitor, Beniamino da Tudela (the Jewish Marco Polo) estimated there were 500 Jews in the city under Swabian rule.

In 1288, when the city came under the House of Anjou, Dominican preaching led to anti-Jewish riots and the synagogue was converted into a church (what is now the church of Santa Maria della Purità, at no. 14, Via del Tempio in the Stella quarter). Conditions improved when the Aragonese kings took power in 1442, and many exiles came to seek refuge in Naples from Sicily, Sardinia, and Spain. In 1510, however, a first expulsion notice was served. Many Jews left the city and only 200 families who could afford to pay the king 300 ducats a year (10,000 in 1535) were allowed to stay. In 1503 the kingdom passed to Ferdinand II of Aragon, "the Catholic," who in 1541 ordered the definitive expulsion of the Jews from the whole of southern Italy. Henceforth, apart from short periods for fairs and markets, Jews no longer lived in Naples and its surrounding area until 1740.

After the ascent to the throne of Charles of Bourbon, Jews were officially invited to come back and live in the Gulf of Naples. Their fame as able merchants led the court to believe they could resolve the kingdom's serious economic problems. To persuade them to come to Naples royal messengers were sent to Livorno (Leghorn) and the Netherlands, with promises of trade concessions and complete freedom of worship. A year later around 120 Jewish merchants had settled in the city. They brought business with a turnover of half a million ducats. This was a respectable figure but nowhere near enough to solve the kingdom's problems. The Jews were not destined to stay long in the city. After the defeat of the Progressist wing at court, which had promoted the operation, a new expulsion edict was proclaimed in 1747. Only in 1830 did a group of Jewish merchants return to Naples. As early as 1831, under the guidance of Isidoro Rouff, a prayer room was opened in the Croce di Malta, a hospice situated in what is now Piazza Municipio.

The revival of Jewish life in Naples owes a great deal to a massive loan that the Rothschild bankers granted the Bourbons to help put Ferdinand I back on the throne when he was threatened by General Pepe's revolution-

Other localities in Campania

Inscriptions, epigraphs, and archaeological finds uncovered during excavations, now kept in various town museums, document an ancient Jewish presence along the coasts of Campania before the fall of Jerusalem and the beginning of the Diaspora. On the basis of this evidence, Jews are known to have lived in Ancient Roman times at Pozzuoli, Bacoli, Marano, the Campi Flegrei area, and further inland at Nola and Capua. Some small inscriptions may still be seen on the excavation walls at Pompeii and Herculaneum, while Jewish objects and frescoes are on display in the National Museum, Naples.

Other groups came to join or replace these early immi-grants in later periods and especially in Salerno and its environs (places like Mercato San Severino) and Amalfi. Benjamin of Tudela, considered one of the most precious sources, provides a picture of the Jewish presence in the Middle Ages. In 1165, he crossed southern Italy, noting there were 500 Jews in Naples, 600 in Salerno, 20 at Amalfi, 200 in Benevento and, heading south to Apulia, 300 in Taranto, and 200 in Trani. Salerno was thus a major center where Jews lived from the 10th century. Their quarter, still visible today, was called the Giudaica and consisted of a long street called Judicavia, closed between "a wall and a low wall." This street went from the church of Santa Lucia to Portanova, behind the Palazzo del Governo.

Synagogue interior. Remodeled in its present form in 1933, the rectangular prayer room is divided midway by an arch. The raised bimah *is in the middle of the room, opposite the ark and surrounded by prayer benches.*

ary troops. In fact at the Lubljana Congress (1821), the Rothschild bank offered to finance the Austrians: Austria was then to give the funds to the Bourbons to pay the troops guaranteeing their return to the throne. The operation was entrusted to Carl, one of the four sons of Mayer Amschel, the founder of the banking dynasty. Noted for his religious devotion, he was nicknamed the *Mezuzah* Baron. In 1830 he moved to Naples, where in the meantime Ferdinand was on the throne again, and opened the first branch of the Rothschild Bank in Italy. This soon became the most important bank in the Kingdom of Naples and in 1841 Carl could set his "brand," a *mezuzah*, on the doorpost of Villa Acton (now the Pignatelli Museum), the finest house on the Riviera di Chiaia. The villa became his residence and one room was used as an oratory and offered hospitality to Jewish guests passing through the city when there were Jewish celebrations.

The presence of the Rothschilds in the city was of fundamental importance for the Jewish group which, in 1861, when the community was officially founded, numbered 630 people. That year some premises were rented at no. 31, Vico Santa Maria a Cappella Vecchia (the same building is used today) to serve as an oratory. Baron Adolf Carl de Rothschild, Carl's son, paid the rent for five years (360 francs a year). The officially opening of the oratory in 1864 was reported as a major event in the city. The first rabbi was Beniamino Artom di Asti.

In 1900, Baron Rothschild died (he had in the meantime left the city). After having been so generous in his lifetime to the Neapolitan community, he was equally generous in his will. He left 50,000 lire to found an Israelite hospital, 100,000 for its maintenance, and 100,000 to found a school, stipulating it should be run by a rabbi. To be able to use this legacy the commu-

nity acquired the legal status of an independent entity.

The generous Rothschild legacy imposed a number of conditions, such as the creation of a school and a hospital (Villa Smith at Posillipo was purchased). But running these facilities soon turned out to be too expensive, and the community had to revise its budget. In 1924 Villa Smith was sold — it had been the hospital since 1902 — and a convention was drawn up for the remaining Jewish inmates with the International Hospital of Naples, which took in foreigners and was non-Catholic. A year later, the premises in Via Cappella Vecchia were acquired — until then they had been rented by Lamberto Foà — thanks partly to a donation from the Ascarelli family.

The building was restored and extended by covering the balconies. The existing prayer room was restructured and reopened in 1933 with new floors, doors, windows, and furnishings (decorated in gold). The community also

The synagogue entrance. The Naples community was the only Jewish group to form again in southern Italy in the 19th century, after being absent since the expulsion of all Jews in 1492.

Silver cup used for the blessing over wine.

looked after the cemetery, amidst great difficulty, and obtained new spaces.

Since being refounded, the mixed Naples group had become as large as 1,000 people. In the early 20th century Jews came from Tsarist Russia, Istanbul, Smirne, Ioannina, Sarajevo, and Salonica. In fact the great fire of Salonica (1917) destroyed the old Jewish quarter, forcing 50,000 Jews to leave the city. Some of them came to Naples, where they created, however, an independent group. With the advent of Fascism and the racial laws, foreign Jews were imprisoned in internment camps, while Italian Jews were requisitioned to forced labor at Tora and Piccilli, near the monastery of Montecassino, in the province of Caserta. Seventeen Neapolitan Jews, who had fled Naples during the war, were deported. At the end of the war the community numbered 534 people; today there are around 200.

The synagogue in the alley

The large apartment with a synagogue at no. 31, Via Cappella Vecchia is now the only Jewish monument that can be visited in the city. Anyone looking for artistic evidence of the Jewish presence will be disappointed. But anyone willing to enter these premises to experience the extraordinary history of this group (as retold mainly by the plaques on the walls) will certainly be impressed. In the heart of old Naples, the building overlooks a courtyard in which there are no outward signs of the presence of a place of worship. The Spanish-rite synagogue is on the first floor, reached after going through the rectangular entrance hall.

The rectangular prayer room is divided in half by an arch. The central *bimah*, surrounded by benches, is in front of the holy ark, set against the eastern wall, opposite the entrance. On the right of the *bimah* is a small wooden pulpit. Branched lamps fitted to the walls lit up the room, which also receives light from two large windows. Resting on wooden columns, the women's gallery is above the entrance. It is reached by an external stair in a room next to the downstairs entrance. The same apartments also have rooms for lectures and meetings, the community secretary's office and the rabbi's house. The American community in Naples (part of a NATO base) has an oratory in Via Scarfoglio, at Agnano. There is no permanent rabbi but officiants come to the festivities from the United States or Israel. Some military people also attend the local synagogue for the festivities.

The Neapolitan cemeteries

There were several cemeteries in Naples. Jewish gravestones from the 4th to 5th century were found three meters (10 ft.) down in 1908 during the construction of the artillery barracks in Corso Malta. The chronicles mention a 13th-century cemetery in the area of Piazza Carmine and Piazza della Croce. The so-called Tomba di Virgilio at Fuorigrotta is also thought to be an old Jewish cemetery. In the 19th century the Rothschilds bought a plot at Posillipo to create a cemetery. But it was only used for a few years, and in 1875 the gravestones were taken to the Poggioreale cemetery. There are around 800 graves in this cemetery, the last dating from 1982. At the entrance there is tomb commemorating the worthy people who on 12 May 1875 acquired the plot: they include Adolf de Rothschild and Isidoro Rouff, president of the community at the time. The most recent cemetery, opened in 1963, is a separate section of the city cemetery in Via Santa Maria del Pianto.

Across the sea to the Ottoman Empire

Trani — together with Oria, Bari and Otranto — was one of the localities in Puglia (Apulia) with the largest and longest-standing Jewish groups. In fact there were Jews in Trani from Roman times until 1541, when all Jews were expelled from southern Italy. The history of the town, therefore, reflects in broad outline the history of Jews in the southern Italian regions.

Merchants and scholars famed throughout the Diaspora lived in Apulia. Like most Apulian towns, Trani was a land of transit in the 15th century also for refugees from Provence, Germany, and Spain on their way to the regions of the Ottoman Empire. There were some cases of attempts at forced conversions (often successful) and serious infamy dictated by popular prejudice. One example of calumny is still recalled today in a procession called the *Sacra Padella* ("Holy Frying Pan"), held in Trani during the Catholic Holy Week: a Jewish woman was accused of having profaned the host by frying it in a pan. This led to a popular riot and the murder of those responsible. Paolo Uccello depicted the episode in 1467–68 for the confraternity of Corpus Domini in a famous painting, now in the National Gallery of the Marches (Palazzo Ducale, Urbino).

The giudecca, *the old Jewish quarter, where many groups of Jews lived until 1492. Their former presence is reflected in the streets names like Via Giudea, Via Sinagoga, and Via della Giudecca.*

Church of Santa Maria in Scolanova. This church was originally a synagogue, but like all the synagogues in southern Italy, it was converted after the expulsion of the Jews. The church is raised above the square and must be entered by going up a flight of stairs on the southern wall.

Synagogues converted into churches

The first *giudecca* (a quarter where the Jews voluntarily lived together) in Trani stretched from the cathedral to the port, within the early Byzantine-Lombard walls. Today part of the district of San Donato, the quarter is a dense network of alleys and lanes reaching as far as Porta Antica. The place names are a reminder of the Jewish past: Via La Giudea, Via Sinagoga, Via della Giudecca, Vico La Giudea, Via Mosé da Trani, and Largo Scolanova.

There were four synagogues in the quarter. But around 1380, at the time of Charles III of Durres, all the synagogues were converted into churches. At the same time 310 Jews underwent forced baptisms (they were called

cristiani novelli — "new Christians"). The new churches were dedicated to San Leonardo Abate, San Pietro Martire, Santi Quirico e Giovita, and Santa Maria in Scolanova. The first two were later demolished but Santi Quirico e Giovita (now Sant'Anna) had already been built over the ruins of a synagogue in 1247, as mentioned by a panel on the northern wall of the church interior: "In the year 5007 after the creation (1247), this sanctuary was built by a group of friends of the congregation, with a high decorated dome, a window providing light and new doors for the closure; the floor relaid and seats installed for the choir. May their piety be remembered before He Who dwells in the splendid heavens." The church has a square plan, dominated by a great dome almost covering it entirely. Not far away is the church of Santa Maria in Scolanova. Its original structure has remained intact. The rectangular interior consists of a single nave. The floor is raised above the street level and must be entered by going up a flight of steps at the side of the southern wall.

The eastern wall interior has a stone aedicule, which once contained the ark. Here the floor is raised by three steps and this was where the Christian altar was placed when the synagogue was converted into a church. In the floor of the basement a great hole was uncovered, possibly the remains of a ritual bath (*mikveh*).

When new Jewish groups arrived in the 15th century, the community moved to a second *giudecca*, at Porta Nuova, on the outskirts of the town.

The cemetery is situated outside the walls beyond the church of Trinità della Cava (now San Francesco) on the right-hand side of the sea road from the historic center to the peninsula of Colonna.

Church of Santa Maria in Scolanova, interior. The rectangular interior consists of a single nave with bare stone walls.

Other localities in Apulia

From Roman times to 1541, Jewish groups lived in the whole region, even in small rural towns far from the main roads. They were often very small groups made up of one or two households ready to move and seek a new home if they were harassed or problems arose about their place of residence. Documented by scholars in over 400 localities, this presence is mainly recorded in place names (Via Giudecca, Largo Giudecca, Via Giudea, Vico degli Ebrei, etc.) and in popular festivities and customs. One particularly interesting case was Oria. The community in this town is thought to have formed after the destruction of the Temple of Jerusalem, when Titus ordered 5,000 prisoners of war to be transferred to Taranto and the Otranto area.

Oria was sacked, however, in 925 by Moors from Sicily, during a raid when most of the population including the Jews were exterminated. The Jewish group was thus decimated and many of the survivors made slaves. They included the twelve-year-old Shabbetai Donnolo (913–985), who was freed after a ransom had been paid by his parents in Taranto. He became a physician and philosopher and the driving force of the Oria Academy of Rabbinical Studies, which attracted scholars from throughout the Diaspora. Paraphrasing a verse of the prophet Isaiah it was said "the Law comes from Bari and the word of God from Otranto."

In the second half of the 9th century Shefatiah ben Amittai, a biblical exegetist and synagogue poet, was the teacher at the Oria Academy. Endowed with thaumaturgical powers, he was summoned by Basil II of Byzantium to heal his daughter and, thanks to his intercession, the Jews in Oria were allowed to freely profess their religion.

Today in Oria there is a large bronze *menorah* on the Porta degli Ebrei ("Jews' Gate"), also called Porta Piazzella or Porta Taranto. Dating from the 15th century, the gate is in the Western part of the town and was the entry to a small quarter (the ghetto or *giudecca*), now called Santa Giudea, set up under Prince Philip II of Taranto. The site of a synagogue has been identified in this quarter near the well of Maddalena, at the beginning of Via di Francavilla. In 1966, this district, together with those of Castello, Lama, and San Basilio, took part in a tournament held in August, preceded by an historic pageant to commemorate Frederick II. The banner of the *giudecca* had a *menorah* on a white and blue background. Two other places must be mentioned on the subject of Jewish Apulia: Sannicandro Garganico and Santa Cesarea Terme. The first was the setting for the unusual conversion to Judaism in 1944 of a large number of inhabitants, proselytized by the self-taught Donato Manduzio, who died in 1948, just when he was about to go to Israel to join a group of his followers who had already settled there.

In the center of Santa Cesarea Terme, on the other hand, there is a Hebrew inscription accompanied by a map of Palestine made before the birth of the State of Israel in 1948. In fact it was inscribed by Jewish soldiers in the Palestine brigade who fought with the British Eighth Army as it headed north during the Second World War. The town council has regularly restored the inscription.

A medieval *mikveh*

Syracuse was the first place in Sicily the Jews came to after Palestine was conquered by Pompey in 59 BC. For the next fifteen centuries, thousands of Jews from all over the Mediterranean were to settle on the island. Indeed Sicily boasted one of the largest concentrations of Jews in the Diaspora.

At that time no Sicilian city or town was without a Jewish family or group, whether for short or longer periods. There were over fifty Jewish quarters — communities that could account for up to twenty or thirty percent of the population, each with synagogues, rabbis, physicians, schools, teachers, forms of self-government, and notables.

Ritual bath (mikveh) in the Jewish quarter on the island of Ortigia. Jews lived on the island for centuries until 1493, when an estimated 1,000 to 3,000 people out of a total population of 12,000 to 14,000 were forced to leave. At the same time around 35,000 Jews out of an overall population of 600,000 left Sicily.

A long period of peaceful coexistence was brusquely interrupted in 1492, when Ferdinand II of Aragon, "the Catholic," issued the expulsion order from his Spanish court. Realizing that this would spell economic disaster for the island, the local Sicilian rulers attempted to block the edict. They managed to win some time, but nonetheless by the end of 1493, all the Sicilian Jews had abandoned the island. They left through the port of Messina, but for many the departure immediately turned out to be disastrous: the groups who had embarked on Calabrian ships were robbed and murdered by the crews. This hasty flight was a real Biblical exodus towards the unknown. According to the estimates of Francesco Renda, the historian who has studied this period of the island's history in greatest depth, in one feel swoop Sicily lost five percent of its population: around 35,000 people out of a total of 600,000.

Some stayed behind and submitted to baptism. They changed their names from Samuele and Abramo to Giovanni and Francesco. Some kept their Jewish surnames (like Jona or de Iona), while others assumed those of the city where they had lived (e.g., de Saragoza and Siracusa). The Inquisition persecuted these "new Christians" for two or three generations to come. They were put on trial for having Jewish tendencies and sentenced to life imprisonment. Their goods were confiscated and some people were even burned at the stake. From Syracuse alone 1,000 to 3,000 left, out of total population of 12,000–14,000. The whole Jewish quarter of Ortigia emptied (the previous quarter had been in the Acradina area).

Other localities in Sicily

A large number of Jewish quarters (over fifty) have been found scattered throughout the island, often with synagogues (later converted into churches), cemeteries, documents and other special objects (such as the *rimmon-im* from Cammarata, now in Palma, Majorca). They are evidence of a very rich Jewish past in Sicily. Today that past is now the subject of careful research and study. The place names found almost everywhere in the island are the starting points for studies (Via Giudecca, Vicolo della Giudecca, Orto della Giudecca, Porta della Judeca, Porta degli Ebrei, etc.). At Agira, in the province of Enna, an old stone ark was found, and in Trapani a synagogue has been identified (now the church of San Domenico). In Palermo the Jews lived in the area of Meschita, where there was a synagogue and ritual bath (*mikveh*). Many more examples could be cited.

To bring together this rich Jewish heritage still scattered in the churches and museums of the island, the Sicilian Regional Government is planning to create a museum in Palermo to house all the major Jewish finds, thus offering the public a fascinating story that scholars and enthusiasts have been rewriting for several years now.

The island of Ortigia

The Jewish quarter on the island of Ortigia is a quadrilateral bounded to the west by Via della Giudecca, to the south by Via Larga, and to the east by the sea. It is cut by a number of parallel streets: Via dell'Olivo, Vicoli II, III, IV alla Giudecca, Vicolo dell'Arco, and Via Minniti. The quarter has the same street layout as it did in the 15th century: low houses (one or two stories), a hospice, a charity house, *mikveh*, and a synagogue (possibly where the church of San Filippo is today), called *meschita* (an Italian version of the Arabic term for mosque).

The *mikveh* in Casa Bianca, at no. 52, Via Alagona, is the only surviving ritual bath of three originally on Ortigia (the other two were under the church of San Filippo Apostolo, the site of the synagogue, and in Vicolo dell'Ulivo).

Discovered by chance in 1989 during restoration work on the building, this ritual bath has become one of the most interesting places for studies of the Jewish quarter. The bath would seem to be from the Byzantine age, and the experts suggest that it may originally have been a Byzantine cistern, transformed into public baths by the Syracusan Jewish group in the Middle Ages. Steep stairs with forty-eight steps, gouged out of the rocks lead to a room with mighty pillars supporting a cross-vault roof, only interrupted by a shaft that evidently provided ventilation and light. All around is a bench, presumably used by people as they waited for their turn.

The bath is made up of five basins, three in the central area arranged in trefoil fashion and two at the sides in more private areas. The whole premises is ten meters (32.75 ft.) down so as to reach the water-bearing stratum supplying the bath. The source was also known in antiquity, as attested by the presence in the area of two ancient Greek wells. The water for the underground basins in Casa Bianca, however, did not come from these two wells. Each basin was filled directly from the source through a crack in the rock deliberately created at the bottom of the basin. The basins are 140 centimeters (55 in.) high to allow for full immersion in an upright position; the bottom is reached by going down eight steps.

Catacombs and headstones

The first Jews in Syracuse used the catacombs of Santa Lucia and San Giovanni as well as many underground caves for burials. They then had a cemetery near Porto Piccolo. After the expulsion, the headstones were used in sea walls for the strait separating Ortigia from the mainland. At the end of the last century, when the sea walls were demolished, twelve Hebrew headstones were brought up from the sea. Of these, three have disappeared, four are kept in the courtyard of the Regional Gallery at the Palazzo Bellomo, and five are set along the entrance path to the catacombs of Vigna Cassia.

With Cagliari and Sassari, Alghero had one of the three largest Jewish communities in Sardinia. It shares the same history as the small Jewish groups scattered throughout the island, whose traces have been lost over the centuries.

The Jews lived in Sardinia in two well-defined periods: under Roman rule and under Aragonese rule. In AD 19, 4,000 Italian Jews were sent to the island by Tiberius' praetorian commander, Aelius Seianus, to combat banditry. At the time Sardinia was divided into two economically distinct parts: on the one hand, the plains of Campidano with fields of grain and, on the other, the

interior highland areas, almost completely wild with woods and outside the control of Rome. The outcome of the military campaign is not known. It definitely ended in AD 35 when Seianus fell into disgrace. Many of those who survived the battles and malaria returned to Rome, while others settled in small groups on the island. Signs of the Jewish presence from those centuries may be found in the catacombs (at Sant'Antioco) and in archaeological remains in excavation sites (lanterns, rings, stelae with Hebrew symbols, and inscriptions).

The second Jewish settlement is associated with the House of Aragon, which had been granted the island as a feud in 1227 by Pope Boniface VIII. But the real conquest of Sardinia began in 1323, with Alfonso of Aragon, although he never exercised full control over the island because of the rebellious local lords of Arborea and the Genoan attempts to win back the north. Aragon, Catalonia, Valencia and the King of Majorca paid for the expeditionary force, whose cost, however, soon spiraled. The Jews of Catalonia (especially the Carcassona family, one branch was to settle in Alghero) granted loans, showing its willingness to help the crown financially. This was to greatly influence the king who later adopted a liberal approach to the Jews. In the wake of the armies, Catalan Jews arrived from Majorca and Provence, but there was no continuity with the earlier groups from Roman times since by then there was no trace left of them.

The Jews remained in Sardinia for one and a half centuries until the fateful year 1492, when they were expelled. Some, including a part of the Carcassona family converted; others (but in fact probably very few, since there were only two cases of "new Christians" dealt with by the Inquisition) became Marranos. Most left the island, thus reconfirming its character as a land of passage. Sardinia was probably too isolated for the Jewish group, accustomed to being forced to take flight and seek refuge elsewhere from one moment to the next.

The Jews' Tower in the city defenses

Most of the signs of the Jewish presence on the island date back to the Aragonese period. At Alghero the Tower of Santa Creu, better known as the "Jews' Tower," was built in 1360 to complete the city's defenses. The construction was funded by the Cagliari Jewish community at the request of Peter IV of Aragon, who promised to honor the name of the donors with a plaque.

The tower is situated just outside the *juharia*, the Jewish quarter which once had a population of 800. The Alghero Jews initially settled near the city walls, to the northwest of the city, at Castellas (or the Castilian Tower). The quarter then expanded inwards to occupy on one side, the stretch of the wall towards the sea gate and on the other the road leading to the bastion of Mirador. Situated around what is now Lungomare Marco Polo, the quarter's main activities were carried out in two streets: Via Sant'Erasmo (formerly Via Santelmo) and Via Bertolotti (formerly Via Carrerò dels Ebreus). The elegant *palazzo* of the Carcassona family, used after 1492 as a royal palace, may still be seen in Via Sant'Erasmo.

In the middle of the *juharia* (also called the *kahal*) in Piazza Santa Croce is the Catalan-Aragonese synagogue. Built in 1381, it was enlarged and restored in 1438, and adorned with the royal crest in 1454. There was also another synagogue, now the church of Santa Chiara, beside Torre Castiglia. The cemetery, or *fossar judeorum*, which in 1381 was in the area called *La Reyal*, was moved outside the city in 1386 to the vicinity of the church of Sant'Agostino, not far from the sea.

Other localities in Sardinia

A Jewish quarter in Cagliari — *juharia* — developed around what is now Via Santa Croce. It was contained within the walls of the castle and at one time even occupied up to a third of the surface area with over 2,000 inhabitants. The Jewish quarter began in the upper part of Via de la Fontana and stretched to Via de Orifanti and the neighboring alleys reaching as far as Torre dell'Elefante.

It is entered from the last stretch of Via Corte d'Appello (formerly Carrer de Orifanti). Not far away is Via della Fontana. Here the fountain of the *aljama* (Jewish group) was guarded by a Christian fountain-keeper and used by all the inhabitants of the castle and people who came from further afield. Next to the fountain, on the side of the castle wall there was an oven, whereas the Balice area, now the university zone, was the site of the public butchers, which included a Jewish counter. Trading took place in Via Stretta (formerly Via Vinaria).

According to some scholars, in the heart of the *juharia*, now Via Santa Croce (formerly *vicus judaeorum*, commemorated by a plaque), there was a second (Catalan-Aragonese) synagogue; the church of Santa Croce was built over its ruins. Other scholars claim the synagogue was on the site of the 17th-century church of Santa Maria del Monte in an area still called *sa sinagoga ezza* ("the old synagogue").

The cemetery, or *fossar judeorum*, was outside the castle walls. Some documents speak of three cemeteries in the Fossa di San Guglielmo and the old quarter of Stampace, while a fourth was not far off at Porta di Palabanda, near the monastery of San Francesco.

The Jewish presence in the city of Sassari has also been studied. The Jewish quarter (at its height the population was 300) was formed around 1345 near Discesa Santa Croce, in the district of San Nicola, and can still be made out today. The area was still inside the walls, but in a peripheral position. When the quarter became too small, the Jews moved outside the alleys opposite the cathedral.

In 1451, to avoid the inevitable mixing of Jews and Christians, the archbishop ordered that all the Jews should return to the quarter. In 1383 a synagogue was built in this area, on the site of what is today the oratory of Santa Croce, not far from the Archbishop's Seminary.

GLOSSARY

ADAR
6th month in the Jewish calendar (February-March).

ALIYAH
[Ascension] 1. The stepping up to the podium in the synagogue to read the *Torah*. 2. The return of the Jews to Israel.

AMIDAH
A prayer of eighteen blessings, the heart of the daily liturgy.

ARON, or ARON-HAKODESH
[Holy ark] It is placed on the east wall of the synagogue (facing Jersualem) and is the receptacle for the scrolls of the *Torah* dressed in its ornaments.

ARVITH
Evening prayer.

ASHKENAZIM
Jews of German or Central and East European descent. They have their own cultural tradition and often speak Yiddish.

ATARAH (pl. +ROTH)
A crown adorning the *Torah*.

AV, or AB
11th month in the Jewish calendar (July-August). The 9th of *Av* is a day of fasting and mourning.

BAR-MITZVAH
[Son of the law] The ceremony marking the 13th birthday of a boy, who has thus come of age and must assume his full religious obligations; after the ceremony the boy may be included in the *minyan,* the quorum of ten men required for reciting public prayers. The same term is also used for the first time a young man is called to read the *Torah* in public. The equivalent ceremony for girls, called *Bat-Mitzvah,* is celebrated on their 13th birthday.

BERACHAH
Blessing, benediction.

BESAMIM
The scents used during the closing cermony on the Sabbath (*Havdalah*).

BESARI
Meat-based kosher cuisine.

BETH KNESSET
Synagogue. Place for meeting, study and prayer.

BIMAH (TEVAH)
A platform in a synagogue from which the Scriptures are read and prayers recited.

CABBALA, or KABBALA
[Tradition] A Jewish speculative mystical tradition begun in France and Spain in the 8th century.

CHALAV
Dairy-based kosher cuisine.

CHALLAH, or HALLAH (pl. +LAHS or +LOTH)
White bread, usually in the form of a plaited loaf, eaten on the Sabbath.

CHAROSET, or CHAROSETH
A mixture of fruit pulp, spices, and dried fruit, consumed during the Passover meal. Symbolically, it is a reminder of the mortar used by the Jewish slaves to build the pyramids in Egypt.

CHUPPAH
The nuptial canopy under which wedings are celebrated.

ELUL
12th month in the Jewish calendar (August-September).

GEMARA
An Aramaic term meaning "supplement." They are commentaries on the discussions mainly held in Aramaic in the schools interpreting the oral doctrine in the six books of the *Mishnah*. The *Mishnah* together with the *Gemara* make up the *Talmud.*

HAGGADAH
[Story] The nonlegal part of the *Talmud* literature (cf. *Halachah*), consisting of an anthology of biblical and post-biblical literature, verse, jokes, and prayer rites read during *Seder*. It is printed with comments, translations, and illustrations.

HALACHAH, or HALAKAH
Jewish traditional law or body of traditional laws.

HANUKKAH, or CHANUKAH
[Dedication] The eight-day festival of lights commemorating the rededication of the Temple by Judas Maccabaeus after the victory of the Maccabees over Antiochus IV of Syria in BC 164.

HANUKKIAH
Lamp with eight candles, plus the *shammash*, symbolizing the eight days of *Hanukkah.*

HASKALAH
[Knowledge, education] The Jewish Enlightenment movement (c. 1750–1870).

HASIDISM, or CHA(S)SIDISM
Popular Jewish mystic movement founded in Poland about 1750. Having given a popular form to the mysticism of the *Cabbala*, it has produced a very rich literature.

HAVDALAH
[Separation] Closing ceremony on the Sabbath that includes blessings on wine, scented spices (*besamim*), and light emanating from a flame.

HESHVAN, or CHESHVAN
2nd month in the Jewish calendar (October-November).

IYAR, or IYYAR
8th month in the Jewish calendar (April-May).

KADDISH (pl. +SHIM)
An Aramaic term meaning "holy" used for a prayer imploring the redemption of the Jewish people. It is recited by the cantor in the synagogue at given times and for funerals and anniversaries.

KETER
Crown of the *Torah,* synonymous with *Atarah.*

KETUBAH (pl. KETUBOTH)
Marriage contract.

KIDDUSH
[Sanctification] A ceremonial blessing recited over bread or a cup of wine on the Sabbath or a festival.

KIPPAH
Skullcap, used by Jews so that they never appear before the Lord bare-headed, as a sign of respect.

KISLEV
3rd month in the Jewish calendar (November-December).

KLEZMER
Typical Jewish folk music from Central Europe.

KOSHER, or KASHER
[Proper] The term for food prepared according to Jewish dietary laws (*kashrut*).

LULAV
A bouquet made of palm, myrtle, willow, and citron (*etrog*), used at *Sukkoth.*

MACHZOR, or MAHZOR (pl. +ZORIM)
[Cycle] Prayer book containing all prescribed holy day rituals for the year.

MAGEN (or MOGEN) DAVID
Another name for the Star of David: a star with six points made of two joined triangles — the symbol of Judaism and the State of Israel.

MAPPAH (pl. +OTH)
Cloth used for wrapping the *Torah* during a pause in the reading.

MASORAH
[Tradition] The critical annotations for the biblical text; it is divided into *magna* ("large"), *parva* ("small"), and *finale.*

MATZAH, or MATZO (pl. +ZOTH or +ZOS)
A biscuit of unleavened unsalted bread eaten during *Passover* as a reminder of the exodus from Egypt.

MEGILLAH (pl. +LAHS or +LOTH)
[Scroll] *Megillath Esther:* Scroll containing the Book of Esther. *The Five Megilloth:* The books of Esther, The Song of Solomon, Ruth, Lamentations, and Ecclesiastes.

MEIL (pl. +LIM)
Ornamental cape used for covering the *Torah.* In the Sephardic tradition, especially in Northern Africa, a wooden case called a *tiq* was used instead of the cape.

MENORAH (pl. +ROTH)
A seven-branched candelabrum used in ceremonies. Already prescribed in the *Torah*, it was part of the furnishings in the Sanctuary, as can be seen in the bas relief on the Arch of Titus in Rome. Today it has a purely symbolic significance and its part of the crest of the State of Israel.

MEZUZAH (pl. +ZOTH)
A piece of parchment inscribed with scriptural passages and fixed to the doorpost of a Jewish house.

MIDRASH
[Search] The exposition and exegesis of a biblical text. *Bet ha-midrash*: study house or rabbinical school.

MIKVEH
Ritual bath.

MILAH
Circumcision. The ritual circumcisor is called the *mohel*.

MINHAH
Afternoon prayer.

MINYAN (pl. +NIM)
The quorum of males (i.e., at least ten over the age of 13) required by Jewish law for a religious service to be held.

MISHNAH
A collection of precepts passed on as an oral tradition and then written down in six sections in Palestine the mid-2nd century. Almost totally in Hebrew, it contains all the essential rules of the oral traditions for civil, penal, and marriage law and the rules for worship in the synagogue and sanctuary. It is the earlier part of the *Talmud* (see also *Gemara*).

MITZVAH (pl. +VAHS or +VOTH)
A commandment or precept. Jews have to obey 613 *mitzvoth*.

NER TAMID
Eternal candle, hung in front of the holy ark.

NISAN
The 7th month in the Jewish calendar (March-April).

PARASHAH (pl. +SHOTH)
The weekly lessons from the *Torah*.

PAROCHETH
Ornamental curtain hung in front of the holy ark.

PARVE
[Neutral] Kosher foods that contain neither meat nor dairy products and therefore can be eaten with either.

PASSOVER, or PESACH
Celebration of the Exodus from Egypt lasting eight days (seven in Israel). Passover opens with the *seder*. During the festivity eating leavened bread is forbidden and *matzah* is eaten in its place.

PURIM
[Lots] A carnival festival on the 14th of *Adar* (celebrating the rescue of the Jews in Persia by Queen Esther), when the *Megillath Esther* is read. During this joyful celebration children wear fancy dress.

RIMMONIM
[Pomegranates] Silver ferrules, usually in the form of pomegranates, which are used to decorate the *Torah*.

ROSH HASHANAH
The Jewish New Year, held on the first day of *Tishri*.

ROSH HASHANAH LA'ILANOT
The New Year of the Trees, also called *Tu B'Shevat*.

SEDER
[Order] A ceremonial dinner with ritual reading of the Haggadah observed on the first night of Passover.

SEFER (pl. SEFARIM)
Book. *Sefer Torah* (pl. *Sifre Torah*): The scroll of the *Torah* containing the Pentateuch (the first five books of the Bible) handwritten in special ink on parchment by scribes. It is used for the lessons on the Sabbath and other festivities. Kept in the *aron*, it is wrapped in the *meil* and surmounted by the *atarah* or *keter* (crown symbolizing the royal nature of the divine law) and two *rimmonim*, while on the side hangs the *tass* (ornamental tray).

SEPHARDIM
[Spaniards] Jews who originally came from the Iberian peninsula after being expelled following the Inquisition of 1492. They mainly settled in other Mediterranean countries and Holland and England. They have their own cultural traditions, and at times still speak some ancient Castilian, which they call *Ladino* or *Spaniolito*.

SHABBAT
The Sabbath, the most important day in the week.

SHADDAI
[The Almighty, God] a medallion or talisman with the Hebrew letters of the word and hung on a baby's crib or round its neck.

SHABUOTH, or SHAVUOT
[Weeks] The Feast of Weeks or Pentecost. It is also the festival of the corn harvest and commemorates the revelation of the *Torah* on Mount Sinai. It falls fifty days after *Pesach*.

SHEMAH
[Listen] The most deeply felt prayer consisting of three passages from the *Torah*, it is recited first thing in the morning and before going to bed.

SHEVAT, or SHEBAT
5th month in the Jewish calendar (January-February).

SHOFAR
Ram's horn, blown during *Rosh Hashanah* and other ceremonies.

SIDDUR
Daily prayer book.

SIMCHAT TORAH
[Rejoicing of the *Torah*] A celebration marking the end of *Sukkoth* and the completion and recommencement of the yearly cycle of *Torah* readings.

SIVAN
9th month in the Jewish calendar (May-June).

SUKKAH
Tabernacle (a kind of booth) in which *Sukkoth* is celebrated.

SUKKOTH, or SUCCOTH
[Tabernacles] An eight-day harvest festival commemorating the period when the Israelites lived in the wilderness.

TALLITH (pl. +LITHIM)
A white shawl with fringed corners, worn over the head and shoulders by Jewish men at prayer.

TALMUD
[Instruction] The main authoritative compilation of ancient Jewish law and tradition comprising the *Mishnah* and the *Gemara*. There are two editions: the Babylonian and the Palestinian (or Jerusalem) *Talmud*.

TAMMUZ, or THAMMUZ
10th month in the Jewish calendar (June-July).

TASS (pl. +SIM)
Ornamental tray for the *Torah*.

TEFILLAH
Prayer; specifically the *Amidah*.

TEFILLIN
[Phylacteries] Two small leather cases containing strips of parchment inscribed with religious texts. They are worn by men (one on the forehead and the other attached to the left arm by special straps) during morning prayer on week days.

TEVET, or TEBET
4th month of the Jewish calendar (December-January).

TIQ
Case or box for the *Sefer Torah* used by the Sephardim.

TISHA B'AV
9th of the month of *Av*, a day of mourning for the destruction of the First and Second Temples of Jerusalem (587-86 BC and 70 AD).

TISHRI
1st month of the Jewish calendar (September-October).

TORAH
[Law or Teaching] In the narrowest sense this is the Pentateuch or the first five Mosaic books of the Bible, traditionally known as the "written *Torah*" to distinguish it from the wider meaning of the whole body of oral teachings of the masters. This "oral *Torah*" has also gradually been written down, especially the *Mishnah*.

YAD
[Hand] A pointer, in the form of a hand at the end of a long stick, used for reading the *Torah* without touching it.

YESHIVAH
A traditional Jewish school.

YIDDISH
Dialect that became a language spoken by Ashkenazim.

YOM KIPPUR
Day of atonement and fasting.

ZOHAR
[Splendor] The title of a classic written work in the mystical tradition of *Cabbala*.

NOTE
The symbol (k) for *kosher* indicates restaurants or food stores under rabbinical supervision. *Besari* means a meat restaurant, *chalav* a dairy-based restaurant, and *parve* a neutral restaurant.

All the addresses and phone numbers listed below have been revised in April 2004.

Piedmont

For guided visits to all the synagogues in the region (except for Casale Monferrato) apply to:
ARTEFACTA – tel./fax 011 8131230
mobile 347 4891662 – info@artefacta.it

Turin

COMUNITÀ EBRAICA, Piazzetta Primo Levi, 12
tel. 011 6692387 / 011 658585/6/7
fax 011 6691173 – comebrato@libero.it

Accommodations
CASA DI RIPOSO, Via Galliari 13
tel. 011 658585/6 – fax 011 6691173
(booking required) (k).

Restaurants
SESAMO'S KITCHEN, Via Saluzzo 23 bis
tel. 011 655548 – fax 011 6503874
Mon–Sat, 10am–7:30pm
(natural and vegetarian cuisine, take-away, and catering on request) (k).
AZIENDA AGRITURISTICA LA MINIERA
DI ROBERTA ANAU
Via delle Miniere 9, Valcava, Calea di Lessolo (TO)
tel. 0125 58618
www.laminiera.it – roberta@laminiera.it
(traditional Jewish cooking).

Kosher products
PANETTERIA BERTINO, Via Galliari, 14
tel. 011 6699527 (bread, buns, pizzas, tarts, biscuits, salami, wine, and frozen meat) (k).
LABORATORIO PASTICCERIA E GELATERIA MEDICO
Via Martiri della Libertà, 4bis
tel. 011 8194319 (*kosher* on request) (k).

Alessandria (section of Turin)
SYNAGOGUE, Via Milano, 7 – tel. 0131 26224

Asti (section of Turin)
SYNAGOGUE AND MUSEUM, Via Ottolenghi, 8
(booking required for visits: Biblioteca Cepros
tel. 0141 593281); 0141 215526
bookshop (booking required for visits).

Biella Piazzo (section of Vercelli)
SYNAGOGUE, Via del Bellone, 3

Carmagnola (section of Turin)
SYNAGOGUE, Via Bellini, 9

Casale Monferrato

SYNAGOGUE, MUSEUM, AND HISTORICAL ARCHIVES
Vicolo Salomone Olper, 44 – tel. 0142 71807
casalebraica@tiscalinet.it
bookshop (only open Sunday 10am–12pm and 3pm–5pm, or by appointment).

Cherasco (section of Turin)
SYNAGOGUE, Via Marconi, 4

Cuneo (section of Turin)
SYNAGOGUE, Contrada Mondovì, 18
tel. 0171 692007 – fax 0171 693290

Ivrea (section of Turin)
SYNAGOGUE, Via IV Martiri, 20

Mondovì Piazzo (section of Turin)
SYNAGOGUE, Via Vico, 65

Saluzzo (section of Turin)
SYNAGOGUE, Via Deportati Ebrei

Vercelli
SYNAGOGUE, Via Foa, 56 – mobile 338 1438521
comebravc.presid@libero.it

Lombardy

Milan

JEWISH COMMUNITY, Via Sally Mayer 2/4
tel. 02 48311001 – fax 02 48304660
comunita.ebraica.mi@libero.it
TEMPLE "HEKHÀL DAVID U – MORDECHAI"
Via della Guastalla, 19 – tel. 02 5512101
CENTER OF CONTEMPORARY JEWISH
DOCUMENTATION (CDEC), Via Eupili 8
tel. 02 316338 / 02 316092 – fax 02 33602728
www.cdec.it – cdec@cdec.it
(library, archives, and video library).

Accommodations
HOTEL PRINCIPE DI SAVOIA
Piazza della Repubblica, 17 – tel. 02 62301
(*kosher* on request).
QUARK RESIDENCE HOTEL, Viale Lampedusa, 11/a
tel. 02 84431 (*kosher* on request).

Restaurants
NUOVA RESIDENZA PER ANZIANI (NRA)
Via Leone XIII, 1 – tel. 02 4982604
(booking required) (*besari*) (k).

ESHEL ISRAEL, Via Cellini, 2 – tel. 02 5455076
(booking required, before 10am) (*besari*) (k).
MIFGASH, Via Montecuccoli, 35 – tel. 02 4156199
(booking required) (*besari*) (k).
PIZZERIA "PIZZA E... CARMEL"
Viale S. Gimignano, 10 – tel. 02 416368
www.carmelbylolita.com
(pizzeria and *chalav* catering) (k).
RE SALOMONE, Via Washington, 9
tel. 02 4694643
(*besari* catering and take-away) (k).
TUV TA'AM, Via Arzaga, 15 – tel. 02 4150331
(*parve-besari* pastries and catering) (k).
GELATERIA FROZEN YOUGURT
Via Ravizza, 5 – tel. 02 48010917
gelatoecologico@ fastwebnet.it
(*parve-chalav*, not *chalav* Yisrael) (k).
CONVIVIUM BANQUETING, Via E. Fermi, 9
20037 Paderno Dugnano (MI)
tel. 02 99048359 – fax 02 99048466
(*kosher* on request).
IL MAESTRO DI CASA, Via A. Boito, 8
tel. 02 72023181 (*kosher* on request).
TOV – CATERING & HOLIDAYS, Via Panzini, 16
tel. 02 466230 – fax 02 4815648
mobile 335 283766 (Sharon Mevorah)
sharonmevora@yahoo.it (*kosher* on request).

Kosher products
DELICATESSE (catering, gastronomy and pastries)
tel. 02 4983893 – fax 02 36508518
mobile 338 8018081 (Paula)
EDEN, Viale S. Gimignano, 13
tel. 02 4122855 – fax 02 48303517 (k).
ERETZ, Via Soderini, 27
tel. 02 4236891 – fax 02 47716507
www.eretz.it (k).
J. MALKI, Via Montecuccoli, 21
tel. 02 4159835 – fax 02 41270307 (k).
ORIENTAL MARKET, Via Caterina da Forlì, 58
tel./fax 02 4042977 (k).
SUPERGAL, Via Bisleri, 16
tel. 02 40091000 – fax 02 40091307 (k).

Judaica and books
DAVAR – JUDAICA & BOOKS, Viale S. Gimignano, 10
tel. 02 48300051 – fax 02 43982598
www.davar.it/ – e-mail info@davar.it
LIBRERIA CLAUDIANA, Via Sforza 12/a
tel./fax 02 76021518 – libclaud@tin.it
BIJOUX DE PARIS – BURMA, Via Manzoni, 12
tel. 02 76005550 – fax 02 794258

Mantua
SYNAGOGUE, Via G. Govi, 13 – tel./fax 0376 321490

Sabbioneta
SYNAGOGUE, Via B. Campi, 13
for visits: Pro Loco – Tourist Office
Via Gonzaga 27 – tel. 0375 52039

Soncino
PRINTERS' MUSEUM, Via Lanfranco, 8
tel. 0374 84883 / 0374 85333 bookshop
Pro Loco, Via IV Novembre 14
tel. 0374 84883 / 0374 85333
prolocosoncino@tin.it

Liguria

Genoa
JEWISH COMMUNITY AND SYNAGOGUE, MUSEUM
Via Bertora, 6 – tel. 010 8391513
fax 010 8461006 – comgenova@tin.it

Veneto

Venice
JEWISH COMMUNITY
Cannaregio, 2899 Ghetto Vecchio
tel. 041 715012 – fax 041 5241862
com.ebra@ve.191.it

JEWISH MUSEUM
Cannaregio 2902/b, Campo del Ghetto Novo
tel. 041 715359 – fax 041 723007
museoebraico@codesscultura.it
(open: June 1–September 30: 10am–7pm;
October 1–May 31: 10am–5.30pm;
closed Saturdays and Jewish holidays, January 1,
May 1, and December 25) bookshop
Guided visits (booking required for groups):
Codess Cultura
English and Italian tours starting each hour,
from 10:30am to 5:30pm (summer);
from 10:30am to 4:30pm (winter).
ANTICO CIMITERO DEL LIDO
visits by appointment or on Sunday
from 2:30pm; closed on Jewish holidays
and in case of bad weather
(bookings: tel. 041 715359 – fax 041 723007
prenotazioni@codesscultura.it
www.codesscultura.it;
next: prenotazioni@museoebraico.it
info@ museoebraico.it – alef@ museoebraico.it)

Accommodations
COMMUNITY CENTER IN THE CASA DI RIPOSO
ISRAELITICA, Campo del Ghetto Novo,
Cannaregio 2874 – tel. 041 716002

(hospitality, *kosher* meals and products;
Shabbat welcome; booking required) (k).
LOCANDA DEL GHETTO
Campo del Ghetto Novo, Cannaregio 2892/2893
tel. 041 2759292 – fax 041 2757987
ghetto@veneziahotels.com
(rooms with timer available for Shabbat,
breakfast) (k).

Restaurants
CAFFETTERIA DEL MUSEO EBRAICO
Cannaregio 2902/b – tel. 041 715359 (k) (*parve*).
GAM GAM, Sottoportego del Ghetto Vecchio,
Cannaregio 1122 – tel. 041 715284
(*besari* restaurant also does Italian cuisine) (k).

Kosher products
PANIFICIO ALBONICO, S. Croce 2268/b
tel. 041 5241102 (k).
PANIFICIO VOLPE, Cannaregio 1143
tel. 041 715178
(bread and various *afiyat* Israel foods) (k).

Judaica and books
FUSETTI & MARIANI, ARTE EBRAICA SHALOM
Ghetto Vecchio 1219 – tel. 041 720092

Padua
JEWISH COMMUNITY AND SYNAGOGUE
Via San Martino e Solferino, 9
tel./fax 049 8751106 – cebra.pd@libero.it

Verona
JEWISH COMMUNITY AND SYNAGOGUE, Via Portici, 3
tel. 045 8007112 – fax 045 8048295
comebraica@libero.it

Trentino-Alto Adige

Merano
JEWISH COMMUNITY AND SYNAGOGUE
Via Schiller, 14
tel. 0473 236127 – fax 0473 206210
meranoebraica@hotmail.com
bookshop (open: Tues–Wed 3pm–6pm;
Thurs 9am–12pm; Fri 3pm–5pm;
for group visits tel. 047 443554).

Friuli-Venezia Giulia

Trieste
JEWISH COMMUNITY AND SYNAGOGUE
Via S. Francesco, 19 – tel. 040 371466
fax 040 371226 – info@triesteebraica.it

CARLO AND VERA WAGNER MUSEUM
Via del Monte, 5 – tel. 040 633819 – bookshop
RISIERA DI SAN SABBA, Ratto della Pileria, 43
tel. 040 826202 / 040 310500

Accommodations
PIA CASA DI RIPOSO A. STOCK, Via Cologna 29
tel. 040 568578 – fax 040 5705590 (lunch must be
booked, short-period accommodation) (k)
piacasagentilomo@libero.it.

Kosher products
Kosher products at Community premises.
LA BOMBONIERA, Via 30 Ottobre, 3
tel /fax 040 632752
(pastry shop with Jewish recipes)
info@pasticcerialabomboniera.it

Judaica and books
LIBRERIA UMBERTO SABA, Via San Nicolò, 30
tel. 040 631741

Gorizia (section of Trieste)
SYNAGOGUE AND MUSEUM "JERUSALEM
ON THE ISONZO", Via Ascoli, 19
tel. 0481 532115 – fax 0481 522056
ass.israele@activeweb.it
(winter opening: Mon, Fri, and Sat, 4pm–7pm;
Tues and Thurs, 5pm–7pm; every second Sunday
of the month 10am–1pm).

Emilia Romagna

Bologna
JEWISH COMMUNITY AND SYNAGOGUE
Via de' Gombruti, 9 – tel. 051 232066
fax 051 229474 – comebrbo@libero.it
JEWISH MUSEUM, Via Valdonica 1/5
tel. 051 2911280 – fax 051 235430
www.museoebraicobo.it
info@museoebraicobo.it
bookshop (open: from Sun thru Thurs
10am–6pm; Fri 10am–4pm; closed on Saturday
and Jewish holidays).

Restaurants
COMMUNITY REFECTORY, Via dei Gombruti, 9
tel. 051 227931 (booking required) (*besari*) (k).

Judaica and books
LA TARLATANA, Via dei Giudei 1/c
tel. 051 237022.
LA CHIOCCIOLA, Via dell'Inferno, 6/a
(objects and ceramic art from Jewish Italy)
tel. 051 220964.

Faenza

Laboratorio Rustichelli, Via Calzi 20
tel. 054 6621285
(pastry with a section of *kosher* products).
Italia Judaica di Roberto Matatia
Piazza del Popolo 14 – tel. 0546 21202
www.italiajudaica.com
robertoesilvia@italiajudaica.it (ceramics).

Carpi and Fossoli

Synagogue, Via G. Rovighi, Carpi
tel. 059 649905
Museum and Monument to the Political and
Racial Deportees to the Extermination Camps
Castello dei Pio
Comune di Carpi tel. 059 688483 / 059 688272
www.fondazionefossoli.org
fondazione.fossoli@comune.carpi.mo.it

Ferrara

Jewish Community, Synagogues, and Museum
Via Mazzini, 95 – tel./fax 0532 247004
Bookings for museum visits: tel./fax 0532 210228
www.comune.fe.it/museoebraico
museoebraico@comune.fe.it
bookshop (open: Sun–Thurs with guided visits
at 10am, 11am, and 12pm).

Modena

Jewish Community and Synagogue
Piazza Mazzini, 26 – tel./fax 059 223978.

Parma

Jewish Community and Synagogue
Vicolo Cervi, 4 – tel./fax 0521 200243.

Reggio Emilia (section of Modena)

Synagogue, Via dell'Aquila, 4
(usually closed to the general public.
Guided visits only, information from
Istoreco association, tel. 0522 437327).
Terra di Danza – tel. 0522 371698
info@terradidanza.it
(Jewish dance workshops and courses).

Soragna (section of Parma)

Fausto Levi Museum, Via Cavour, 43
tel./fax 0524 599399
www.museoebraicosoragna.net
info@museoebraicosoragna.net
bookshop (open: March–October, Tues–Fri
10am–12pm, 3pm–5pm; Sun 10am–12.30pm,
3pm–6pm; closed Mon and Sat and August;
visits also by appointment).

Tuscany

Florence

Jewish Community, Synagogue, and Museum
Via L.C. Farini, 4
tel. 055 245252 – fax 055 241811
www.firenzebraica.net – comebrfi@fol.it
(museum open: April–May, Sun–Thurs
10am–17pm, June–August, Sun–Thurs
10am–6pm; September–October, Sun–Thurs
10am–5pm; November–March, Sun–Thurs
10am–3pm; Fri 10am–2pm
Cooperativa Servizi Culturali Sigma
tel. 055 2346654 – fax 055 244145
cscsigma@tin.it – also for the Siena synagogue).

Accommodations
Casa di Riposo Settimio Saadun, Via Carducci 11/b
tel. 055 241210 / 055 2479883 – fax 055 244044
casasaadun@fol.it
(lunch on booking, possibility of
accommodation for short stays).

Restaurants
Ruth's, Via Farini 2/a – tel./fax 055 2480888
(*chalav*) (k).
Il Gelataio De' Ciompi, Piazza dei Ciompi
(ice-cream parlor) (k).

Kosher products
Falsettini Bruno, Sant'Ambrogio Market
tel. 055 2480740 (meat) (k) .
Polleria Giovannino, Via dei Macci, 106
tel. 055 2480734 (meat, salami, wine, and
canned food) (k).
Kosher Market, Via dei Pilastri 7ar
tel/fax 055 240508
www.koshermarket.it – info@koshermarket.it
Natura Si – Natural foods Supermarket
Viale Corsico, 19/23 – tel. 055 366024
Jean-Michel Carasso (catering), caspafe@fol.it

Livorno

Jewish Community and Synagogue
Piazza Benamozegh, 1 – tel./fax 0586 896290
www.comunitaebraica.org
info@comunitaebraica.org
Museum, Via Micali, 21
(guided visits: Cooperativa Amaranta, Gilda
Vigoni, tel. 349 2564537 – mobile 339 3422139).

Kosher products
Corucci, Counter 25, Central Market
tel. 0586 884596 (meat) (k).
Panificio Lo Giudice, Via delle Commedie, 9
tel. 0586 894532.

Pisa
JEWISH COMMUNITY AND SYNAGOGUE
Via Palestro, 24 – tel./fax 050 542580
com_ebraicapi@tin.it
guided visits: Alef Tav – tel. 050 9711383

Pitigliano (section of Livorno)
SYNAGOGUE, MUSEUM, AND OVEN
Antico Ghetto, Vicolo Marghera
("Little Jerusalem" Cultural Association
tel. 0564 616006 – fax 0564 616077;
Pro Loco – tel. 0564 614433).

Kosher products
PANIFICIO DEL GHETTO E PASTICCERIA
Via Zuccarelli (traditional Jewish pastries).
CANTINA COOPERATIVA SOCIALE
Località Vignagrande – tel. 0564 616133
(Pitigliano *kosher* wines: Rosso della Piccola
Gerusalemme, Bianco di Pitigliano D.O.C.) (k).

Siena (section of Florence)
SYNAGOGUE, vicolo delle Scotte, 14
tel. 0577 284647
(guided visits: Cooperativa Servizi Culturali
Sigma – tel. 055 2346654 – cscsigma@tin.it).

Kosher products
SAVINI MASSIMO, Via di Salicotto, 23
tel. 0577 283140 (meat) (k).

Marches

Ancona
SYNAGOGUES, Via Astagno, 10
tel./fax 071 202638 – comeban@libero.it

Pesaro
SYNAGOGUE, Via delle Scole o Via Sara
Levi Nathan – tel. 0721 67815.

Senigallia (section of Ancona)
SYNAGOGUE, Via Commercianti, 20.

Urbino (section of Ancona)
SYNAGOGUE, Via Stretta, 45.

Lazio

Rome
JEWISH COMMUNITY, Lungotevere Cenci
(Temple) tel. 06 6840061 / fax 06 68400684
www.romacer.org
info@romacer.org

MUSEUM, Lungotevere Cenci; bookshop
(open: October–May 9am–5pm; June–September
9am–6pm, Fri 9am–2pm, Sun 9am–12.30pm)
(bookings for museum visits: tel. 06 68400661;
bookings for visits to the historical archives:
tel. 06 68400663 – museo.ebraico@romacer.org).
UNION OF THE ITALIAN JEWISH COMMUNITIES
BIBLIOGRAPHIC CENTER
Lungotevere Sanzio, 9 – tel. 06 5803670.
OSTIA ANTICA EXCAVATIONS
Viale dei Romagnoli, 717, Ostia Antica (Rome)
tel. 06 56358099 – fax 065651500.

Accommodations
PENSIONE CARMEL, Via Mameli, 11
tel. 06 5809921 (k).
PANTHEON VIEW – BED & BREAKFAST
Via del Seminario 87 – tel. 06 6990294 (k).
IL GIRASOLE, BED & BREAKFAST
Via del Boschetto, 13 – mobile 349 1820287.
GRAND HOTEL PARCO DEI PRINCIPI
Via Frescobaldi, 5 (Villa Borghese)
tel. 06 854421 – tel./fax 06 8845104
(*kosher* banquet on request).
HOTEL CAVALIERI HILTON, Via Cadlolo, 101
tel. 06 35092000 – fax 06 35092134
(*kosher* banquet on request).
SHERATON ROMA, Viale del Pattinaggio, 100
tel. 06 54537382 / fax 06 5940813
(*kosher* on request).
ST. REGIS GRAND, Via V.E. Orlando, 3
tel. 06 47091 – fax 06 4747307
(*kosher* banquet on request).

Restaurants
GIGGETTO AL PORTICO D'OTTAVIA
Via Portico d'Ottavia, 21/a – tel. 06 6861105
(Jewish *trattoria* right in the old Ghetto).
PITIGLIANI, Via Arco de' Tolomei, 1
tel. 06 5800539 (*besari*; booking required) (k).
LA TAVERNA DEL GHETTO, Via Portico d'Ottavia, 8
tel./fax 06 68809771 / 68212309 (*besari*) (k).
IL CARROCCIO, Via del Carroccio, 9
tel. 06 44237018.
LE BON TON CATERING, Via Casoria, 19
tel. 06 7026889 – fax 06 7026920
(*besari-chalav*; booking required) (k).
YOTVATA, Piazza Cenci, 70
tel. 06 68134481 (*chalav*) (k).
GAN EDEN, Via Eleonora D'Arborea, 40
tel. 06 44231457.
ORIENTAL FOOD KOSHER, Via Livorno, 8/10
tel./fax 06 4404840 (*besari*) (k).
ZI' FENIZIA, PIZZA AL TAGLIO
Via S. Maria del Pianto, 64 – tel. 06 6896976
(*besari*) (also open for Motzae Shabbat) (k).

DAL POMPIERE, Via S. Maria dei Calderari, 38
tel. 06 6868377 (traditional Jewish dishes).
EVANGELISTA, Via delle Zoccolette, 11/a
tel./fax 06 6875810 (traditional Jewish dishes).
PIPERNO, Via Monte de' Cenci, 9
tel. 06 68806629 – www.italy.net/piperno
(traditional Jewish dishes).
PIZZA E FESTA, PANINOTECA
Via Portico d'Ottavia, 1/b– tel. 06 6893235 (k).
KOSHER PIZZA, PIZZA AL TAGLIO, Via L. Magrini, 12
tel. 06 5590790 (besari) (k).
KOSHER BISTROT, PANINOTECA, via S. Maria
del Pianto 68 – tel. 06 6864398.
KOSHER DELICE, PANINOTECA, via G Boni, 18/a
tel. 06 44202626.
PASTICCERIA BOCCIONE, via Portico d'Ottavia, 1
tel. 06 6878637.

Kosher products
BERNASCONI, Piazza Benedetto Cairoli, 16
tel. 06 68806264
(bar with *kosher* pastries on request).
SCIUNNACH – LABORATORIO PASTA ALL'UOVO
Via A. Lo Surdo, 27/a – tel. 06 5565760.
KOSHER POINT, Via O.M. Corbino, 17
tel. 06 5584363 (k).
LE-PESACH KOSHER products at BETH EL
(distribution), Via Padova, 42
tel. 06 44242857 (k).
KOSHER BISTROT, Via S. Maria del Pianto, 68
tel. 06 6864398 (k).
KOSHER DELIGHT, Via Silvestro Gherardi, 16/18
tel. 06 5565231 – fax 06 5595335
(delicatessen) (k).
SCARFÒ, Via Padova, 84/86/88 – tel. 06 44291117
(bread and biscuits).
TORNATORA, Via Oderisi da Gubbio, 27
tel. 06 5593658 (pastries and gastronomy).
MACELLERIA BABANI BEN DAVID
Via Lorenzo il Magnifico, 70
tel. 06 44243959 (meat).
DI PORTO, Via Damaso Cerquetti, 2
tel. 06 5346992 (meat).
DI VEROLI, Via Galla e Sidama, 51
tel. 06 86207971 (meat).
GEPE-GEAN, Via Stamira, 2/b
tel. 06 44244055 (meat).
OUAZANA, Via S. Gherardi, 44/a – tel. 06 5565231;
Via G.Boni, 18/a – tel. 06 44202626 (meat).
PASCARELLA KASHER, Via Cesare Pascarella, 36
tel. 06 5881698 (meat).
SPIZZICHINO, Via del Forte Bravetta, 148
tel. 06 66157796 / 06 7803676 (meat).
TERRACINA, Via S. Maria del Pianto, 62
tel. 06 68801364 (meat).

Judaica and books
LIBRERIA MENORAH, Via del Tempio, 2
tel. 06 6879297 – menorah@menorah.it
(bookshop specializing in Jewish material).
BIJOUX DE PARIS – BURMA, Via dei Condotti, 27
tel. 06 6798285 (gift shop).
YUD JUDAICA, Via del Portico d'Ottavia, 1/a
tel./fax 06 6876555 (gift shop).
YUD PREZIOSI, Via Napoleone III, 49/51
tel. 06 4466777/ fax 06 4466477
yudsalv@libero.it (preziosi).

Campania

Naples
JEWISH COMMUNITY AND SYNAGOGUE
Via Cappella Vecchia, 31 – tel./fax 081 7643480
c.e.napoli@virgilio.it

Apulia

Trani
TRANINOSTRA CULTURAL ASSOCIATION
Corso Imbriani, 61 – tel. 0883 491605
www.traninostra/traniweb.it

Sicily

Syracuse
MIKVEH OF CASA BIANCA ALLA GIUDECCA
Via Alagona, 52 – tel. 0931 22255
www.allagiudecca.com
allagiudecca@hotmail.com

Sardinia

Alghero
THOLOS CULTURAL ASSOCIATION – tel. 079 978090
ITALY-ISRAEL ASSOCIATION – tel. 070 308398

SELECTED BIBLIOGRAPHY

Architettura judaica in Italia: ebraismo, sito, memoria dei luoghi, Palermo, Flaccovio, 1994.

C. BERTOLA, *Vita e cultura ebraica. Documentazione fotografica sulla presentazione ebraica in Piemonte nei secoli XVIII e XIX*, edited by Giorgio Avigdor, Regione Piemonte – Archivio delle tradizioni e del costume ebraici "Benvenuto e Alessandro Terracini", Turin 1983.

N. BIDDAU, *Gli spazi della parola. Sinagoghe in Piemonte*, Turin, Elede, 2002.

S. BONDONI, G.BUSI (ed.), *Cultura ebraica in Emilia-Romagna*, Rimini, Luisé, 1987.

F. BONILAURI, E. MAUGERI (eds.), *Cimiteri ebraici in Emilia-Romagna*, Rome, De Luca Editori d'Arte, 2002.

F. BONILAURI, E. MAUGERI (eds.), *Museo Ebraico di Bologna. Guida ai Percorsi Storici*, Rome, De Luca Editori d'Arte, 2002.

F. BRANDES (ed.), *Veneto. Jewish Itineraries. Places, history and art*, Venice, Marsilio, 1996.

N. BUCARIA, *Sicilia Judaica*, Palermo, Flaccovio, 1996.

R. CALIMANI, *Storia del ghetto di Venezia*, Milan, Rusconi, 1985.

R. CALIMANI, G. SULLAM REINISCH, C. VIVANTE, *Venice. Guide to the synagogues, museum and cemetery*, Venice, Marsilio, 2001.

V. COLORNI, *Judaica minora*, Milan, Giuffré, 1983.

E. CONCINA, U. CAMERINO, D. CALABI, *La città degli ebrei. Il ghetto di Venezia: architettura e urbanistica*, Venice, Albrizzi, 1991.

G.S. CUSIN, P.C. IOLY ZORATTINI (eds.), *Friuli-Venezia Giulia. Jewish Itineraries. Places, history and art*, Venice, Marsilio, 1998.

C. DE BENEDETTI (ed.), *La sinagoga degli argenti. Arte e spiritualità ebraica a Casale Monferrato*, Turin-Florence, Pluriverso, 1991.

S. DELLA PERGOLA, *Anatomia dell'ebraismo italiano*, Assisi-Rome, Benedetto Carucci, 1976.

G. DISEGNI (ed.), *Sopra la volta il cielo. Viaggio tra i beni culturali ebraici*, Florence, Giuntina, 2002.

R. DI SEGNI, *Guida alle regole alimentari ebraiche*, Rome, Lamed, 1996.

Ebrei a Torino. Ricerche per il centenario della sinagoga 1884-1984, exhibition catalogue, Turin, Allemandi, 1984.

U. FORTIS, *Ebrei e Sinagoghe*, Venice, Storti, 1984.

U. FORTIS, *Il Ghetto sulla Laguna*, Venice, Storti, 1987-1993.

M.L. GIRIBALDI SARDI, *Asti. Guida alle sinagoghe e al museo*, Venice, Marsilio, 1999.

M.L. GIRIBALDI, M.P. VILLANI, *Il ghetto, la sinagoga. Viaggio attraverso la cultura ebraica ad Asti*, Turin, Lindau, 1992.

V. GIURA, *La Comunità Israelitica di Napoli (1863-1945)*, Naples, ESI, 2002.

P.C. IOLY ZORATTINI (ed.), *Gli ebrei a Gorizia e a Trieste tra "ancien régime" ed emancipazione*, Udine, Del Bianco, 1984.

I. KAHN, D. LISCIA BEMPORAD (eds.), *La Nazione Ebrea di Livorno. Itinerari di vita*, exhibition catalogue, Livorno, Graphis Art, 1992.

L. LEVI, *Che cosa è l'antisemitismo? Per favore rispondete*, Milan, Mondadori, 2001.

D. LISCIA BEMPORAD, A. TEDESCHI FALCO (eds.), *Tuscany. Jewish Itineraries. Places, history and art*, Venice, Marsilio, 1995.

M. LUZZATI, *Le tre sinagoghe. Edifici di culto e vita ebraica a Livorno dal Seicento al Novecento*, Comune di Livorno – Turin, Allemandi, 1995.

G. LUZZATTO VOGHERA, *L'antisemitismo. Domande e risposte*, Milan, Feltrinelli, 1994.

B.V. MANN, *I ta lyà. Duemila anni di arte e vita ebraica in Italia*, exhibition catalogue, Milan, Mondadori, 1990.

B. MIGLIAU, PROCACCIA M., with S. REBUZZI and M. VITALE (eds.), *Lazio. Jewish Itineraries. Places, history and art*, Venice, Marsilio, 1997.

A. MILANO, *Storia degli ebrei in Italia*, Turin, Einaudi, 1963.

M.L. MOSCATI BENIGNI (ed.), *Marche. Jewish Itineraries. Places, history and art*, Venice, Marsilio, 1999.

M.L. MOSCATI BENIGNI, *Sinagoghe di Urbino & Storia del ghetto*, Comune di Urbino, Urbania 1996.

Museo della Comunità ebraica di Trieste Carlo e Vera Wagner, Florence, Alinari, 1992.

Museo Monumento al deportato politico e razziale nei campi di sterminio nazisti, Castello dei Pio, Carpi, 1973.

L. PADOA, *Le comunità ebraiche di Scandiano e di Reggio Emilia*, Florence, Giuntina,1993.

L. PICCIOTTO FARGION, *Il libro della memoria. Gli Ebrei deportati dall'Italia (1943-1945)*, Milan, Mursia, 1991.

F. RENDA, *La fine del giudaismo siciliano*, Palermo, Sellerio, 1993.

A. SACERDOTI, *Gli ebrei italiani. Chi sono, quanti sono, come vivono*, Venice, Marsilio, 1997.

A. SACERDOTI, F. BONILAURI, A. TEDESCHI FALCO, V. MAUGERI, and L. MORTARA OTTOLENGHI (eds.), *Arte e cultura ebraiche in Emilia-Romagna*, exhibition catalogue, Milan-Rome, Mondadori-De Luca, 1988.

A. SACERDOTI, G. BOURBON, *Casale Monferrato. Guida alle sinagoghe e al museo*, Venice, Marsilio, 1996.

A. SACERDOTI, L. FIORENTINO, *Guida all'Italia ebraica*, Casale Monferrato, Marietti, 1986.

A. SACERDOTI, A. TEDESCHI FALCO, with V. MAUGERI (eds.), *Emilia Romagna. Jewish Itineraries. Places, history and art*, Venice, Marsilio, 1992.

A. SACERDOTI, A. TEDESCHI FALCO, *Lombardia. Itinerari ebraici in Italia. I luoghi, la storia, l'arte*, Venice, Marsilio, 1993.

A. SACERDOTI, A. TEDESCHI FALCO, *Piemonte. Itinerari ebraici in Italia. I luoghi, la storia, l'arte*, Venice, Marsilio, 1994.

R.G. SALVADORI, *La comunità ebraica di Pitigliano*, Florence, Giuntina, 1991.

R.G. SALVADORI, *Breve storia degli ebrei toscani*, Florence, Le lettere, 1995.

B. SEGRE, *Gli ebrei in Italia*, Milan, Fenice 2000, 1993.

Shalom Trieste – gli itinerari dell'ebraismo, exhibition catalogue, Comune di Trieste, Trieste 1998.

P. STEFANI, *Gli ebrei*, Bologna, Il Mulino, 1997.

M. STOCK, *Nel segno di Geremia. Storia della comunità israelitica di Trieste dal 1200*, Bologna, Istituto per l'Enciclopedia del Friuli Venezia Giulia, 1979.

L. TAS, *Storia degli ebrei italiani*, Milan, Newton & Compton, 1987.

A. TEDESCHI FALCO (ed.), *Liguria. Itinerari ebraici in Italia. I luoghi, la storia, l'arte*, Venice, Marsilio, 1997.

A. TEDESCHI FALCO, *Ferrara. Guide to the synagogues and museum*, Venice, Marsilio, 1999.

S. VINCENZI, *Il ghetto. Bologna. Storia e rinascita di un luogo*, Bologna, Grafis, 1993.

L. VOGHERA LUZZATTO, *Una finestra sul ghetto. Stefano Incisa e gli ebrei di Asti*, Rome, Carucci, 1983.

C. VIVANTI (ed.), *Storia d'Italia, Annali 11, Gli Ebrei in Italia*, 2 vols., Turin, Einaudi, 1996-1997.

N.G. ZAZZU, *Sepharad addio*, Genoa, Marietti, 1991.

N.G. ZAZZU, R. URBANI, *Gli Ebrei a Genova. Esposizione fotografica di documenti archivistici dal XII al XVIII secolo*, Genoa, Marietti, 1984.

Photolitograph
Fotolito Veneta, San Martino Buonalbergo (Verona)

Printed by
Grafiche Nardin, Ca' Savio Cavallino Treporti (Venice)
for Marsilio Editori® s.p.a. in Venice

EDITION

YEAR

10 9 8 7 6 5 4 3

2008 2009 2010 2011